THE
KUAN YIN
TRANSMISSION™

THE KUAN YIN TRANSMISSION™
HEALING GUIDANCE FROM OUR UNIVERSAL MOTHER

Published by Blue Angel Publishing®
80 Glen Tower Drive, Glen Waverley
Victoria, Australia 3150
Email: info@blueangelonline.com
Website: www.blueangelonline.com

Cover artwork by Zeng Hao
Edited by Jamie Morris

Blue Angel is a registered trademark of Blue Angel Gallery Pty. Ltd.

ISBN: 978-1-925538-60-1

FOR ALL HER CHILDREN

THE
KUAN YIN
TRANSMISSION™

HEALING GUIDANCE
FROM OUR
UNIVERSAL MOTHER

ALANA FAIRCHILD

BLUE ANGEL®
PUBLISHING

CONTENTS

INTRODUCTION

I wrote this book because of a request from the Universal Mother. I have known her and loved her for a very long time. She has helped, guided and protected me, whilst nurturing my potential (sometimes through challenge, always through grace) so I can continue to grow into the fullness of my being. I rely upon her for all things. My relationship with her is sacred and nourishing. Although this relationship with her is natural for me, I realised it was not so for many others. I knew she wanted to be close to all her children. It is my purpose in this work to help that happen.

What does the name *Mother Nature* conjure up for you? Perhaps you think of the whole earth as our living planet, or perhaps you instantly think of trees or mountains, birds flying free or delightfully strange insects. To me, Mother Nature is all those things, and she is also the body we inhabit and the human soul.

In the same way Mother Nature has numerous and ever-evolving faces—which may appear as different as a cactus and a rabbit, for example, yet are all *her*—so too does the Universal Mother have numerous and ever-evolving faces.

The innate power of the mother is to grow, love and nurture beings into fullness. The bond with the mother is common to all humans, irrespective of the quality of the relationship, or absence thereof, with one's biological mother. I believe our disrupted and oftentimes wounded relationship to our mothers—and that of our mothers with their own mothers—can be healed by the Universal Mother. The benefits that come from such healing are profound. They include the capacity to be truly oneself — feeling loved, seen, accepted and empowered to live a unique life path that honours one's inner truths—as well as the ability to transform the inner seeds of divine potential into a vibrant, quirky, beautiful soul garden of sacred expression.

In the spiritual traditions of ancient India, the mother is said to be the first guru, the one who protects and guides you and sets you on your true path in life. In that culture, the sacred feminine energies are called *shakti*, which loosely translates as *power*. She is the capacity to get things done. When our connection with the Universal Mother is intact, open and receptive, we experience healthy growth on all levels of our being — emotional, psychological, spiritual and physical. We dream of what is in our hearts, and life moves us to bring those dreams into fruition.

We need her, and she needs us, too. Together, we can create, birth and manifest from the heart in such a way that all beings benefit. We may worry that pursuing our fulfilment could be selfish, perhaps causing detriment to another, as when we prosper through another's loss, for example. There are certainly times when this happens. However, when we are connected to the Universal Mother and learn how to nestle into her guiding grace, her skilfulness and compassion flow through us. When her genius is at work in a human, the development and expression of that human helps all beings. The happiness of that human supports the happiness of others. We can trust her when we don't know how things are going to work out or what is going on. We can also trust her when we think we *do* know how things are going to work out and what *is* going on. We can trust her.

Trust is the spiritual trip switch. It opens us and creates willingness and receptivity to grace. The purest spiritual realms of enlightened activity, grace and blessing are constantly offering themselves for the benefit of all beings. When we trust, we connect. When we connect with the Universal Mother, we receive. No matter what our human experience with our human mothers may have been, we can trust that the Universal Mother is generous, present and not subject to the natural limitations we humans must grow through. She is endlessly resourceful and creative in her responsiveness. We can never avoid challenges in our lives. The only way to overcome an obstacle is to outgrow it. We may think that means a lot of hard work on our part. Sometimes it does. More often, we can allow the Universal Mother to foster our growth, allowing us to manage what looked to be a mountain as though it were a molehill. Everything seems more manageable when we lean into her. The hook, a spiritual tool often depicted in the hands of divine beings such as Tara (another face or emanation of the Universal Mother), symbolises the reach of the deity. To be effective, a hook needs something to latch on to. Our confidence and trust are rings the hook can catch so we may be drawn out of our suffering and into the luminous grace of the deity.

The moments when I really feel the Universal Mother are the ones that most move me. This is when I know she is not an abstract principle nor a fantasy figure but a living, loving, vibrant being with the capacity to be an effective force of love, protection, guidance and blessing in our lives. This does not mean that we lie on the sofa eating crisps, expecting her to do all the spiritual work. We do need to reach for her. We need to learn how to open to her, to take her hand. We need to understand this is not about giving up ownership of our lives to a greater power nor about becoming like infants. It is about stepping on to our path more courageous, bold, compassionate, fearless and feisty than ever before. It is about spiritual growth. Genuine spiritual growth has substance. Its subtlety may prevent us from consciously recognising its effects, but nonetheless, there is change, there is healing, there is empowerment. This is the forte of the Universal Mother and her blessing in our lives.

Part One

Getting to Know our Universal Mother

The first eight chapters of this book are an introduction to many faces and facets of Kuan Yin, our Universal Mother. Many people don't realise they already know and have encountered her throughout their lives. My journey into her wild, resourceful and tender heart has been so beautiful and life changing that I wanted to share it with you. Through the stories and guidance that I share in this book, I hope you will recognise your own connection with her, as well as open your heart to an even deeper relationship. If you do so, your life will never be the same again. She is the path to happiness, peace, protection and fulfilment that is a nurturing *reality*. She is that which we are truly seeking.

CHAPTER ONE

KUAN YIN:
ASK, AND HELP SHALL BE GIVEN

As a goddess, an ancient divine being and an enlightened spiritual guardian, Kuan Yin offers unlimited protection, intervention and assistance to all beings. Having attained enough spiritual growth, enlightened beings operate in a field of unity, clarity and wisdom. Their actions are pure and so infused with higher wisdom that they can help others without causing further problems. If you've ever tried to help someone but, made things worse in the process, you'll know that good intentions are not enough. They are an excellent start, and we want to cultivate a helpful attitude towards others, but it is when good intentions combine with a high level of spiritual growth that the results are most effective and a win-win for all. That doesn't mean the ego will like the result of what manifests. But whilst the ego might struggle—to let go of a false idea of superiority, for example—the soul will be coming to life and that is best for all. Our connection with the Universal Mother and our trust in her wisdom supports us on our path as a healer (an energy healer, therapist, bodyworker, teacher with heart, parent with awareness, one who wants the world to be a better place, etc.) and to do our best work (which is actually her work).

Millions of people around the world love Kuan Yin. She is sought as a compassionate mother who provides safe refuge from our problems and helps us find our way through confusion and suffering into clarity, happiness and peace.

At the first moment of suffering, compassion was also born. Since then, Kuan Yin has been devoted to the welfare of every being. It doesn't matter to her if you are Buddhist, Taoist, Christian, Muslim, Pagan, if you claim no religion at all or are an atheist. Buddhism teaches that Kuan Yin chose this realm of manifestation—the earth, the realms connected to it and all beings within those realms—as her spiritual responsibility. She declared that her spiritual purpose would only be fulfilled when every being suffering in this realm was liberated into happiness and peace. She chose to be the protector, guardian and healer for each and every one of us, including humans, lost souls, animals and every other being. As wisdom is one of her key traits, I believe her spiritual intention is entirely realistic, and the enormity of her task gives us a sense of the vastness and power of her being.

Kuan Yin is very gentle, extremely powerful, resourceful and consistent. Her watchful presence is unwavering. I have experienced her grace firsthand many times. She has protected me from people's unscrupulous behaviour, helped me avoid physical danger, provided guidance in my personal life and overseen my working life. She is there for me, for all of us, constantly, unconditionally and with generosity and grace. The positive change she brings continually astonishes me, no matter how many times I experience it personally or see it in the lives of others. Her kindness and effectiveness are buoyant encouragement to let go of fear, doubt and uncertainty and take peaceful refuge in her spiritual grace with absolute trust. The *Buddhist Sūtras* (sacred scriptures) teach us that Kuan Yin is a saving goddess who will help even those who seem most lost. Under the Universal Mother's watch, no-one is left behind. No being is too far gone nor is any circumstance too difficult for her assistance.

The *Lotus Sūtra* is a sacred scripture associated with Kuan Yin. Known as the teaching of the Universal Gateway, the twenty-fifth chapter of the sūtra speaks of Kuan Yin as a benevolent and accessible pathway to spiritual salvation. As an enlightened being dedicated to the liberation of all beings, she is known in Buddhism as a *bodhisattva*. That is a term for a being who uses their spiritual strength to assist others on their path, and in doing so strengthens themselves spiritually. In the *Lotus Sūtra*, the bodhisattva assumes 33 different forms to save people from harm. We will explore those forms in Chapter Three (a nice numerical synchronicity, as 333 is a divine signature of enlightened beings, also referred to as *ascended masters* in various Western spiritual traditions).

Kuan Yin's kindness is so great that one does not need to learn difficult practices, become particularly virtuous, eat certain foods (or avoid certain foods) or become a master of meditation or anything else to benefit from her help. This doesn't mean she is indulgent. It means she knows that human beings trying to become perfect tend to accomplish the opposite! One only needs to consider the fall from grace and the scandals that so many spiritual leaders go through. We need to do our part to grow and live into our potential, but demanding perfection or superiority from ourselves or others is not an expression of wisdom. The ancient Greeks shared their understanding of this in the story of Icarus, who fashioned wings of wax and flew. He loved flying so much, he tried to fly to the sun. I've had dreams of flying. It feels amazing, so I understand his enthusiasm. The symbolism of flight is something we can all relate to. It brings the exhilaration of being temporarily free from otherwise natural and healthy limits. The Icarus-urge can capture us with fantasies of being superhuman, whether that means partying until the wee hours without a thought for the next day or living on adrenaline, thinking we are immune from the need to rest and the sickness that follows if we do not. Of course, what goes up must come down, as those who have had any lesson in humility will know — including Icarus, whose wings melted as he approached the sun and the realm of the gods. It didn't end well for him, as you can imagine. As it turns out, the superhuman is simply human, after all.

The teaching here is that humans are not meant to be gods. We are meant to be human! The Divine within us does not eradicate our need to go through human experiences — the joys as well as the challenges. This is a good thing. Numerous spiritual traditions recognise the human journey as the best for making spiritual progress and approaching enlightened bliss. It has an even better success rate than being a god (according to many Eastern traditions, not all gods are enlightened and not all enlightened beings are gods). We can take that desire to fly high and use it for wiser purposes than avoiding our humanity. We can use it to develop our divine nature through a connection with supportive higher beings. We can allow our sacred relationship with the Universal Mother to help us thrive as spiritual beings having a human experience. We can take delight, we can grow, we can release fear and become a light on this planet. All this is possible for human beings. And we don't have to be perfect to attain it.

Calling Kuan Yin's name with a sincere and believing heart is enough to invoke her assistance. Her response is unconditional. Status, gender, religion or past mistakes are no impediment to her blessing. It is easier to grow spiritually if one is not constantly concerned about material wellbeing, so the benefits of calling upon this divine being are understood to be material as well as spiritual. If financial or other material matters are the main issues you need to heal to overcome obstacles, then she will grant the relevant blessings. This is her unconditional love and wisdom at play. The practices outlined in this book and throughout *The Kuan Yin Transmission*™ can connect you with Kuan Yin in such a way that her presence in your life becomes a beautiful, living and vitalising grace.

Kuan Yin is often pictured wearing white flowing robes and either standing or seated upon an open lotus or with her feet resting upon uprising dragons. This imagery is meant to communicate her purity of heart. She never judges nor turns away, no matter how many times we have found ourselves in the same situation, helplessly repeating our mistakes. She understands how hard it is for humans to break habits of negative thinking and self-defeating behaviours, even if our intentions are good. She recognises how compelling our problems can seem to us, especially when we fixate on them. She knows how to break negative patterns and gives us fresh chances, again and again, if need be.

When we are willing to call upon Kuan Yin sincerely and with complete trust, our life can change dramatically for the better. Although this is simple, most of us have been conditioned to believe in the opposite approach: analyse the problem, then control it until it gives way to what we want to happen. This may work temporarily, but a lot of the time it just makes matters worse. "What you resist persists," as the expression goes.

Trusting Kuan Yin is an easier and more effective way to solve problems. It does require that we grow our spiritual muscles, so we are capable of trusting. For some people, that can be a terrifying prospect, and it is nearly impossible to overcome habitual grasping and the desire to control. Kuan Yin knows this and can help even the most doubtful heart surrender. There only needs to be the slightest inclination, the simple willingness to say her name with a genuine desire for her help. All else will crumble under the power of her grace.

Kuan Yin is frequently depicted with a vase that is said to hold either pure water or healing nectar. In Buddhism, the vase symbolises a holy vessel that contains blessings of wellbeing, abundance, purification, healing and so forth. A Buddhist would call Kuan Yin's vase a *treasure vase*, in that it holds all precious treasures and will provide whatever is needed.

Not long after the release of *The Kuan Yin Oracle*, I undertook a tour through rural Australia. I was facilitating healing circles dedicated to Kuan Yin. Singing her mantras or sacred prayers and channelling guided meditations, I walked about a circle of people gathered to connect with her, feeling filled with her grace. Occasionally, if guided to do so, I would rest a hand in blessing on a participant's shoulder or arm. At one stage, I felt strongly guided to approach a participant, place my hand lightly on her shoulder and gently sing Kuan Yin's mantras, intending that the energy in the sound move into this woman's heart. I did this for a few moments before I felt guided to move on.

After the meditation, the participants shared their experiences. I was intrigued by what that woman had felt. Just after I had sung the mantras, she distinctly felt drops of water on her bare foot. As she still felt the warmth of what she assumed was my hand upon her shoulder, she also assumed I must have knocked over her water bottle, which was near the base of her chair. When she heard me singing from the other side of the room, she had the startling realisation that I had moved on to work with someone else and that neither the warm hand nor the water on her foot had anything to do with me!

I believed the hand at her shoulder and the water drops for which there was no physical explanation were manifestations of blessings from Kuan Yin's own hand and from her treasure vase. Since this woman had yet to learn anything about Kuan Yin and her iconography, these manifestations couldn't be explained away as wishful thinking as she knew nothing about vases, blessings or anything else — although, it was a different matter after the class. Perhaps she needed a startling sign of divine presence, so she could have more faith in Kuan Yin than in the problems she was struggling to resolve. This woman was also open-minded and open-hearted enough to receive such a sign without becoming afraid or doubtful. She simply felt incredibly grateful, awestruck and humble. So, such a blessing was given to her.

It is important that we do not compare our experiences with that of another nor make the erroneous assumption that if someone receives a more dramatic experience of a blessing, then the Divine Mother must love them more or that they are more spiritually advanced. That is such nonsense! For each, the blessing shall be best for the circumstances. There is a beautiful teaching in the tradition of Tara (an emanation of Kuan Yin whom we will meet later in this book) that every being is Tara's child. Not one of Tara's *children*, Tara's *child*. Singular. There can be no preference and no preferential treatment or competition for affection or resources when there is just one. All are assisted to the capacity they can receive. As we grow spiritually—and remember, simply calling her name is a way to bring that about—our capacity to receive increases and hence our capacity to give also increases.

I want to be clear that neither our capacity to receive and give, nor the maturity of our relationship with the Universal Mother, means we will automatically have powerful visions or experiences of her, such as I have described above. Spiritual experiences of that nature are not essential for growth and are not necessarily indicators of spiritual advancement. I don't dismiss the beauty of such moments, and part of my work is to help you be open to such beautiful experiences because I feel they can be enriching and encouraging. However, I don't want you to assume your own or someone else's spiritual capacity is based on having visions or other spiritual encounters. I like to share my own beautiful experiences as encouragement and to reinforce the understanding that the Universal Mother is with us all and capable of much grace. I believe this is why I keep having such experiences, not because of some spiritual superiority, because I don't believe such a thing exists.

Many people do express unique spiritual gifts and abilities, but these creative and fascinating expressions may or may not coincide with advanced spiritual development. I believe the most reliable measure of spiritual growth is how we act. Are we kind, compassionate, wise and free within ourselves and with others? How does our presence affect others? Do we generate fear or confusion? Do others tend to relax and open their hearts when they are with us? Visions and other experiences can be helpful, but they can never replace the development of the heart, which is the true purpose of spiritual growth. This is not an invitation to judge ourselves or others, but rather a loving suggestion to enjoy what can come of this work, whilst taking care not to become overly dazzled by intensely beautiful experiences, nor distracted from what really matters.

Sometimes, Kuan Yin is pictured holding a willow branch. Over thousands of years and across many cultures, the willow has been seen as a protective talisman during dark times. It was thought to bring relief from pain and to trigger healing and recovery. It has symbolised the ability to bend without breaking, thus representing inner strength and the feminine power that allows us to trust we will be okay, even in circumstances we cannot control, and which feel oppressive. Therefore, the willow is a sign of hope that Kuan Yin will lift us out of suffering and into peace. When we are in physical, emotional or psychological pain, the promise of relief can help us let go of fear and concern and allow our healing to happen more swiftly.

As mentioned earlier, Kuan Yin is typically depicted either holding or standing upon a lotus blossom which represents innate spiritual purity. This means that neither Kuan Yin nor the 'Kuan Yin part of us' in our hearts can be made 'bad' nor be deserving of judgement, suffering or disgrace. A saying I heard growing up, "You've made your bed, now you have to lie in it," refers to bearing the consequences of our actions. The Eastern word for this is *karma*. Imagine a parent and child in their garage. As the parent rummages around looking for some important files, the child escapes their attention, climbs a ladder and lays their curious hands on a gun that has been gathering dust on a high shelf for years, all but forgotten until that moment. Maybe it still has a bullet in it, even though the owners thought it was not loaded. The child grabs hold, but the gun slips, hits the ground, fires, and some harm is caused. The result could be damage to an old painting or someone could be killed. There are certain repercussions that far outweigh what is required for learning to take place.

Kuan Yin's protection will never prevent our learning, yet her intervention can transform a situation from devastating to instructive. There are far too many potential dangers in this world, to our hearts and minds, not to mention our bodies, for any of us to be without her. We cannot always know why things happen the way they do, nor can we know what hidden blessings are lurking in otherwise dire circumstance. I believe that with sufficient spiritual skill even great tragedies can be worked through to increase wisdom, courage, commitment or compassion, but I am very much a fan of things not needing to be more difficult than absolutely necessary. And I imagine how much more graceful life would be if we could learn our relevant lessons in a gentler way. I believe the Universal Mother's compassion is such that this can be accomplished.

Kuan Yin's lotus is also a message that the mud won't stick, as the expression goes. So, no matter how much someone may unconsciously act out their own suffering by blaming us, under Kuan Yin's protection, we won't be touched. For sensitive beings, who tend to feel other people's emotional energy and struggle with strong boundaries, Kuan Yin is truly a saving grace.

She teaches that there is a spiritual nature within us that is always stainless, pure and of the light. We may find that hard to believe sometimes — about ourselves or others. Yet, Kuan Yin's lotus flower reassures us of this. It encourages us and asks us to remember what is real. She can help every being realise this part of themselves. This affirmation of our innate, unwavering innocence can help us let go of nightmares of guilt, shame, doubt and anxiety.

Earlier on my personal growth journey, I realised that even though I sometimes really wanted to judge others because I found them annoying or astonishingly mean, if I was to grow spiritually, I shouldn't do it. So, I undertook the process of becoming less judgemental as a discipline as part of becoming a better clairvoyant, better healer and, generally, a better human. When I found myself judging someone or myself, I tried to have more empathy and let the judgement go. I would tell myself that everyone has bad days. Recalling the last time I did something I wasn't proud of would help me feel more compassion towards the object of my disgruntlement! It was an effort, but it did help me to feel kinder and more peaceful in my heart, which I preferred to feeling riled up over someone doing something I didn't consider right. Eventually, I found not having to judge others—or myself—for their behaviour, unexpectedly freeing. It became more natural, and I less often needed to go through the process above to find peace. Judgement puts us in a prison of sorts, and compassion sets us free. It is no wonder that one of the protections afforded by Kuan Yin is freedom for those who are imprisoned in any way.

In one story of Kuan Yin, she manifested as a Chinese princess called Miaoshan. Miaoshan was a bit of a handful. Like any free-spirited being, she rebelled against forces of oppression and control. She incurred her father's wrath by refusing to marry the man he intended for her. What was in her heart was to live a religious life as a nun. Her father's outrage at her continual thwarting of his will led him to order that she be executed for insubordination!

Such severity and violence against those asserting spiritual independence was common in times gone by. I have met several people who are scared to stand up for their true spiritual beliefs. I believe this is due to unresolved past life experiences of being judged, ridiculed, ostracised, excommunicated and, in some instances, tortured or even killed for defying social, political or religious conventions.

Even now, under the guise of political correctness or religious principle, some people attack those whose viewpoints doesn't match their own. This is not Kuan Yin's way. Her way is respectful. It invites us to step out of suffering and into beauty, healing, peace and freedom. She shows us ways to be courageous and effectively overcome ignorance and hate without fuelling the fire. Spiritual healing is about freedom and happiness for all. Taking vengeance or destroying someone, or judging, attacking or criticising another, has nothing to do with spirituality, even if someone slaps a 'spiritual' label on it or says it serves a greater purpose. The end does *not* justify the means on the spiritual path. If we cannot see another way, then we have yet to hand it over to the Divine so a way with spiritual integrity can be created or shown to us.

With such purity in her heart, it turned out Miaoshan could not be killed. Much to his frustration, both the executioner's axe and his sword shattered into a thousand pieces when he tried, and the arrows that were fired at her veered away. He tried to use his hands, and even then, he could not take Miaoshan's life. It was rather a difficult day at work for him.

Out of compassion for the executioner, whom she realised would meet an ill end of his own if he failed in his task, Miaoshan forgave him for trying to execute her. She took on his karma, so he could be free of it. This gave him a real chance to change, rather than remaining trapped under the weight of the negativity he had created. The same idea exists in Christianity with the teaching of Jesus dying on the cross for the sins (which we could perhaps also refer to as negative karma) of humanity. Both traditions recognise that humans can get themselves into trouble, that our capacity to create problems can be greater than our capacity to resolve them, and thus, there are times when we need spiritual intervention.

I believe the aversion many feel towards Jesus is not about him, but about actions that have been carried out in his name by human beings who have fallen prey to the misconception that spiritual superiority exists. The pain this has caused is far reaching, affecting individuals and our culture. The misreading of sacred scriptures in any tradition leads to disaster. In relatively recent history, misinterpretation of scripture has resulted in appalling actions that, if seen with clarity, would be recognised as striking at the heart of the being who inspired the religion, and not in any way supporting the spiritual truths they wished to teach. Personally, I think the true heart of any religion is found in the practice of its mystics. For example, I believe Rumi, the Sufi mystic, expresses the most beautiful, passionate heart of Islam's teaching on surrender to the Divine.

As shown by the mystical vision of Julian of Norwich, who saw Jesus as a mother—and then meditated on the deeper meaning of that for twenty years—Jesus Christ can be experienced as an expression of the Universal Mother. The *Christ consciousness*, as a New Age devotee would refer to it, is an expression of the Universal Mother. She is not limited to one of her faces but shines through them all. Her heart *is* Kuan Yin, the goddess Isis, Mother Mary, Kali and Tara, amongst others. If it is Jesus who opens your heart to divine love, wonderful. If your heart seeks sanctuary in other divine beings (instead or as well as) that is also wonderful and appropriate and blessed and just as it is meant to be for your life journey.

It is interesting that the five emanations of the Universal Mother—Kuan Yin, Tara, Isis, Mary and Kali—are those who were clearly destined to be included in this work. I didn't choose them. Their appearance in all my notes and in a series of synchronicities and emails from other people confirmed their inclusion from the very beginning. I believe the Universal Mother is meeting the deep, if not fully conscious, need of many souls on Earth at this time. In the rising of the sacred feminine, she brings us generosity, grace and goodness, which support our increased capacity for courage and rebirth. The Universal Mother will take forms that work for all beings, as long as human confusion and violence continues.

The dark side of religion can create tremendous pain, which may manifest as anger, fear or judgement. As Hindu Saint Ramakrishna said, "Religion is like a cow; it kicks, but it also gives milk." While a religious path may be a beautiful (or challenging but still ultimately helpful) facet of your life path, your spiritual journey need not be compromised by the absence of a religious path. The absence of a religious path may even enhance your journey. This depends not on the perceived value of the religion but on what is needed for your spiritual growth.

Our souls know what we need. Just like our bodies crave foods that contain vitamins or minerals we are deficient in, or the way the innate intelligence in cows guides them to feed on the most nutritious grasses, we are drawn to what nourishes us. This may exclude, perhaps, the occasional slip into a chocolate binge or other 'learning opportunities' like dating a string of people who are bad for you. The Universal Mother shows herself in various forms—male and female, fierce and tender—because we each have different needs to be met in different ways. If we trust that, rather than second guessing it, our 'learning opportunities' can be softened into greater grace.

Let's return to that feisty and magical minx Princess Miaoshan. After taking on the executioner's negative karma, she descended into the hell realms. In some stories, she rode in on the back of a supernatural tiger, as one does. However, rather than suffering there, she played music and sang and began transforming hell into paradise, liberating many souls by purifying their karma and opening their way to heaven. One of Kuan Yin's titles is *Universal Gateway*. This reflects the effect of Kuan Yin's energy in our lives — she transforms darkness into light. She becomes the spiritual portal through which we can leave a life of suffering and experience a new way. She was so effective at liberating others that Yama, the Tibetan lord of the hell realms, promptly demanded she leave whilst he still had a hell to govern. So, Princess Miaoshan ascended to blissful realms, no doubt singing and dancing all the way. Kuan Yin, however, continued to manifest herself in various forms to assist all in need.

The *Buddhist Sūtras* teach that there are 33 forms the bodhisattva of compassion can take, but I believe that number is symbolic, that there are unlimited forms. The master number 33 signifies the endless creative power, devotion and service of the Divine. You can learn more about that in my book *Messages in the Numbers* if you wish. I do feel the 33 forms have special relevance and are powerful, so I've outlined them in this book. There's a difference between thinking the Divine Mother can help us with anything and reading the ways the wisdom traditions from which Kuan Yin emerged into human awareness has articulated her powers. I feel exposure to such teachings can help generate a more unconditional quality of trust in our hearts.

Some teachings say all forms of compassion are Kuan Yin in disguise. That could include saints, goddesses and the kindly stranger who lets you know when you've dropped your wallet. When we practice compassion, we grow the presence of Kuan Yin

within us and our world. I like this teaching because it is simple, practical and effective.

As articulated in the Buddhist tradition, the emanations of Kuan Yin manifest in whatever gender or personality is needed. I love the freedom in that. She is unrestricted in her capacity to assist. She may show up as a gentle mother or tender father to guide us, a best friend to encourage or a warrior to empower us. Maybe we need a king to inspire us to take full responsibility for our lives, or our own version of a ferocious but protective monster, more fearsome than our greatest fears, to chase away the darkness and give us the courage to step up — like Sully in the animated movie *Monsters, Inc.*

In Tibet in particular, Kuan Yin is known not as a divine mother, but as a divine father bodhisattva or saviour being called Avalokiteshvara (in Sanskrit) or Chenrezig (in Tibetan). Some Tibetan teachers see Kuan Yin as a combination of Chenrezig and Tara (another Tibetan goddess whom I see as an emanation of Kuan Yin). Other Buddhists (especially, in Japan and China) see Kuan Yin as the Chinese version of Avalokiteshvara, which is how I personally experience her and what historians generally take to be the case. Kuan Yin is known by many different names: Kannon in Japan, Quan Am in Vietnam and Guan Yin in Malaysia, for example.

No matter the tradition this divine being comes from, the many names of Kuan Yin translate the same. Essentially, the name means, *the one who hears the cries of the world.* The story associated with this meaning tells us that Kuan Yin was so luminous with spiritual grace and purity of heart that she was ready to ascend into heaven, never to return to the realms of suffering again. As she was about to step over the edge of the world into complete bliss, she heard a sound that tugged at her heart. It was the cries of the world she was hearing. She made a vow to postpone her final ascension until all beings were freed from such suffering.

Kuan Yin is typically pictured with two arms but can also be depicted with a thousand arms and sometimes, also, with eleven faces. There is a story about how Maha Kuan Yin of a thousand arms and eleven heads came into being. Despite her great effort, there were still so many beings suffering. Kuan Yin's arms could not move as effectively and efficiently as she wished. Amitabha, the Buddha of Infinite Light who is often pictured sitting in Kuan Yin's headdress, provided her with one thousand arms, so she could reach all those in need. Amitabha also granted Kuan Yin eleven heads (a sacred number that signifies divine blessing and calibration into higher consciousness) so she could more easily see and hear those who needed her help. In some stories, it is said that Tara (a powerful goddess and emanation of Kuan Yin, with numerous emanations of her own in various colours—green, white, orange, red, blue and black—which we will explore later on) rose up out of Kuan Yin's tears of compassion.

The number 1000 is symbolic (so you don't have to worry that you or a loved one in need of her help might be the 1001st in the queue). Her multiple faces and arms signify the ways the Divine's unlimited and responsive nature overcomes the limitations that humans tend to perceive.

There is something profoundly encouraging about knowing that whatever we need, whatever will work, the Universal Mother can and will provide for us. Just as different physical problems can be resolved with different medicines, different kinds of suffering need different kinds of assistance. In Tibetan shamanism, this would be called *dza* — the spontaneous arising of divine qualities in response to what is needed.

We don't have to be afraid of feeling need, vulnerability or even the desire to have certain things in life. The problem is typically our attachment—our clinging to the how and when and where and with whom—which creates the suffering. But asking for help and then allowing the Universe to 'do its thing' can bring far greater benefits than simply the fulfilment of one person's desire. Remember earlier we talked about the genius of the Divine being able to simultaneously serve all needs rather than some at the expense of others?

Many years ago, I decided I wanted to venture beyond Australia and teach in the United States. Actually, I decided I wanted to teach all over the world, which began to happen in due course. The United States, however, took a while. It wasn't until a vibrant young American woman who worked in a metaphysical centre in California bought a set of my oracle cards that things began to stir. She was so moved by them, that she stocked them in the store, told everyone about them and, finally, declared to her colleagues that she was, and I quote, "... going to manifest the shit out of Alana Fairchild coming here." Her intention and desire were the pull I needed to fulfil my vision, and my desire and intention were the pull she needed to manifest her vision. Unbeknownst to either of us, others felt the same way. When I finally began working in the United States, beautiful souls told me they had been praying for me to teach there. Mutual need generated the motion, opened the channel, created space for the divine response and set things in motion.

In the fulfilment of your soul, lies the seeds for the fulfilment of all souls. Understanding this eradicates the need for guilt or holding oneself back from receiving. Rather than creating a license for unchecked greed, which comes from the fear that you will not receive so you must 'take' as much as you can by any means and at any cost, this shift in attitude can help us let go more easily. This, in turn, creates more space to receive what is rightfully meant for us, which, in turn, will benefit others. Such results are typically so much more wonderful than our limited perspective can imagine in even our most optimistic and inventive moments.

I believe that dza, the divine outpouring in response to need, manifests in all areas of human existence. Our human need that cries out—saying for example, "Why isn't there a cure for this disease?"—generates the spiritual grace necessary for discoveries in medical science. The intense desire for effective treatment (in patients, in researchers, in doctors, even in pharmaceutical companies which may be more motivated financially than spiritually) magnetises the needed awareness from the spiritual planes into human consciousness. Breakthroughs happen, understanding unfolds and a new way is found.

Does this mean the Divine doesn't give us what we need or want until we beg for it? No. The Divine is constantly bestowing blessings because that is its nature. But our desire gives us the motivation, the nudge we need to open ourselves and reach for it. When our desire for change becomes greater than our need to have things remain within our control, the Divine is given space in which it can manifest something new on our behalf.

Otherwise, it's as if we are sitting under a rainfall of divine nectar with our mouths closed, distractedly playing on our phones, whilst it runs off us uselessly. When we recognise we are thirsty, we will realise the need and opportunity for quenching that thirst, open our mouths and take it in.

The spiritual tragedy of many otherwise privileged people is ignorance of their own suffering. Suffering can be remedied by the Universal Mother, but how can a person be encouraged to take medicine if they do not even acknowledge that they are ill? As my grandmother used to say, "You can lead a horse to water, but you can't make him drink."

There is a rare medical condition where a person cannot feel physical pain. This may seem beneficial to those who only associate pain with negativity. However, living with such a condition is fraught with danger. Pain indicates that something is not okay. For example, it tells us to quickly remove our hand from a hot object to avoid being burned. In the modern world, many people suffer from an equivalent condition on an emotional level. They are numb to their authentic inner pain. Without the capacity to recognise our pain (physical or emotional), we cannot know we are suffering and therefore cannot know that we need to change our course and seek a remedy. It may seem blissful to be ignorant, but the harm done by unchecked suffering will continue even if we are not aware of it. This causes inner and outer havoc until we have no choice but to face it, by which time it may seem intimidating to tackle or even impossible to overcome.

In the example of suicide, it is often the case that no-one saw it coming. A person who takes their own life may appear to be a vibrant and engaged member of society, they may have attained the type of success to which others aspire. It is assumed that they have made it, and by our generally superficial mainstream priorities, perhaps they had indeed done so. Yet, when the state of the soul is not honoured, pain will be accumulating inside, even if the person themselves cannot recognise it.

That is not the problem of the individual, but of a spiritually-deficient culture in which the inner reality of the soul is neither sought out nor understood. When everything seems fine on the surface, it is not necessarily because all is well within the soul. It seems like the pain of the individual, but they are experiencing a side effect of what is going on in our human collective. It is akin to how a condition of the blood may manifest in a condition of the skin. You may not understand the cause by looking at the surface of the skin and treatment of the symptom never resolves the actual cause, which is condition of the blood. If you clear and heal the blood, there is no condition of the skin to contend with anymore, as the system has become healthy.

Pain is not something to be ashamed of, but rather something to be explored to unearth the truth hiding at its core. To feel pain, we need the courage and willingness to connect with our bodies, with our inner soul truths, to what is really going on in the depths, to not judge ourselves or others by how 'together' we appear to be on the surface. That is a soul journey in itself.

It is not enough to be in touch with that pain. There also needs to be spiritual space where our truths can be expressed and held. In modern culture, recognition of the importance of such space and the knowledge of how to cultivate it, is generally absent — unless one has been trained as a therapist or healer, for example. Even if you understood how helpful it is, without access to your own inner spaciousness, it is impossible to hold space for others. You cannot give what you don't have. Connecting with the Universal Mother can teach us how to grow our capacity to experience and hold sacred space within ourselves and for those around us. As we are guided on our authentic soul journey, qualities like compassion, wisdom, courage, goodwill and generosity of spirit are developed.

Society's general inability to access or hold compassionate space for suffering, with respect and non-judgement, contributes to a collective disconnection from the inner reality of the soul. To understand this, think about a time when you didn't know you needed a hug until someone opened their arms to you, and suddenly a genuine need for reassurance and comfort rose to the surface. Maybe you didn't know what you felt until you were held in loving arms, safe enough to let yourself *feel*. Now, imagine living in a society where even the concept of giving a hug was not understood, let alone practiced. You would be the same person, with the same inner need, carrying on through life, keeping all that feeling and any connected pain and confusion inside — until it accumulated to the point that it could no longer be held within. It might then manifest externally, in more extreme cases as disease or acting out in some terrible way such as harming oneself or others.

The spiritual quality of consciously-held space is even more powerful than a hug. It is the permission to be real, honest, open, and to feel safe and held in doing so. Such spiritual space may be defined as unconditional love with presence, patience, non-judgement, discernment, fearlessness and wisdom. It is so powerful and so important that despite its invisible and intangible nature, healing cannot happen without it. If one does hold such a space, healing can happen even if nothing else is said or spoken about.

Sacred space is a powerful field of energy. It empowers us to recognise and deal with what is really going on. I believe the absence of this space is evidence of the societal spiritual dysfunction behind the high rates of suicide. The pain within the heart of someone who is suicidal is the pain that, as a society, we are yet to understand, acknowledge and integrate. As we honour, learn about and practice holding compassionate space for ourselves and others, we can begin to heal the underlying cause of suicide, depression, terrorism, and so on. As Kali, the Universal Mother is particularly adept at helping us learn how to cultivate spiritual spaciousness within and around us.

Being able to feel the pain *and* have it held in a compassionate and wise spiritual space is the way for dza, or divine remedy, to flow. Without connection to authentic pain, we cannot heal. We cannot even recognise that we need to heal and therefore cannot reach out to receive dza. The gift of the Universal Mother is that in being in touch with our pain brings us into her remedy. Rather than avoiding it until it builds into tragedy, we move through it and gain blessings of wisdom and freedom in the process. Like any real spiritual attainment, there is much that we can do individually, according to our capacity, but we can only accomplish this great task of healing together.

We shouldn't hold back from asking the Universe to help us, others, anyone and any being in need. Asking supports the process of dza. It helps open a channel of grace for the greater benefit of all beings.

This is why it is important not to fall into the trap of believing that if your life improves others will suffer. That belief is based on a consciousness of lack, which belongs to the world of ego and is inaccurate. Poverty consciousness believes there is not enough to go around. It focuses on separation — the idea that someone can only win at another's expense. In spiritual terms, this is just not possible. That would be like saying you can restore the health of one organ by cutting out another organ. Spirituality reminds us that we are all part of one body. When any individual part wins, our overall health improves.

We don't have to understand or predict how dza is going to work in order to trust in it. The spontaneous divine outpouring is not only compassionate, but wise. In that wisdom, it can work without the obstacles we tend to focus upon. We only need to open the channel, to provide the space and make the request. The Divine handles the rest. In our willingness and surrender, we become the fingertips of the divine hand, moving in harmony with a higher intelligence who knows how to get things done.

Getting things done means that gentle Kuan Yin will sometimes strap on her combat boots and show up as wrathful goddess Kali to confront any demons in our minds that need to be brought under control. Unless you are a Hindu or Buddhist, you may not be familiar with the idea of a divine being suddenly switching it up and emanating him- or herself in a different form. If negative forces threaten the beloved ones under a peaceful deity's protection, they can become a wrathful badass version of themselves.

The Hindus are, to my mind, the most fantastic purveyors of this multifaceted, shapeshifting, divine-emanation worldview. As a child, I loved their various gods and goddesses. It never occurred to me to feel conflict with my Christian upbringing. Similarly, whilst I respected my beloved grandmother's Catholic religious path, I didn't feel any sense of separation from God, Mother Mary, Jesus—or Kali and the slew of other divine beings I loved—when I renounced all religious affiliations as a young woman at university. My spiritual path deepened as a result. I realised that my natural love for divine beings in all religious traditions wasn't blasphemous or weird, it was just open-minded ... a gift, even. That open-mindedness helped me understand this could be the case for others, too, if they were so inclined.

So, if we weren't born Buddhist and don't particularly feel a desire to convert, we can still connect with Tara, Buddha or Kuan Yin. Likewise, if we weren't born Hindu, we can connect with Kali or the rock god and intoxicating pleasure-creator known as Krishna. Same if we weren't raised Catholic but feel drawn to Mother Mary, perhaps to the astonishment of our Christian friends or pagan relatives! It is absolutely fine. Or, if we weren't born Christian, and don't want to convert to Christianity but just want to love Jesus, that is fine, and an effective spiritual path, too.

The Divine puts no boundaries or limitations upon us in terms of how we love God. What matters is that it is genuine to our hearts, not what anyone else thinks about it. The Divine is constantly evolving and expressing itself in myriad forms, so every being can become happy and free. The only limitations are those we create and impose upon ourselves and each other.

Kuan Yin can assist us at a spiritual level, helping us let go of judgement and, perhaps in doing so, gain some wisdom. As we become less attached to how we think things should happen and, instead, trust in the flow of life itself, we become happier. Kuan Yin can purify us and help us overcome negative emotional and psychological conditioning, so we aren't torturing ourselves internally by interpreting everything that happens or doesn't happen to mean something dire about who we are — that we are undeserving, unworthy, abandoned, neglected and so forth. She can help us find the equanimity and trust required to weather the storms of life, whilst being willing to take chances and live more fearlessly from the heart. Kuan Yin can help us become more vital, alive and free. She is an inner healer and guardian.

She is also known in some forms—namely, White Tara, whom we will meet in this book—as the Wish-Fulfilling Gem. In masculine form as the four-armed Avalokiteshvara, the gem is depicted as a crystal and held between his hands in front of his heart. Hinduism and Buddhism abound with the notion of blessings for wish fulfilment: wish-fulfilling gem, wish-fulfilling cow, wish-fulfilling tree, wish-fulfilling chakra. Perhaps this is because the fulfilment of our wishes, far from turning us into ego-driven brats, can help us realise the fundamentally abundant nature of the Universe so we can stop grasping so hard. We may realise we have so much already, and there is so much more available to us, that we shift into gratitude. This relaxes the heart and mind, so we can tune in to our inner guidance more easily and create a more loving life path in this world.

Kuan Yin is a spiritual being who helps us at a spiritual level, but she is also a very involved, effective, physical-world healer and is able to assist us in very practical ways. She has forms specifically associated with protecting us when we are under attack

and with generating material prosperity, so we don't worry about money and can get on with what Buddhists and Hindus considered the rather more important work of our spiritual practice.

She has helped me with everything from my love life (and trust me, that has *really* needed some help over the years) to my finances, career and even finding the best place for me to live. She helps me deal with every possible practical issue I am willing to hand over to her. I got over the mental obstacle that some things were not spiritual enough to request her assistance for by recognising that the less I worried about mundane matters the more energy I had to complete my creative projects to assist people on their spiritual path. So, from finding parking spaces, to dealing with conflicts, to the timing of my day, to summoning the integrity, courage and clarity to make tough decisions in life, she is there, shining a light and creating a way forward for me to take, if I so choose.

My spiritual guidance asked me to create this project two years before the writing commenced. I accepted it but had no idea what it was going to be. I needed to follow many twists and turns—including a visit to Tibet—so I could learn all I needed to bring it through.

In Tibet, I had to contend with governmental regulations, along with the needs of thirty people from all over the world who had come on retreat with me. It was an amazing, and sometimes deeply challenging, experience for us all. I will talk about the sacred moments of blessing, which imparted the empowerment for this program, at the end of the book as a nice little end note from which we can part with the joy and grace of spiritual light in our hearts. However, there were a few hairy moments in between! Times like those—when I am feeling most vulnerable and need some intervention—are the moments when I really see the Divine at work in my life. These moments illustrate why we don't need to be scared when we aren't in control. They are the moments when the doorway opens for the Divine to step in and show us heart-melting, reassuring grace. The times when we feel the most vulnerable can become the times when we are the most spiritually empowered.

Leading a retreat through Nepal and into Tibet was challenging on a number of levels. The altitude, especially in Tibet, was a lot to physically deal with. (I'll spare you the details of the emotional distress that arose from the 'rudimentary toilets' in the wilds of the Himalayas.) The erosion of the Tibetan culture was psychologically difficult to witness. Nonetheless, the spiritual energy of the Himalayas—and the lake and glacier we visited, in particular—radiated the most astonishing purity I had ever experienced on this earth. I have been fortunate enough to visit an abundance of powerful sacred sites in Australia and India, yet Tibet took the notion of sacredness to an entirely new level. India feels like sacred ground to me, and Tibet feels like sacred space. I mention this, because I don't want to put you off if you feel drawn to visit Tibet. That draw, just like an attraction to India, is a call of the soul and, when answered, a call I believe can result in the dispensation of life-changing grace. Travelling there does require courage and spiritual protection, however. Whilst we felt safe, we were challenged at moments by various bureaucratic requirements. Some of this I expected, but, given that the retreat was dedicated to an emanation of Kuan Yin known as Tara, I knew she would help us manage the processes.

The rules and regulations required to enter Tibet changed so often we didn't know whether the paperwork the travel advisor gave us one day would be acceptable to the Chinese government officials the following day. This caused more than a modicum of stress for my retreat manager, who was doing his best to make sure a large group of people from various countries had the most up-to-date paperwork.

Standing before the immigration officer at the entry point into Lhasa, even though he was friendly and professional, felt intense. I handed over my paperwork and passport, which he briefly surveyed and stamped, but then he gave me one of the forms back. He said, "If you return to China, remember, if you are on a group visa," which was a requirement for our group to enter Tibet, "you don't need this white form." He suggested I toss it in the bin, which I did. I idly wondered why he had told me that, when the rules changed so often it would likely be a different story if I did return, but I mentally 'filed it away' nonetheless, and proceeded through immigration.

During our retreat, which began in Nepal and finished in Tibet, we had an altar set up. I had arrived in Nepal earlier than the rest of the group. I typically do this. It helps me get a sense of the spiritual energy of a place, especially when I have not visited previously, and it also allows me a chance to adjust to the time zone and altitude and whatever else is necessary for my mind, body and energy field to hold the additional weight of the group field, once the retreat officially begins.

I loved wandering about the streets of Kathmandu. Although it is a dusty and chaotic place, and downtown Kathmandu has dangerously high levels of air pollution (many people wear surgical masks on the streets), the area of Thamel, where I stayed, was relatively calm and clean, yet still vibrant and crazy enough to feel like Nepal. The blend of Indian and Tibetan cultures, along with Nepal's unique quality, made it a most fascinating place to visit.

I attended some yoga studios when I was in Nepal, but mostly did my own private *vinyasa* flow practice in a small, dedicated studio within the hotel complex where I was staying. At the front of the studio was a statue of a divine being. He held an object between his palms and wore a beatific smile under his half-closed eyes. Although the hotel was fully booked, whenever I went to do my yoga practice, I had the room entirely to myself. It was just me, the noise of cats prowling in the alley behind the studio, my yoga practice and this beautiful, big brass statue of a mysterious Buddha.

The deeper I went into my practice, with the spiritual energy of Nepal supporting the process in a palpable way, the more I felt the statue emanating a presence of overwhelming love. I began to look forward to my yoga practice, not just for the usual benefits it brings to my body and mind, but because I was going to spend time with this being. I recognised that the statue had been blessed at some stage, because its energy was very active. It filled the space. I was no longer doing a solo yoga practice in that small studio. I was communing with a divine being of limitless love—I was hanging out with a great and true friend. I was surprised at how personal it felt.

One day, at the end of my practice, I was resting in *savasana*, which means *corpse pose*. This is where you lie as still as possible on your back, allowing the effects of the yoga *asanas* (postures) to integrate. In that state of deep quiet and restfulness, I became aware of a white and pink light gathering above my head. It was heart-meltingly beautiful. Just feeling it, watching it, being in it was bliss. After some time passed, I realised the energy was the heart energy of the divine being in the room with me. I then also realised I had been communing with this same being for years! In Nepal, the divine presence was so amplified (and yet still so gentle) that it startled me, and it took me a few moments to realise the being was actually Kuan Yin. I could tell by the feeling of it, whereas I couldn't tell by the form of the statue of an unknown Buddha, lovely as he was.

I sat up from my savasana with hands in prayer, gazing at the statue through new eyes and with a sense of wonder. I just knew without knowing that the statue was Avalokiteshvara and that he held the wish-fulfilling gem between his hands. This was Kuan Yin, too.

I was overcome with the emotion of just how much this being loves us all. I wanted to share the moment with others. I knew I'd write about it in this book, eventually, but I also wanted to share it on social media, so I took a picture of the statue. As I went to upload the photograph from my phone later that day, I noticed the number of the photo on my phone just happened to be 3303. There was that sacred number three again.

My experience inspired me to go out and find a crystal just like the one Avalokiteshvara—or Kuan Yin—was holding, for the altar at the retreat. I knew if it was meant to be, I would find it, even though it was a peculiar shape. It wasn't round like most crystal balls nor an egg-shape either. It was a perfect Shiva *lingam*, an oval/bullet shape that would fit between my human hands just as the crystal fit between Avalokiteshvara's hands in the statue. A short walk around the corner, and I spotted it in a store window. Wondering if I was going to have to go through the much-dreaded bargaining process after being quoted ridiculously inflated prices (Thamel is known for being a tourist trap), I was pleasantly surprised that the whole encounter was relatively quick and painless. Somehow, the Divine empowered me with respectful but effective bargaining techniques I had not been able to summon previously (nor would likely be able to summon again).

This lovely but not particularly noteworthy crystal attracted an unexpected amount of attention, which I would have preferred to avoid, but which also helped me practice trust. To leave China at the end of the retreat, before flying to the United States to complete a teaching tour, I had to take two flights — one from Lhasa to Beijing and one out of Beijing. I had packed the crystal in my carry-on luggage, feeling that it would be less prone to damage than if it was packed in my checked bag. As I went through the checkpoint to have my carry-on luggage scanned, my bag was pulled aside, and a gruff customs officer called me over. I opened my bag under her instructions, and she grabbed the crystal, unwrapping it and holding it up to the light. I had a sudden flash of intuition that she was considering how she might confiscate it. I silently began repeating Tara mantras in my head.

"You cannot have this in your carry-on luggage," she began, but before she could finish the sentence, her colleague came over from the scanning machine and said, "It's fine this time, just keep it in your bag and don't take it out." I wasn't sure what the danger could be with a piece of crystal on board a cabin. Maybe there had been a crackdown on psychics doing mid-air predictions! I kept my musings to myself, silently thanked Tara for her intervention and swiftly repacked my bag, agreeing to follow the customs officer's instructions. When my flight landed in Beijing, having learned from my experience, I unpacked the crystal from my carry on and packed it into my checked baggage. Given that I had to go through the entire check-in process again to get out of China, which left me with a very short time to make my flight, I was glad I did. As I passed through the next series of security checkpoints, I noticed a sign I had never seen before: *No crystal balls in carry-on luggage*! If I hadn't had the earlier experience, which led me to remove the crystal from my carry on, I would not have had time to go back, relocate my luggage (if that was even possible) and repack it. The crystal may well have been confiscated after all. I breathed a thankful sigh of relief for the previous encounter and for having had the common sense/intuition to take it to heart, so I was able to proceed drama-free through the next security checkpoint.

Then it was a matter of getting through immigration to leave the country. I expected leaving China would be easier, offering fewer hoops to jump through, with visas and such, than we'd had to get in. Turns out it was the opposite. As I approached the immigration officer's desk and handed over my paperwork and passport, she asked me for the white form I had thrown away at the immigration point when I first entered China.

Suddenly, that apparently random piece of information the immigration officer had given me upon entry into China came back to me. Turns out it wasn't random or useless at all, but an important piece of information I would need in a future situation. I believe the Divine grants us this sort of 'preventative grace' often. We just don't always recognise it.

"You don't need the white form on a group visa," I said calmly. The customs officer didn't seem to like this response. Concerned she was going to deny my right to leave the country, I silently began to chant Tara mantras. A short moment later, another customs officer walked right by me. The first official with my paperwork slammed the group visa form against the glass partition at the front of her cubicle and called out something to him. "Yes, of course! It's fine!" he happily replied in English, before continuing on his way.

She waited long moments before stamping my passport. I silently chanted the whole time, and eventually I was free to leave. I later found out that a retreat participant who had decided to stay on for several days after the retreat had similar issues but was actually detained. They had to go through a process of reissuing paperwork and was not able to leave the country for three days. Without Tara providing what I needed before I even knew I needed it, my own experience could have gone rather differently. I hope the retreat participant who was detained is practicing her Tara mantras to minimise any future dramas or avoid them altogether. I share the Tara mantras with you in Chapter Five.

Kuan Yin, as Tara, as Avalokiteshvara, and as you'll see in this book, as Mother Mary and Goddess Isis, and as many other forms, is able to help us in so many practical ways. Let us explore some of those specifically, in the next chapter.

CHAPTER TWO

THE TEN SACRED PROTECTIONS OF KUAN YIN

ALTHOUGH KUAN YIN'S POWER IS UNLIMITED, THE *LOTUS SŪTRAS* reveal ten specific deliverances Kuan Yin provides for those who call upon her name. The language is peculiar to a Tibetan cosmological viewpoint, featuring references to evil beasts and great infernos but with a little lateral thought, we can see how those protections are incredibly relevant to our everyday lives.

THE FIRST PROTECTION: PROTECTION FROM DANGERS OF FIRE

The protection from fire can be interpreted literally and symbolically. Spiritually, the symbolism of fire can relate to purification. For example, when we undertake a physical detoxification program, do inner emotional work with a therapist or journal or say mantras to purify our minds so we are able to meditate with less mental distraction. Even meditation on its own will begin a mental and emotional detoxification process as the 'karmic rubbish' we carry around as repeated anxious or judgemental thought patterns rises to the surface to be witnessed and, with Kuan Yin's assistance, purified and released. We are also purifying when we undergo shedding processes in our lives, perhaps by walking away from toxic relationships or negative habits.

No matter how we are purifying, these processes can be difficult. Various symptoms can arise. They may take the form of physical discomfort as toxins are released and eliminated. They may also appear as a natural resistance to the process of healing and the resulting change which may take us into unfamiliar and uncomfortable territory. Maybe our sense of identity has been caught up in certain abusive patterns and we aren't sure who we will be and how we'll relate to others (or how they will relate to us) if we evolve into a more clear and empowered way of being. So, we can resist—or altogether avoid—the purification process from deep-seated fears which may manifest or increase our suffering as we release what has been.

Whether that resistance feels like it comes from within or from those who don't want us to change, Kuan Yin can help. Spiritual protection during such a time can ensure the purification process can run its course and provide the greatest benefits for all, whilst taking the edge off—or, in some cases, completely eliminating—the more challenging aspects of the process. We can be become warmed enough to cook, in a spiritual sense, but not be painfully burned.

Fire can also symbolise jealousy, anger, vengeance and passion. Spiritual protection from these emotions provides us with a layer of psychic defence that allows us to maintain equilibrium and, protect our mind from becoming susceptible to negativity. Those emotions may be our own or our projections towards others. Perhaps someone is jealous because they are insecure about some aspect of their own lives. Comparing themselves to you, they torture themselves with thoughts that they are lacking in some way. This sad state of being may be too difficult for them to process, so they react without awareness, perhaps angrily trying to tear you down to ease their own pain. Or perhaps you have fallen into this miserable trap yourself. It's no fun, no matter which side of the interaction you are on.

Several years ago, I was asked to speak at a metaphysical festival and facilitate some events in rural Australia. As I would be away from home for a prolonged period, and because I was realising my romantic relationship at the time needed to end, I felt quite vulnerable. I found meditating on Tara (as mentioned, an emanation of Kuan Yin) each morning helped enormously to support me personally and professionally. The work was proceeding well, and I was happy with what was taking place.

It was not my first visit to the area. The year before, I had attended a festival there, singing and providing healing and workshops, which had gone very well. However, the energy in that place was difficult to manage. It was an active mining town. Mining tends to open not just the earth but issues for those that live in such places — at least that is my experience of working in several Australian mining towns. A number of the miners were struggling with depression, addiction and rage. Their wives were often dealing with the combination of having an abundant income and enjoyable material lifestyle but a deficiency of emotional intimacy with their spouses. These women sometimes sought the beauty of New Age teachings to support them as they processed the complexities of what was going on in their heart, their marriage and their town. In short, it was not an easy place to be, nor was it easy to handle the energies there. I suspect this is part of the reason so many lightworkers and healers end up living in these parts. They tend to go where they are needed.

During my first visit to that town, I met a very well-known metaphysical practitioner. This woman had appeared in the local media and had a reputation for being a great psychic. She approached me, full of enthusiasm for me and my work. I was delighted to meet such a positive spirit, and we chatted a little, and then I went on with my work. When I returned the following year, it was a different story. This woman had not had an easy year. Her finances were a particular issue. I could empathise. I was raised in a family where financial fear was palpable, and it had left a mark in my soul that took many years of inner work to heal. I knew only too well what it felt to fear for your material wellbeing. I also knew how marvellous the Divine is at solving any issues we have — but the journey to trust can take some time.

One morning, during my meditations on Tara, I had a particularly intense and blissful experience of her. I couldn't explain it, because I wasn't doing anything differently. I just accepted it as a gift and felt grateful. A short time later, I saw the woman who was organising the workshops for me at her computer. She had a pained expression on her face. "You are not going to like this," she said, "but I think you should see it." The psychic woman, who had once idealised me, had gone to the other extreme (as tends to happen when one puts you on a pedestal; the urge to kick it out from underneath you eventually follows suit!). At the exact moment I had been in bliss with Tara, she had been posting some particularly nasty and vitriolic comments about me on social media. I don't often experience trolling—I've been fortunate in that regard—but it does happen, and this was one of the uglier examples of it. I was saddened, but I recognised it was her issue. I felt I needed to respond to it, calmly and clearly. And I did so, making the connection between Tara's increased energy in my meditation and the time the post was written. I felt it would be okay. I was protected.

The following day, it happened again. Again, it coincided with an unexpected and sudden surge in Tara's blissful energy overcoming my heart with great joy in meditation. It was so long ago that I cannot remember if I responded to the woman again or not, before then blocking her on social media. I wished nothing but the best for her, but I wasn't interested in engaging with someone who had no interest in taking responsibility for their own feelings and pain and was instead attacking others. I couldn't help such a person. I have no idea what happened to that woman. I never heard from her, nor about her, again. I hope there is peace in her heart.

Passion can be a marvellous fire in our bellies, inspiring us to be courageous and creative in the manifestation of our most exciting inner visions. I personally find I am willing to move mountains for what (and whom) I love. This sort of passionate energy could bring much benefit to the world. It could benefit the children who see their parent/s empowered and open to life. It could help in the fulfilment of your spiritual destiny and thus benefit all the beings your fulfillment will assist. However, if that passion takes over your life to the point that your relationships fail, that peace of mind, patience, trust and equanimity cannot prevail, then your fire may be burning so bright that you are creating imbalance — burning yourself out, instead of radiating your inner light. That may lead to unnecessary illness and suffering. This, then, is another example of a situation in which Kuan Yin's spiritual protection regarding symbolic fire can assist us by preventing such difficulties and helping us develop equanimity right alongside our passion. Passionate people, such as myself, can be impatient and easily frustrated. It goes side by side with all that inner fire! Learning how to create peace and equanimity within one's own heart and mind gives us the steadying influence we need to last the long haul in manifesting our vision and not giving up in dramatic declarations of defeat.

The sūtra goes like this:

If there are people who wish to harm you
by pushing you into the great pit of inferno,
think of the power of Bodhisattva Avalokiteshvara;
the inferno pit will be transformed into a water pond.

—*Lotus Sūtra* 25: 2.3

THE SECOND PROTECTION: DELIVERANCE FROM DANGERS OF WATER

There is the literal need for protection in the realm of water. Drownings, tsunamis and flooding are very real threats to person and property for many of us. Mother Nature can be fierce! Even so, our need for deliverance from the symbolic dangers of water are far more commonplace.

The water element in Tibetan medicine relates to the skin, purification and the healing of diseases such as cancer. Hydration is essential for our wellbeing. Clean drinking water is not always readily available. Even though I live in Australia, which has a relatively high standard of living, for health reasons, I purchased a water filter. A separate protection for poisons is outlined in the *Lotus Sūtra*, however, which implies that this protection must relate to something more.

Water signifies the literal fluids of our physical bodies and the health of our oceans and rivers, which in turn have a profound effect on the cleanliness or disease of our physical bodies, and, therefore, cleansing and purification on a physical level. Water also signifies emotional and psychic cleansing, which also (eventually) influence our physical bodies. I don't mean just in the sense that a negative mindset will make you feel grumpy or tired. Over time, a psychic wound will fester unless it is treated. We may not be aware of its existence until it manifests in a physical problem — unless we meditate or do inner healing work on our emotional states and begin to sense where our energy field is consistently out of balance.

I have personally had deeply unconscious wounds surface as states of imbalance in my body. In working with my body, I needed to recognise and repair the emotional foundation for my physical health to return. It didn't matter how much I worked on the physical, unless I also worked on the emotional side of things, I couldn't break free from the negative pattern.

Emotional healing can be challenging. Even identifying a deeper disturbance can require a fair amount of emotional intelligence — let alone knowing how to reconfigure your mind and emotional patterning to stop repeating the past and create a new way. Habit has a powerful psychic gravity which is a force to be reckoned with. Without spiritual assistance, I am not sure any true and lasting shifts can be made in most cases of deeply-embedded emotional wounding. Kuan Yin's protection from the dangers of water helps us heal our emotional life so wounds from this or other lifetimes no longer keep us enslaved in self-defeating behaviours.

On a more everyday emotional level, Kuan Yin's protection regarding waters can also address the dangers of 'drowning' in confusion, feeling overwhelmed and therefore trapped in indecision, procrastination or exhaustion. These emotions can prevent us from having the necessary inner resources—such as energy, clarity, courage and conviction—to step forward and really live. Without such spiritual protection, we may end up hiding in the stultifying familiarity of what we already know, plagued by insecurity and uncertainty about how to break free and grow and explore untried avenues.

The significance of all of this can be very subtle. Kuan Yin may clear diseases from the astral or watery psychic levels before they manifest into physical disease without us ever being aware of it. She can also heal diseases that have to do with pollution of waters which have already shown up in our bodies or our world, for example, as disorders of blood, lymph, skin, kidneys and other organs and functions of filtering and elimination. Many people who live relatively health-conscious lives still need regular energy clearing to deal with the challenges of modern life. These trials include the ingestion of chemicals and pesticides, as well as stressors on the body related to artificial light and incoming radiation from electronic devices. The body has an amazing capacity to process these things, but we often need help to reconnect to our innate healing potential and overcoming the disconnection from natural powers of regeneration that modern living tends to foster.

The protection against the dangers of water also shields us from being deceived or disturbed by the workings of collective emotional energies. Anytime you watch a news report and feel inner panic or other intense emotions, like fear, anger or rage, you can be certain you are not the only one being emotionally triggered. Without spiritual awareness and protection, we are often unaware that our emotions are manipulated and amplified by collective energies. We may believe there is every reason to feel anger or fear, without realising we have a choice. We can either be overcome by emotional reaction, getting swept up in mass panic, or recognise all such moments as opportunities to do our best to not only calm ourselves, but to realise that, in doing so, we become a calm port in the emotional storm for others.

Reflecting upon our emotions—perhaps by tapping into the wise message they are communicating and then letting them go—rather than collapsing into panic, rage or depression, requires that we have enough space between the triggering moment and our reaction. In that space, we can become conscious of what is taking place. Then we are able to do something constructive with the experience. In that moment, which Kuan Yin can help us access, we have an abundance of choices including the choice to take the higher road, so to speak, acting with integrity, generosity, courage, forgiveness and strength.

"We are all churning our karma," as one of my precious Tibetan teachers says. We are distilling our true essence and working through the challenges of our life journey. Our issues will seem tough at times. Although someone else's path may appear more easily resolved, that has nothing to do with how they experience it. Likewise, even though well-meaning people tell you what they think you should do, when it comes down to it, you are the one living your life. We *can* respond to others with the compassion that helps them discharge emotional intensity, so that they can find a way through suffering into peace and clarity by touching into their own inner wisdom.

Water symbolises our participation in a collective field. Just as an individual drop of water is also part of an ocean, rainfall or river, our energy fields are part of the greater collective field of life itself. In this unified field, we are open to many influences — some uplifting and conscious, others more challenging and disruptive to our wellbeing. For instance, you could walk into a shopping centre feeling energised and clear, but leave feeling confused, cranky and drained. Or perhaps you have been eating healthily and feeling good, but then you spend time with a certain person and all you want to do afterwards is binge on junk food.

In the latter case, Western psychology would say one of your underlying wounds has been triggered by that person and causing you to binge on junk food. In the Tibetan world of spirits, a shaman may say you have been overtaken by a hungry ghost (a lost spirit who is trapped in karmic attachment to earthly experiences). In this case they are attached to food, but it can also occur with addiction to alcohol, mood-altering substances, or even certain emotional states such as rage.

I experienced the hungry ghost phenomena when walking past a pub in the trendy, inner west suburb of Balmain in Sydney. I was overcome with an urge to go inside and drink. This was shocking because I rarely drink, and I don't particularly enjoy it. It would never occur to me to reach for a glass of wine at the end of a stressful day. I have been blessed with a disinterest in alcohol for which I am grateful, having seen the pain alcohol addiction has caused so many. But that moment shook me to my core because I realised that if the spirits congregating around that pub, desperate for a fix of alcohol, could trigger such desire in me, who has zero interest in alcohol (and therefore found it easy and painless to walk on and not act on that passing whim), what would happen to full-blown alcoholics in such a moment? How difficult would it be for them to resist temptation, when it was fuelled not only by their own pain, but by other energies still pushing for a fix? Oh, my goodness! I felt so much compassion for the struggles of such people and for such tormented spirits. Thank heavens for Kuan Yin's ability to intervene, heal and protect all such beings, when we call on her to do so.

The sūtra says:

If you are drifting in a great ocean and facing imminent danger
with dragons, fishes, and other demons,
think of the power of Bodhisattva Avalokitesvara;
the waves will be unable to swallow you.

—*Lotus Sūtra* 25: 2.4

The Third Protection: Deliverance from dangers of falling

It's easy to imagine that, in the Himalayas, a fall could be much more than an embarrassment. When I was leading a spiritual retreat up into the Himalayan region of Tibet, we spent a very special day visiting a sacred lake and stunning glacier. These were at high altitude; this glacier in particular is above the level of Everest base camp. The road to reach such heights is long, winding and steep. As our transport proceeded higher and higher, the plunging drop on the side of the mountain road became more terrifying to witness. Our group gasped at the sight of an abandoned car perilously perched on the very edge of a ravine. How it had not tipped over and plummeted into complete destruction, I cannot say, but I suspect the third protection of Kuan Yin was at work. The car's precarious position explained why a retrieval team was yet to remove it. One couldn't help but imagine what it must have been like to have been in that car, about to plummet to certain death, only to have it stop suddenly, allowing the occupants to somehow scramble back up to the road, safely. As we continued our ascent, the multitude of *mani* stones, stones with the six-syllable Kuan Yin mantra painted on them, seemed even more luminous with grace.

In numerous Eastern religions, Mount Meru, represented as an enormous golden mountain, is considered the central pivot through which the Universe unfolds. When witnessing the splendour of the Himalayan ranges, which include particularly sacred mountains, like Mount Kailash (which some believe to be the physical emanation of the spiritual presence of Meru), it is easy to understand why mountains symbolise great spiritual heights and divine powers of creation.

Teachings about Meru say that pure, divine beings live upon its peak, and that within the mountain lies the heavenly kingdom of Shambhala. While Meru contains many different levels of heaven, as one moves down the mountain, various levels of hell exist within it, too — complete with the beings that dwell in the hell realms. But the mountain has powerful guardians to protect the Universe from beings that may seek to cause disturbance to others. Tibetan cosmology includes much detail about this mountain and its significance, but for now it is enough to understand it in terms of the third protection of Kuan Yin, the protection from falling — both from physical falls, such as the driver of the car would have experienced, as well as more symbolic falls.

The various heavens and hells sit inside Mount Meru like layers in a cake. Western occultists visualise them in a similar way — just not in vertical layers, but more as layers wrapped around a central axis, like Russian nesting dolls. The idea of vertical layers, like a cake, help us understand progressing spiritually as taking steps to higher levels. We can imagine it like the game *Snakes and Ladders*, which you may have played in childhood. If you were lucky (or, from a Buddhist view, you had cultivated good karma), your throw of the dice would yield a number that led you to a ladder, and you could go up several levels. Our real-life version of this could be karmic brownie points gleaned from a kind action, a prayer of devotion, an offering to the divine ones to help another out or simply doing our personal spiritual practice. We accumulate enough positive energy to generate a fortunate spin of the dice, and up we go. Things get easier, problems resolve, and we feel on top of the world. We are stepping up a level or two on Mount Meru.

However, let's say that, for whatever reason, perhaps through simply being human, we stumble. We get triggered into negative patterning and before we realise it, we spiral into what could become a destructive streak that threatens to undermine our previous efforts. In *Snakes and Ladders*, our bad luck (or in Buddhist-speak, a karmic trace of negativity arising) would result in us throwing a number that leads us to the head of a snake, and we begin to slide down into negative behaviour. Then, our feelings of grace, light and *I've so got this!* suddenly become, *What the hell went wrong? Why am I back here again?* So, we need Kuan Yin! We need her third protection from the dangers of falling.

Sometimes, we take what might be called a wrong turn. It could also be called a learning opportunity (especially if you are ever the optimist), but even on your most radically optimistic days, you could agree there are certain learning opportunities you'd rather not have to endure if they could be avoided. I am all for the more gentle and graceful path whenever possible and Kuan Yin is, too. I wonder about struggles that arise in my life at times. I can learn from them, sure, but do I need to experience them at all? Is my spiritual protection working for me? Then this thought pops into my head: *This could be an entirely different situation—and not for the better—if there was no spiritual protection around me.* That helps to shift my attitude to one of gratitude and trust, which in turn allows for a swifter resolution of the situation. So, whilst we may still stumble from time to time (I personally think this helps to keep us humble and compassionate), Kuan Yin creates a sanctuary of protection around us that helps such a 'trip' be no more than a reminder to pay more attention rather than being the beginning of a very painful descent into the hell realms of the psyche, where suffering just begets further suffering.

This third protection also addresses the ill will of others. The sūtra gives an image of someone pushing you off the edge of Mount Meru, which is rather the opposite of a helping hand! The idea of being suspended mid-air (which you'll see in the sūtra below) means that the karmic outflow of another's negative action towards you will be blocked. So, you might experience the nudge, but not the plummet. It breaks negative karmic cycles, which is an extraordinary spiritual power not even the gods have been able to attain.

A story about Shiva, the badass, wrathful Hindu deity of destruction and spiritual enlightenment (and one of the forms of Kuan Yin, as you'll see in Chapter Three), tells of a devotee who was cursed to die at a certain age. Shiva couldn't change the man's karmic destiny of dying at that age, but wanting to protect his devotee, he manifested magic that would keep the man at an age prior to that of his destined age of death. Thus, Shiva slowed down time and conquered death via some impressive celestial conjuring.

Kuan Yin's ability to keep us suspended in mid-air symbolises halting the negative consequences of another's actions. This is particularly relevant for those who feel they are labouring without relief under karmic legacies of their ancestors—dealing with family issues that won't seem to heal and cause pain or struggle for all—or for those in the public eye who suffer from trolling or gossip. Kuan Yin's third protection is a blessing indeed, protecting our growth and gains on the spiritual path, and defending us from sabotaging forces to ensure those gains continue to accumulate and multiply for the benefit of all beings.

The sūtra puts it like this:

If you are at the summit of Mount Sumeru,
and someone pushes you off the edge,
think of the power of Bodhisattva Avalokitesvara;
you will be suspended in mid-air like the sun in the sky.

—*Lotus Sūtra* 25: 2.5

Individual freedoms are better respected in some countries than in others, but the threat of the abuse of power and of citizens is inherent in any political system, even those which claim all decisions are made for the protection of the people. Abuse of minorities by those in power is more visible now than ever, as is our sadly limited ability to eradicate such behaviour from our world. We are so in need of Kuan Yin's assistance to address the countless cases of human rights violations where people are tortured, imprisoned and even killed for their beliefs.

Then there is the less obvious, though still dangerous, political, cultural and social damage caused when innate goodness and respect are superseded by so called politically correct rules that amount to little more than moralistic bullying with a sugar-coated title. This is the mess that takes place when humans are not encouraged to find and live by their own spiritual centre and are instead conditioned to look to external sources for moral guidance on how to behave. If we value and encourage spiritual maturity within ourselves and within those in our sphere of influence, such as our children, we can create a genuinely respectful culture, with enough discernment to prevent wisdom from being overcome. We can do this best by choosing how to live. And, Kuan Yin can help us clean things up so the voices of the soul which can bring something of value into this world will not be drowned out by the clever and destructive voices that can so easily manipulate flawed systems.

This protection highlights how little we can rely on appearance or compelling language. I learned that fairly quickly in law school. You can argue any side of a case and be equally compelling. That is the dangerous quality of pretty poisons. On the surface, they look or sound right, but if you ingest them, they will harm you. That something seems right on the surface or can be justified by argument does not indicate its true value. One can only assess *that* by its effect in our being and through that, in the world. Is more love created? More kindness? More openness, trust and maturity? If not, then either the ideal is off-centre or the method of bringing it to life, which is just as important, is not on point.

People, governments, social justice groups and political groups can get so caught up in the limited viewpoint of their own agendas and rationalisations that they fail to see they are becoming worse than the very forces they were fighting. Because they seem to be fighting for good, they accept any means to their end. This is always a dangerous practice. The moment one allows essential spiritual integrity to be violated in pursuit of a 'higher cause', it is no longer a higher cause.

So, we need Kuan Yin's protection for obvious abuses of human rights and for the great causes that are fought for by brave souls seeking to change and heal the world, but who end up creating war rather than solutions. While we should not minimise the potential heroic glory of their intentions, I've seen some activists behave abhorrently towards others and feel justified in such actions. Yet, they are perpetuating unkindness, abuse, disrespect, harm and hate — the very things they are trying to eradicate. As any parent knows, it is futile to try to guide a child by telling them to do as I say, not as I do. But we can successfully accomplish noble goals of healing transformation without sabotaging our ultimate aim. Kuan Yin can protect us from be being derailed from our goals by helping us be more skilful and effective in our approach and find ways which really assist all beings in need.

There are political dangers inherent in societies where human beings interact on the basis of power rather wisdom and compassion. I think most people could cite examples of power games and abuses of authority that weigh heavily over their hearts, causing stress, anxiety and pain. This pain may come from dealing with a vindictive divorce, in which our children are used as emotional pawns to 'win' more in court, or from feeling victimised by an inflexible administration in one's strata management or from the helpless rage we experience at the rising price of petrol. We can lose our peace of mind in an instant over such events, and in such a way that nothing constructive comes from it (such as an inspired creative solution). These incidents, all in some way political, can eat away at our trust in the powers of goodness.

I had an interesting experience of this myself when I purchased a dress from a seller on eBay. I unpacked the dress, checked that it had no tears, cut off the sales tag and placed the dress on a hanger to air out. It was then I realised there were marks through two portions of the silk.

Although I had a legitimate reason to request a refund, I had a sinking feeling in my gut. Buying and selling on eBay is riskier than purchasing in a store with a regular returns policy. A return requires a dispute resolution process in which you argue your case, and the eBay team makes the final adjudication. It can take weeks of back-and-forth emails. If the other party doesn't have a respectful attitude, and one doesn't particularly enjoy conflict, it can be an uncomfortable experience or a downright anxiety-inducing process. Nonetheless, my intuition prompted me to initiate the return process, so I sent a polite email, with pictures, to the seller, explaining the situation. She refused to refund the item and, over the following days, tried every possible avenue to avoid the refund, including making various accusations. One was I had bought an exact replica of the dress and tried to return that, instead of the one she'd sold me! I felt a combination of astonishment, amusement and was also anxious about the increasing ridiculousness of her suggestions — anything to avoid taking responsibility for selling a defective item.

You may wonder how this relates to political protection. Well, during our exchanges, the seller announced she was a 'power seller' on eBay. This means she has a very high turnover on eBay and also that she generates a considerable income for eBay. She informed me she had her own account dispute manager specifically to give her advice. I recognised that she was trying to intimidate me. I then had a flash of intuition: *She's trying to bully me, even though she knows that she is in the wrong, and the Divine wants her to learn a lesson about not being above ethical behaviour.* I felt I was being asked to continue with the process, so she didn't become further corrupted by her own power drive. It was a startlingly detailed insight, and it did give me some comfort during the unpleasant email exchanges that unfolded.

At one stage, she told me she was handling the process for the return, and I believed her. My intuition came to me a day later letting me know she was not doing anything. She was trying to make me wait so the timeframe for legitimate returns would close, and she'd avoid the return on a technicality. I enquired with eBay as to whether a return had been lodged by the seller and, of course, it had not. I then followed up on the paperwork myself.

It was a good learning experience for me. I had to keep my mind clear and focused on Kuan Yin, so as not allow anxiety or anger to seep into my heart because the process—which could have been so simple—was being drawn out and made complicated by the seller's attitude and behaviour.

Finally, the prescribed time frame for 'working things out' with the seller passed, and eBay was willing to step in and determine the case. It could take several days and, given the seller's actions with me, I expected all those days to be part of the process. The first day of the adjudication period was my birthday. I was giving myself a birthday present of tattoos. Kuan Yin's mantra was going on the inside of my left forearm, where it connected to my heart energy. I felt that would assist me in receiving her grace. I felt a second tattoo, of Tara's symbol on my right wrist, would support me in sharing that grace with others through my actions in the world. I was also getting tattoos on either ankle, again with personal meaning to me. The tattoo process was painful, but I meditated through the discomfort, repeating Kuan Yin's mantra and offering the pain to her as an act of devotion. I spent a total of four hours meditating on Kuan Yin on my forty-fourth birthday, getting four tattoos dedicated to her work, which was what I had dedicated my own heart to my entire life, really. It felt deeply meaningful to me.

When I finally stepped out of the studio (I'd never visited it before and had been delighted to find it populated with Mother Mary statues tucked into various nooks and crannies), I checked my phone and realised that, at the moment the tattoos were finished, an email had come in from eBay. If these four tattoos were giving me Kuan Yin's field of protection, as I intended with the carefully selected placements and designs, then even though it was quite early in the decision-making process, eBay may have decided in my favour. Turns out, that is exactly what happened. Kuan Yin's gift to me was the reassurance that no matter what appears to be, she is looking out for the highest interests of us all. If we trust her, she will be a guardian for each of us.

The sūtra says:

If you are suffering from the punishment of government,
and your life is about to end by execution,
think of the power of Bodhisattva Avalokiteshvara;
the sword will be splintered into pieces.

—*Lotus Sūtra* 25: 2.8

THE FIFTH PROTECTION: DELIVERANCE FROM PRISON

Imprisonment can be a state of mind, as much as a state of body. Perhaps your life has been touched by a loved one who was interned or detained against their will, sent to prison for a crime which they may or may not have committed. Or maybe you have been moved by the plight of prisoners in some way. I know of a healer who works in prisons, doing his part to calm the anger, fear and violence that tends to be perpetuated in such places. His work benefits more than the inmates and the prison environment. It helps calm the surrounding areas, stabilising the energy of the neighbourhood in which the prison is located. As all true spiritual work does, the benefits flow on to benefit all beings.

The deeper symbolism of imprisonment in this sūtra, as it applies to many of us, relates to the symbolic prisons within which we are shackled without awareness or acknowledgement most of the time. These prisons are made of our own stories, our habits and our beliefs. When we are deeply wounded, they can keep us trapped in a repetitive horror story of fear, loneliness and abuse.

When we believe these nightmares to be the only available reality and see them as a higher truth of sorts, the prison door slams shut. When we believe the situation is inevitable, unchangeable and beyond divine intervention, we deny ourselves the ability to receive, to transform, to be blessed and be liberated. Or, perhaps, we think divine assistance could help, but believe the Divine has more important matters to attend to than our suffering.

This idea of putting ourselves in prison reminds me of a beautiful poem by Hafiz, a Sufi poet and mystic. He paints a vivid picture in this short poem.

The small man builds cages everywhere he goes, whilst the sage ducks his head when the moon is low, dropping keys all night long for the beautiful, rowdy prisoners.

To me, 'the small man' is akin to our ego, the part of us that says *no* and looks for reasons to be afraid, to keep things as they are and to block growth.

There is a jeweller I visited for the occasional jewellery repair. I found it incredibly frustrating to deal with him. His first response to any repair was to list all the reasons it couldn't be done. Since I am the exact opposite—tending to say yes to things and later allow the way to be shown, with faith it will be possible—the first time, his attitude puzzled me. On the second occasion, it annoyed me. On the third occasion, it infuriated me! In the interest of contributing to world peace, rather than adding to the levels of anger in the world, I found another jeweller.

The new jeweller was capable of seeing the world more as I did, and delivering the results I needed, too. Whilst the first jeweller had a valid way of seeing the world, according to his upbringing and beliefs, it shut down the possibility of my being able to repair, change or create my jewellery the way I wanted. I disliked this 'shutdown' of my creativity intensely! It felt like my wings were being clipped, and what really bugged me was that I knew it wasn't necessary. Sometimes our creative flights of fancy really do need to be put on hold for a higher purpose, and that I understand and respect. However, there was no higher purpose, here. It was simply a clash of mindsets. I knew there would be others who would be more open-minded and see the same situation differently: same jewellery, same request, different attitude, different outcome.

When I am around someone who does not have the same openness of mind that I have, it feels like everything we try to do together grinds to a halt. It's not about delays as taking time for things to percolate can be part of the creative process. It is like the creative bird of spirit never even gets permission to take flight. The sense of flow and movement and ease and accomplishment of tasks I am used to suddenly dries up like a sun-scorched river bed. No matter how great the idea or how genuine the interest of all involved, a fundamental mismatch in openness of mind means one person is going to feel uncomfortably pressured, and the other will feel trapped or held back.

The prisons of the mind can be dark places where addiction and self-hatred are fostered. Less extremely, they can simply limit what we think we can or cannot attain during one lifetime. We may know we are holding ourselves hostage to unhelpful or harmful beliefs which are relics from childhood conditioning and are not meaningful to us as adults who are free to choose our own destiny. Yet, we cling to them like a drowning man holding on to a raft. Why? Perhaps due to a fear of change because change can require so much hard work. It can seem exhausting before we even begin. When I am reading for people and guidance comes through with a practical suggestion, they sometimes respond with, "I don't want to do any more work — I am SO TIRED!"

I understand, but when something comes through from a divine source, the action suggested will yield the kind of results that break a cycle. It's a different kind of work, not only in effect but in experience, too. There is work that depletes and work that brings energy. We still need rest because we are organic beings, yet it is rest after fulfilling work, not futile effort, and the work itself brings the rewards that are sought. That can be incredibly vitalising.

The protection of Kuan Yin is with us if we wish to receive it. She will shelter us from painful mindsets which are locked into unhelpful patterns and support us to open to and enjoy the process of discovering what is possible, which is typically so much more than we imagine. We can think of Kuan Yin as the liberator. She is the way out. We can trust in her. We can allow her to set us free. That requires us to release ourselves from prison, which may mean no longer believing someone else holds the power to keep us from our destiny. It requires letting go.

My very first romantic relationship was a brief but intense affair. I ended it when I realised the man I had been seeing had also been seeing other women. We weren't exclusive, so that wasn't an issue in itself, but when I intuitively sensed what was going on and asked him to confirm it, he flat out refused to talk about it. I understood he had reasons for behaving in such a way, but I couldn't be in a relationship with someone who refused to communicate with me on matters that were important to me. Without trust and communication, it wasn't a healthy relationship.

It was a difficult position for me to work through. I was seeking closure, but it was one-sided. I wanted to process things, and my former sort-of boyfriend did not want to acknowledge anything about the conflict. So, I decided I would heal my experience of the relationship without him. I was optimistic that this breakup (my very first) would be complete, and I would feel free and clear to move on with my life. I wrote him some letters which I never sent, as they were about me expressing on an energetic level what he refused to talk about on a human level. I got angry, I felt sad, I cried, I felt betrayed and abandoned, and then I felt peace. I forgave him. I wished him the best and let it go.

Not long after that, I met my first serious boyfriend and had my first long-term relationship. He loved me with a very pure heart and we talked about absolutely everything, including the reasons for our amicable breakup when that time was upon us. If I had doggedly remained stuck in the idea that I couldn't be free until the first man was willing to give me the closure I needed, I would have been trapped — chained by fetters that would have prevented me from moving forward in my life. When that former sort-of boyfriend eventually tried to contact me some months later, then wrote to me, and then showed up on my doorstep, I was polite—and I would like to think kind—but completely disinterested in pursuing anything further with him. I would have felt that way even if I hadn't been in a relationship with my new boyfriend.

Kuan Yin manifests in a spirit of forgiveness that frees us. Spirit does not require outer circumstances to change for us to be freed, although they typically do as a result of our inner shift. The point is, we don't have to wait for something to happen to free us. Kuan Yin frees us from within, and the rest unfolds as a consequence.

The sūtra tells us:

If you are being locked in a prison,
and your hands and feet are being bound by chains and fetters,
think of the power of Bodhisattva Avalokiteshvara;
you will be released and freed.

—*Lotus Sūtra* 25: 2.9

In my twenties, I met a woman whom we'll call Cynthia. She had short blonde hair, a pretty face and looked something like a pixie with a slightly wicked curve to her lips. She was an intrepid adventurer into all things psychic—which is how we met—and when I read for her, in between asking questions, she would pepper in anecdotes of her previous psychic encounters. I did a few sessions for her over the years, and they were always memorable.

She once told me of the time she saw an ad in a newspaper for 'activation of talents' with a psychic healer with an 'inherited gift.' I wasn't exactly sure what that entailed when she told me, and neither was she at the time, but that didn't stop her wanting to find out. So, off she went to this mysterious psychic healer to see if her piqued curiosity would result in something wonderful. Cynthia soon found herself sitting opposite this self-proclaimed psychic healer in a darkened shed in the woman's backyard in an outer Sydney suburb. There was a crystal ball on the table and robes over the woman's head. The woman didn't report much of note, and Cynthia was feeling a bit let down, when, suddenly the woman became very animated, declaring that Cynthia had a curse upon her. I believe she described it as the evil eye. She then requested a large sum of money to remove the curse. Cynthia might be open-minded, but she wasn't a fool, and she left in a huff ... although her quest for psychic adventure did not seem to ebb after the experience.

I personally believe the vast majority of psychic healers (and others practicing in this gloriously idiosyncratic and quirky New Age/metaphysical field) are genuine, and that Cynthia's experience was likely more of an income-generating exercise than a genuine insight. However, that doesn't mean 'curses' belong solely in the realm of charlatans and have nothing to do with daily life.

We can unintentionally place potentially damaging curses on ourselves and others through what we say, in our heads and aloud. These might be things like, "I will never find love," or "She will never get better," or "My ex will always be a nightmare to deal with." We could unwittingly curse a child by making negative declarations about their future when we are angry. For example, if a child lost their job, the fear of not being able to protect them from the challenges of life might cause a parent to say something in anger, perhaps like, "You'll never amount to anything!"

We may not realise that our negative prophecy is setting things in motion in that person's head and heart, because our modern society doesn't tend to have such an understanding. We are taught to consider the notion of curses as silly superstition that only effects weak-minded people. But words can fertilise goodness in our lives. Conversely, they can become poisonous seeds of doubt, fear, anxiety and criticism. It matters not whether you believe this. It happens, anyway. For instance, in a stressful moment of parenting, we might automatically say something to our child and suddenly realise we have become our mother, repeating exactly what was once said to us. When the prophecies of parents are visited on another generation decades later, for better or worse, we can see that words have more staying power than we typically realise. This is a common example of how we absorb words and have them affect our behaviour.

Kuan Yin's protection is there for us, whether we are talking about the patterns of negative thinking that can become akin to unconscious curses; the unwillingness to forgive, which over time creates a kind of poison in our hearts; or the negativity directed towards us by gossip, slander or other unintentionally or intentionally negative practices.

This protection is basically a kind of divine mirror. It deflects and returns what others put out, rather than allowing an innocent bystander to be hit with their painful projections. There are crystals that absorb negativity—black tourmaline, for example—and crystals that deflect and return negativity, like black obsidian. Personally, I leave deflection up to the Divine Mother's wisdom and just focus on protecting myself, rather than taking the offensive. That's my personal preference. Unless more direct action is truly necessary, I prefer to surround myself with energy I love—diving into writing a book, for example—as a form of protection, as it connects me deeply to Kuan Yin. If it comes to my attention that someone is trying to cause me trouble, which has happened a few times over the past several years, I don't inflame the situation by focusing on it or the person behind it. I put my mind into the sanctuary of the Universal Mother as best I can. In that process, I may also vaguely notice when the negativity someone has sent my way begins to wither and lose strength, because the 'reality' of it ceases to be a reality for me. Kuan Yin becomes the fullness of my reality, and I continue with my life.

The beauty with this approach is that if you have a compassionate heart (and, given that you are reading this book, it is extremely likely you do), when you call in the presence of Kuan Yin for yourself, she will also touch others who are thinking about you in loving ways. The Universal Mother loves all and serves the spiritual growth of all. She doesn't send curse-giving people off to hell. If they are behaving in such a way, they are likely living in a kind of hell already. Instead, she works her spiritual magic to help them heal. If you are to experience an attack of negativity, you can transform it into a bonus by encouraging yourself to seek deeper connection with Kuan Yin. As a result, the person caught up in painful negativity will be connecting with her, not you. She is of such an enlightened nature that any connection with her, even that of negative intention, can evoke healing. The choice is still theirs to make, but through your spiritual skilfulness in self-care, you are giving them a chance to connect with the Universal Mother. What a precious gift!

The poisonous herbs mentioned in this sūtra may seem to belong to another era, but I feel their significance extends Kuan Yin's protection to unclean substances — anything from drugs cut with unknown substances to impure food with toxins. I knew of a very powerful Chi Gung master—truly a gift and light on this earth for so many—

who nearly died from a case of severe food poisoning. He was blessed with enough grace to heal himself, but it was so severe that his life and his light on our planet was nearly lost. What a dreadful turn of events that would have been. So, one can recognise the need for this sort of protection and be grateful that it exists.

The sūtra puts it like this:

If there are people who wish to harm you
by curses or poisonous herbs,
think of the power of Bodhisattva Avalokiteshvara;
the effects will be bounced back to the originator.

—*Lotus Sūtra* 25: 2.10

THE SEVENTH PROTECTION: DELIVERANCE FROM DEMONS

In the modern worldview, demons could be a symbol of psychological darkness. Some spiritual traditions consider them to be chaotic beings that need healing. It doesn't really matter how we define demonic energy or are uncertain it even exists, Kuan Yin will protect us nonetheless.

We all have the potential to be swept up by our own dark side. I once heard the ego described as the part of us that looks first for ourselves in a photograph to see if we look good. I knew a woman who would post the most unflattering photographs of people on social media, tagging them for everyone to see, provided she looked good in the image. Her pride and vanity were greater than her sensitivity or care for the others depicted in the photograph. That's one example of the ego at work.

Anyone might find greed, vanity or pride lurking inside. Every human could be said to have a potential demon and a potential angel within their heart. The question is not whether there is darkness within, but whether we can focus on growing our light, so we always have a choice as to how we behave. If we are of feisty temperament and someone does something that really annoys us, we may feel our anger arising. Yet we may still have enough compassion and equanimity to allow our negative reaction to fall away, without lashing out at the object of our temporary irritation and without judging ourselves, either. Maybe we even learn something valuable from our temporary flash of anger — that we need a rest or setting some cleaner emotional boundaries in that relationship, for example.

At other times, when the darker side of our nature feels too powerful to overcome with our goodness, we need to grow our compassion, work on our light and build up more spiritual muscle. If we treat the experience as a sign to continue or increase our spiritual practice, even being the worst version of ourselves will not swallow up our light. If our vilest nature is nurtured—encouraged through meanness, gossip, being ruthless rather than kind or putting off prayer or meditation again and again—that darkness may eventually grow to the point that we are willing to cause harm to others as long as our own needs are met. Such a corruption of our inner light, obscured by growing darkness, makes it harder to access our innate goodness of our spirit.

Darkness can grow through our treatment of others as well as through our treatment of ourselves. Compassion that doesn't extend to yourself lacks sustaining and protective power. If you strive to be kind to others but neglect self-care, you'll struggle to keep your light strong enough to deal with the occasional bouts of negativity that arise within and around you. Self-care—such as honouring your need for rest, setting healthy boundaries and providing time for nourishing practices such as exercise, yoga, prayer and meditation—strengthens the soul. Taking care of yourself is not an act of ego. Ego denigrates us or another. The path of the soul nurtures us and from our regularly replenished inner well, we have more that is positive and helpful to share with others.

Emotional energies such as greed, hate, fear, anger and pride can become sources of pain for ourselves and others. However, with sufficient soul we can use them as tools for transformation, growing generosity and equanimity, passion, determination, discipline, devotion and respect, and creating greater light for all in the process. Even the most negative emotions and mind states can provide valuable information. Anger may tell us our boundaries are not being respected. Fear may tell us we need to listen more closely to our inner self. And pride may be letting us know we have lost connection with the most valuable parts of ourselves, the real nature within, which is without arrogance or vanity. These are all forms of emotional intelligence which can be distilled from the darkness and transformed into light. If we cannot quite summon the spiritual strength required to greet our dark side and ask how it could be expressed in a constructive way, we only need speak Kuan Yin's name. She will cover the deficit, and more. This grows our inner light and helps us contend with our less luminous moments with more wisdom.

Deliverance from demons doesn't mean we will never encounter negativity. We need to recognise the darkness that exists within and in the world. Our choice is how to handle it. Kuan Yin can assist us to do so skilfully and without experiencing or creating otherwise avoidable harm to ourselves or others. Potentially harmful energies—whether in the form of our own thoughts gaining momentum and derailing positive changes we are making or in the form of other beings acting from fear—cannot touch us when we are under Kuan Yin's protection.

If you feel oppressed in spirit, unable to find your lightness of heart, your joy or a sense of delight in life, it is a good idea to call upon Kuan Yin to clear the possibility of something untoward blocking your path. This might be an obstacle in your own mind or it could be that you are worn down by external sources of negativity. Once you have taken sanctuary in spiritual protection, you will regain your natural spiritual strength and ward off negative influences. When this healing is underway, you'll find things are flowing and that you are dealing with the occasional challenges as they arise and learning something from them, all the while feeling a sustained, underlying connection to a nourishing divine grace.

In the vibrant Buddhist teachings, some enlightened divine beings appear 'disguised' as the scariest of demons. These fierce deities have hearts of gold. They just assume a ferocious appearance to accomplish their enlightened activity. You may feel drawn to these ferocious forms if you are dealing with a lot of negativity in your life. During my most challenging times, I loved Kali—a ferocious emanation of the Universal Mother—with a passion. Although I need her only occasionally these days, my love for her has never waned. Having a complete badass as a spiritual guardian can instil unwavering confidence in an otherwise tentative mind. There's nothing quite so emboldening as knowing an unconquerable ally is in your corner, willing to fight for you and help clear any obstacles in your way.

These wrathful deities are sacred badasses. They are more fearsome than our greatest fears. Thus, they give us a chance to not let our fears dominate us any longer and to trust in their greater (and kinder) power instead. The wrathful manifestations of Kuan Yin include forms of Tara, such as Black Tara (also known as Kali), Blue Tara and semi-wrathful deities (partly badass, partly peaceful) whom I particularly love. Semi-wrathful deities include Orange Tara and also Red Tara, in the form of the enchanting sorceress Kurukulla. We will meet all these enlightened divine goddesses later in this book.

With the Divine Mother's help, we can get on with the practice of growing our soul, including dealing with our dark side, without it being harder or more confusing than it need be. When we take sanctuary in Kuan Yin, saying her name with trust in our hearts, even the most disturbing energies are neutralised, and we are kept safe in her light.

The sūtra says:

If you face harm from vicious rakshasas,
poisonous dragons or various demons,
think of the power of Bodhisattva Avalokiteshvara;
no-one will dare to harm you.

—*Lotus Sūtra* 25: 2.11

For a Tibetan, a hungry snow leopard might pose such a threat to physical survival as to be classified as an evil beast, no matter how magnificent such an animal may seem to our hearts. In Australia, a comparable threat to physical wellbeing might be from one of the numerous snakes or spiders which populate our wild lands. We may respect these animals, even consider them a soul-totem, but if faced with their aggression, a Kuan Yin buffer would most certainly be welcome!

This protection also refers to safeguarding against the potentially destructive effects wrought by deeply wounded human beings who have become so contaminated by negativity that they have lost connection to the goodness within their soul. Although some people may seem inherently evil, I believe that all human beings possess the same spiritual seeds of goodness, grace and light. Through unresolved wounding, the potential for negativity can increase, so that some people can indeed act like evil beasts.

In the Netflix series *The Good Witch*, Cassie, the lead character, is good and kind, but not always understood by the less mystically-inclined members of her community. She is visited by her long-lost sister, Abigail. Abigail and Cassie look somewhat alike, and both are able to influence those around them. They both have a highly developed intuitive grasp of the deep inner workings of other people and have a knack for playing on those inner drives to accomplish their intentions. Whilst Cassie uses her intuitive insights to help people, Abigail uses her uncanny understanding of what drives people to generate discord and chaos. She walks into a room, homes in on whatever aspect of ego someone is demonstrating—pride, doubt, anger, greed, hate, fear—and increases it, fanning the flames with remarkable effectiveness. And, quickly, things fall apart. So, where Cassie's influence is healing, Abigail's is harmful. The writers of the series, and the actress who plays Abigail, manage to portray her manipulations as distorted expressions of her need for attention and love. That doesn't excuse what she does — that still needs to be dealt with. And the way to deal with it involves Cassie's particular skill of healing.

It is tempting to judge people who are particularly damaged and doing truly dreadful things in the world—weaving poison wherever they go—as evil and cast them aside. Certainly, setting a strong boundary which ends any contact with such people might be wise. However, you can have compassion for them, whilst doing so. We cannot always know what a person's path has been and how they have come to be as they are; certainly, if they are acting out evil intent in the world, their soul has been severely damaged. Holding a light of compassion (which in no way equates to allowing any abuse to continue) ensures the evil infecting their soul doesn't contaminate ours. This is one of the protections Kuan Yin offers us. We can hold the light strong within our hearts, even when faced with someone who has become so corrupted that it is hard to sense the beautiful essence of their innermost heart under the dominating activity of their ego. In fact, the strength of that compassionate heart-fire might be enough to stimulate the dormant seeds of their heart within their being.

In the Netflix series *Rita*, feisty Danish school teacher Rita has seen and learned a lot through her many years working in high schools. A young student teacher 'adopts' the hard-nosed Rita as her unofficial mentor. The inexperienced young teacher Hjørdis is quickly out of her depth with the students. One student in particular distresses her. The girl, who dresses in black with torn fishnets and facial studs, radiates an aggressive vibe that intimidates the young teacher. When Hjørdis turns to Rita for support, she laughs. "It's not the scary-looking kids who are the trouble makers," she says. She points to a meticulously dressed, studious young girl, who has not a blonde hair out of place, "Those are the ones you have to worry about." Hjørdis doesn't understand what Rita means. Later, when the little blonde angel turns into an absolute devil, determined to destroy Rita's career and happiness when she discovers that Rita and her father are romantically involved, Hjørdis is no longer quite so swayed by appearances.

The more we grow our light, the more we want to share it with the world and the more visible we become on a spiritual level — even if our everyday life seems the same as it was before. You may not know how much your light is assisting others, yet as you grow your inner light and safeguard it, keeping it pure and strong in your heart, it cannot help but light up the darkness. Some years ago, I received an email from a woman I had never met. In her email, she explained she had once dreamed of a woman talking to her, giving her guidance and reassuring her that everything was going to be all right. Years later, when she was listening to a CD of meditations I had recorded, she recognised my voice as the voice of the woman from her dream. She then sought out a picture of me. Lo and behold, there was the image of the woman from her dream. At the time of her dream, none of my materials had been created, let alone published. Back then, I was a psychic doing readings for people. I cared enough about the Divine to connect consciously each day, which proved sufficient for my light as a healer to help people. Whether or not you ever hear such stories, you can nonetheless trust that your light is powerful and makes a difference.

Kuan Yin ensures we are protected from negative forces which may try to keep our light from shining as brightly as it can. Early on in my career, well-meaning individuals often discouraged me from continuing my work. For a long time, I laboured without knowing if I would attain any success in my field. I had a big vision and found disappointment hard to deal with, which was not an ideal combination of personality traits for 'keeping the faith' in the absence of immediate results. In my heart I knew that I loved working with divine beings, that they helped people and that I wanted to continue dedicating my life to such work. I wanted to thrive, grow my work and reach many people. I had no idea how that could happen or if it ever would. But I did know not to allow negativity to undermine my determination and willingness to persist. Even when those around me held no faith or interest in my heart's purpose, and I wasn't a hundred percent sure if I was being realistic in my ambitions, with Kuan Yin's protection, I continued. Although there is still much to be completed to bring my vision to life, I am in a position in my life where I can look back and recognise the wisdom in being so determined and seeking the spiritual sanctuary required to stick to my path, even when it all seemed so uncertain.

Kuan Yin's protection helps us to safeguard our minds. She can protect us from negativity, but we must decide of our own freewill what we are going to make of the path we are travelling. There are numerous reasons why we may go through a dark night of the soul. One may well be to learn that our divine connection with the Universal Mother is strong enough to sustain us through experiences we wouldn't otherwise be able to handle. If someone had told me I'd need to undergo certain experiences, I'm not sure I would have believed I was capable of doing so. However, I managed to come through the challenges with flying colours, and the experiences have ultimately been of spiritual benefit for me and those with whom I share my work. Only undergoing those experiences will reveal our true capacity. It is reassuring to know Kuan Yin is always with us if we ask and that she will shield and protect us, so we can move through our journey without being derailed. We have it within us to succeed. She wraps her light and grace around us to ensure we have the opportunity to do so.

The sūtra reassures us thus:

If you are surrounded by evil beasts
with sharp fangs and fearful claws,
think of the power of Bodhisattva Avalokiteshvara;
they will quickly flee and scamper away in all directions.

—*Lotus Sūtra* 25: 2.12

THE NINTH PROTECTION: PROTECTION DURING DISPUTES OR WAR

Although it can be hard to imagine, for many, ongoing war is simply part of life. When one of my most beloved Tibetan teachers journeyed with a small group through the wilds of the Himalayas, the worst problem they faced was not wild animals or lack of water, but the threat of bandits who would not hesitate to rob and kill them. Their journey took many weeks. They travelled on foot with a small number of horses and set up camp along the trail in places where they hoped to avoid detection, yet the threat of bandits lurked around every corner. Eventually, they passed through a small village where they were informed by the locals that bandits had recently been seen in the area. During their travels, my master performed a Tara practice using a small *damaru* (drum) and her mantras. Tara, as I've said, is an emanation of Kuan Yin, but she is also a multi-faceted goddess in her own right and is especially looked to for protection and swift action. This particular Tara practice was dedicated to the safety and protection of his group as they travel.

Every night, the master would retire to his tent and practice. After several nights, the members of his camp noticed what seemed to be little sparks of fire radiating from the master's tent, coinciding with the rhythmic beating of the drum during his ritual. The sparks grew in intensity until, one night, even the master, deep in meditation, noticed. The group decided it was a divine sign, so when the sparks were bright, they kept watch for bandits throughout the night. However, no bandits came.

The master continued his practice, and then one night there were no sparks at all. The group decided to be very careful that evening, because surely a sudden change must mean something. Remaining on alert, they hid themselves just as a group of bandits came riding by! Fortunately for all concerned, including all the students my master would later teach, they were undetected.

The camp members continued on their journey, taking note of the evenings when the sparks were bright on the master's drum, sleeping well and conserving their energies. On the evenings when there were no sparks, they knew the sign was to be careful, and so they did not sleep and instead placed themselves in hiding until it was safe to move on again. I am happy to report they safely completed their journey, and this amazing master was able to continue with his life's work.

I love this story for a number of reasons, including how courageous this beautiful, happy, funny, good-natured, unassuming Dzogchen master is in person. It was amazing to hear these stories and connect them to such a joyful being. This gives hope that even the most difficult circumstances need not corrupt the beauty of our hearts. The other reason I enjoy this story is that it illustrates the creative and resourceful ways the Divine can guide us to take care of our needs. Tara knew the group needed sleep, but there were also times when they needed to hide. Rather than allowing them to wear themselves out with the exhaustion of endlessly keeping watch, she helped them navigate their way to safety.

When I am going through a situation in my life that involves uncertainty, my natural tendency is to want to sort it out as swiftly as possible. I also know there are times when one just has to wait for the experience to run its course. I may not know why, but if something isn't resolving itself promptly, there are reasons for that. Some karma or other has to unfold, and it may involve me, or it may not. So, rather than run myself ragged trying to fix something that cannot be resolved at the time, I've learned to practice letting go.

My prayer to the Divine is often something along these lines: "If I need to know something, please let me know. P.S. I'm leaving all of this situation in your capable hands." Then I deal with what is right in front of me, doing what I can and surrendering the outcome to a greater power. When it is time for me to act, I get a nudge. It happens often that something I'd completely forgotten about or considered a done deal suddenly comes to mind. If I forget it again, in the middle of the night, or in meditation, or at some other random time, there it is again. Almost every single time that happens, it has been an important matter which needed to be resolved at that time. The resolution happened in moments, and all that energy could then be directed into whatever I was working on, like a new oracle deck. Rather than adding more stress to the world, I was able to add more beauty. I liked that very much.

Whilst war is a terrible reality for many, even in the relative calm of places at peace, this protection remains relevant. Being 'in the wars', as my grandmother used to put it, can refer to a series of bad days, weeks or months during which you may feel as if you are under attack. Maybe there is a recurring drama in your family or other relationship, or a dispute over property or custody or finances. My training as a lawyer taught me battle tactics. I've seen enough dysfunctional divorce proceedings to know they can become an emotional and psychological minefield for all involved. There is a reason people speak of 'battling' for child custody. There is an expression that is used in the Australian media to describe someone who isn't from a privileged background and must struggle more than most to overcome challenging odds: The little Aussie battler. If one is being bullied at work or school, it might feel as though war is being waged against you, likewise if you are being trolled on social media. Showing us the best ways to deal with these situations, helping us to find the courage, humour and self-love necessary to handle what is happening with dignity and grace is Kuan Yin's specialty. She helps us move through such situations without losing our integrity, self-respect or self-worth.

Earlier, I described the divine protection I experienced during an unpleasant eBay dispute regarding the return of a damaged dress. At one point during our email exchanges, the seller—who was doing everything she could to refuse the return—sent me a picture of a dress. It was by the same designer, in the same style, but with a slightly different print. The photograph showed the price tag attached and came with this message: "Can you please confirm the garment arrived just as pictured." I sensed her intention instantly. She had realised that she didn't have photographic proof the tag had ever been attached. As the removal of the tag was the main basis for her refusal to provide a refund, she was afraid that she couldn't refute me if I lied and said that the tag had never been attached to the garment.

Even if it meant I would lose the dispute, I was not willing to lose my integrity by being shifty and exploiting her absence of evidence by claiming the tag was never attached. I wasn't about to sink to deception or trickery. I made a clear request for the Divine to sort this situation out. I was aware there could be some karmic reason why the decision would go in the seller's favour and if I owed her karma from a past life, I was quite happy for it to be resolved. I liked to cross things off my to-do list, which was already too long by half. No matter which way the decision went, I wanted to feel good about how I handled it and how I conducted myself. When the decision was given in my favour, I felt a sense of trust that it was meant to be that way, according to a will higher than my own, and the situation felt karmically clean. Whilst this was a tiny and temporary 'war', I appreciated the assistance of the Universal Mother immensely.

In whatever ways we may feel at war, under weighty judgement or attack, the sūtra offers us this:

> *If you have disputes before the court,*
> *or are fearful in the midst of the war,*
> *think of the power of Bodhisattva Avalokiteshvara;*
> *all enemies full of resentment will retreat.*
>
> —*Lotus Sūtra* 25: 2.21

THE TENTH PROTECTION: BESTOW CHILDREN OF GOOD FORTUNE

This protection, a blessing of future happiness and success for one's children, can bring peace to a parental heart. It promises the continuation of a legacy of happiness passed down the ancestral line. Any parent who has seen the worst of themselves in their child's behaviour and cringed would gratefully embrace this protection, which ensures the best of what they have to offer, and more, will flourish amongst their descendants.

In the Christian tradition there is the expression, "the sins of the father visited on the son." I would describe this as the negative karmic inheritance we have to deal with should our ancestors be incapable or unwilling to do so. The souls of our ancestors are connected to our own and to the souls of our descendants in such a way that soul qualities, as well as genetic material, are passed along the family line. In something of a relay race for our souls, we carry the baton from our ancestors when they have gone as far with an issue as they can. If we cannot reach the finish line under our own steam, bringing an issue to final resolution and closure, then our children and their children will continue running the race. The teaching from Native American culture to make choices that will sustain benefit for the next seven generations reflects an understanding of the spiritual responsibility we carry for our legacy.

The legacy of negative karma that falls on the shoulders of a soul group incarnating as a family could relate to the keeping of secrets—a history of unacknowledged abuse for example—that prevents healing and resolution from taking place. Each soul will need to deal with an unconscious attraction to abusive patterns. This may manifest in the abuse of others or be internalised as self-abuse. The wounding is recreated, over and over again, moving down the generations until someone has the skilfulness to begin to break the pattern. Then, over the generations, with each soul doing their part, the karma can begin to dissolve and ultimately be healed. This often requires the courage and willingness to stand up to one's family to bring out the truth and allow karmic healing to continue. That can be tough on everyone involved, and one must understand the deeper spiritual significance of what they are attempting to accomplish through such a process. It can be done with kindness and respect, but there will likely be resistance and pain before there is letting go and healing. Such souls are the ones who are picking up the baton in the relay race and covering a lot of ground towards the finish line.

The beauty of this sūtra of protection is that it promises a completion of the race. It promises that divine favour, blessing and generosity shall touch the heart of the child, the future legacy-bearer. As this blessing will resolve the karmic inheritance handed down the ancestral lines, many souls will benefit from it. Every future relative and every past relation, as well as any person who would have a relationship of any sort with one of those souls in any incarnation, will all be touched by the blessing. Darkness is lightened for potentially thousands of people through one simple prayer.

The karmic inheritance we pass down the line is not only about wounding. It also concerns talents and gifts, which were developed, or not, in previous generations. A sensitivity to music or art, an innate connection to dance as a form of emotional expression, a talent with words or design, these can all be karmic inheritances, along with strength, kindness, respect and boldness of spirit, just to give some examples. It is possible, through our own healing and spiritual growth, to offer a legacy to our descendants that truly improves their lives, giving them the benefits of our sometimes-hard-won wisdom and the opportunity to further develop the spiritual capacities our ancestors accessed.

The idea that our fulfilment can bring fulfilment for all is based on an understanding of spiritual unity. In a dualistic view of the world, where the ego believes it is separate and can profit at the expense of another, there is devotion to the idea of the dog-eat-dog world. This idea is neither helpful nor realistic. It fosters an unnecessary and inaccurate anxiety for those who have enough compassion to care about the plight of others. They may believe their happiness, success and abundance denies someone else the same fruits, as though resources were limited and there were not enough to go around. The ego may see things this way, but, hopefully, by now, we understand the perception of the ego is distorted. If we are aware of the connections between all living things, we see that, in spiritual unity, we are the one child of the Universal Mother. Therefore, our divinely-bestowed success enhances the success of all beings.

If you are praying for the blessing of your true higher purpose and sacred work in the world, whatever that may be, you are not denying the path of another, nor competing for limited resources. If you open your heart to divine intervention, you are not secreting it away from others in need. When it comes to divine light, it is not this *or* that, but this *and* that ... and that, and that, and that, to infinity.

The more we connect to, are infused with and radiate that light, the more benefit we gain in our own hearts and lives, and the more able we are to support others on their path, although we may not realise just how much of an effect we are having for the greater good. Goodness takes every opportunity to multiply. Our heart need only creak open the tiniest bit—with hope or trust or faith or gratitude—for the light to find its way in and emanate outwards from within our innately good hearts. This is a double blessing of light shining within and around us.

The sūtra blesses us with this grace for the benefit of all:

If there are women who wish to give birth to a son, they should worship by giving offerings to Bodhisattva Avalokiteshvara, who will bestow them a son blessed with good fortune, virtue and wisdom. If they wish to have a daughter, they will have a beautiful and adorable daughter blessed with accumulated benevolent roots.

—*Lotus Sūtra* 25: 1.11

Chapter Three

The Thirty-Three Forms of Kuan Yin

Kuan Yin is not limited to 33 forms. She is unendingly resourceful in her responsiveness to the needs of sentient beings. If she needs to manifest her intervention as a book that opens your mind, or a cat that stumbles into your life and opens your heart, then she will do so. She will unveil her message through a tree that provides comfort and a sense of grounding, a sublimely beautiful rainbow that brings you hope, as the vital clarifying piece of information you need to heal an illness and more. One of my favourite ways she shows up in my life—although I am grateful for the myriad ways she assists us all—is when, in meditation, I sense the bliss, love and beauty of her being, accompanied by a vision of her light. In such moments, I cannot help but say to her, "Whatever you ask of me, I shall willingly do it. I will follow you anywhere. May all beings know you as I know you in this moment."

The *Lotus Sūtra* describes 33 forms of Kuan Yin. I am sharing these forms with you for the same reason that I explored her ten special methods of protection. Even though she is not limited to these methods and forms, exploring them can help us understand how vast her reach is in our lives and, thus, help us break through our self-created, limited ideas about the ways the Divine Mother can show up and support, guide and protect us. We often fail to ask for divine help because we don't believe that the Divine could help us with our worldly concerns. Maybe, with the possible exception of the parking-space angels, we feel material-world matters, everyday stresses and concerns which seem selfish are not appropriate to take to her in prayer. But this entire worldly realm—with all its problems—is *her self-chosen realm* of spiritual endeavour. She wants to assist us all, and she has the power to do so. All we need do is ask.

The difficulty in obtaining divine grace in our lives is never about whether the Divine is reaching out to us or capable of lifting us. The difficulty lies is in our ability and willingness to open to that grace, to believe in it and to claim it in our hearts. The difficulty is that we tend to place more faith in the perception of our problems than in the higher states of divine love. As we build a personal relationship with Kuan Yin and begin to experience her helpfulness and capacity firsthand, we start to shift our faith and make our own way easier. Instead of blocking divine assistance unintentionally, we learn to consciously open ourselves to grace. We learn to undo the I-must-do-it-or-it-won't-get-done mentality and, instead, partner up with the Universe. Grace in action creates confidence. We learn to flow from an empowered state, rather than a controlling mindset. We find we can more effectively and more easily help not only ourselves, but others, too.

These forms of Kuan Yin help us understand some of the many ways Kuan Yin may appear in divine disguise to assist us. Remember, these are not limitations on her supernatural powers or unconditionally loving grace. These prompts are simply meant to help us open our hearts and minds to expect and accept her showing up freely and generously in our lives. As we resonate with her different forms, we will find ourselves growing closer and more open to her divine presence, however it appears in our lives.

1. WILLOW LEAF KUAN YIN

The willow tree is flexible, its branches softly rustling on the gentle wind. The element of wind in Tibetan medicine is about movement, flow and creativity. Wind brings life. The psychic winds in Tibetan medicine are akin to the energies, *prana* or *chi* in the New Age, Ayurvedic and Taoist traditions. Willow Leaf Kuan Yin expresses the flexibility of the Universal Mother in the ways she reaches us and gets things moving in our lives.

Through its medicinal properties, the willow also represents the relief of pain and illness—be it spiritual, emotional, psychological or physical. We can grow through the experience of pain by learning to listen to our body and read its signals—noticing when we need to make changes in our habits of lifestyle and thinking, for example. Pain can signify toxicity in our bodies or in our relationships and requires us to take action to resolve it. Perhaps, our pain signifies a need for rest, so we can heal. Maybe it is helping us realise we don't take enough 'divine down time' to nurture ourselves on a regular basis. Experiencing pain can help us develop a greater capacity for compassion and wisdom, so we can become a much-needed source of comfort and strength for ourselves and others. Pain can teach us patience, and through it we can learn about the healing process. There are many benefits that can come when we work through our pain.

There are also times when our pain becomes so great that it transforms into tremendous suffering and we struggle to break free. Then, it can be hard to articulate the real source of our pain and treat it. We may be willing to do the work on ourselves but just not know how to begin. Or perhaps we have been working hard to create the needed changes but aren't making the progress we wished for. Exhaustion and a sense of despair or defeat may loom large and bleak over our inner horizon.

I have experienced Kuan Yin's ability to step in, clear the storm clouds and reveal the bright dawn of new light. She can lighten the burden, oftentimes eradicating it completely, and assist us in processing the experience. Kuan Yin will never block our learning, but, in her great compassion, she can transform the process of it into a gentler and more loving path through the darkness into the light.

2. Kuan Yin upon the Dragon's Head

Dragons are curious creatures. They exist not only in stories and imagination, but as real, yet ethereal, beings. I heard a fascinating story from a man who had a powerful spiritual practice. One day, as he was meditating in a deeply relaxed state, he felt himself leave his body and move into another reality. He explored this reality for a little while, and then he saw a strange, dark creature warily eyeing him. As the creature emerged from the shadows, he realised it was a dragon. Being a fearless sort of fellow, he reached out to touch it. The dragon, apparently disliking that, pulled away, snorting slightly, and promptly disappeared back into the shadows!

The dragon is a potent symbol, particularly in Chinese culture, representing qualities such as leadership and authority. But the most compelling quality of the dragon is power. Traditionally, the Chinese have considered the dragon the most powerful of all creatures. Kuan Yin seated upon the head of a dragon symbolises her supernatural spiritual power being even greater than that of the most powerful of all creatures. The *Strength* card in the Tarot features a feminine being wrestling a lion (and she appears to be winning the battle). Here, even in her gentle form, Kuan Yin likewise overcomes an apparently more powerful creature.

There are times when we convince ourselves our troubles are such the Divine couldn't possibly help us. We may think the spiritual beings who love us aren't interested in our financial wellbeing or our fear of a certain health condition. Yet, not only are they interested, they are also willing and able to assist us. Kuan Yin's great desire to free us from suffering is mind-bending. For most of us, myself included, it is a continual, sacred work-in-progress to allow the full extent of her grace to manifest in our lives.

In Taoist philosophy, the Universe is composed of *yin* and *yang* energies, the two fundamental forces of creation, which are constantly interacting with each other. We might call them sacred feminine (yin) and sacred masculine (yang) energies. Dragon represents the yang energy, which is bright, open, expansive and dynamic. It causes energy to rise and expand. It is characterised by drive, action, pursuit and reaching. It is achievement and the constant 'on' of technology.

Yin is powerful, too, but in a different way. It is quiet, introspective, dark and magnetic. It causes energy to gather and ground. It is also capable of enormous accomplishment, but in a way that may seem like we aren't doing as much — or anything at all! The yin method of manifesting is about the law of attraction, about magnetising what we want into our world, rather than going out and making things happen.

Both yin and yang are part of life. The problem for many of us is they tend to become imbalanced. Our tendency to overdo the yang side of things can stem from our distrust and disconnection, and results in many illnesses, both mental and physical. Most of us need to replenish our over-exerted yang energies and balance them with regular, quality yin downtime through meditation, yoga, reflection, relaxation and getting enough sleep. Kuan Yin upon the dragon's head is a much-needed healing goddess for our yang-obsessed modern era, promising she can show us the way to a wiser and more healing way of being.

3. Kuan Yin Holding the Sūtra

As a little girl, I had a fantasy that when I died and went to heaven (I never even considered going anywhere else), I would sit at God's feet, and he would patiently answer all my questions about the Universe. A peculiar fantasy, perhaps, but the thought of it calmed my child's mind and evoked peace. There was something so wonderful about the promise of understanding everything I could ever want to know, especially when the mean-spirited behaviours I witnessed in some of the children at my school troubled my heart and confused me greatly.

I once took a huge malamute dog, that belonged to my boyfriend at the time, out for a walk. It weighed more than I did and wasn't particularly well trained. It was more like the dog was taking me for a walk (or run, actually, as it bolted down the road towards the park and I did my best to keep up with him). Sometimes life can feel rather like my experience with that malamute dog. Instead of us feeling that we are in control, we can be swept up in what is happening, feeling like that is very much outside of our control and it takes all our skilfulness to simply keep up!

If it's any consolation, those tend to be the times when we are growing, and that is a good thing. Yet, it is not always easy to have faith that things are going to work out. In such times, I would turn to my spiritual guides for help, and they'd often explain things to me, helping me cultivate a higher perspective. This perspective gave me the comfort that everything was going to be okay and the courage to do what I could to move things in the right direction and surrender everything else. At other times, I needed to go through something without the support of my spiritual guides. This was necessary, so I could practice self-reliance and independence of mind. In such circumstances, my guides would become silent. I still knew they were 'there' and loved me. I just needed to figure out some things for myself. I always felt happy when they were back online, because I enjoyed our spiritual conversations and because their 'reappearance' meant I'd passed whatever 'earth school' test I had been undertaking at the time.

Kuan Yin holding the Sūtra shows us that the knowledge we need will be given. Whatever teachings, nudges, precious pieces of information could lead us to a healing breakthrough, for example, will be given in the best way, at the best time. A sudden sign from the Universe might appear, an oracle-card reading might make it all clear or a sudden insight might bubble up from within during a dream or meditation, or yoga practice. There is no need for panic or despair during those moments when we feel we are on our own and bumbling inelegantly through the uncertain passages of our life journey. We just need to keep tripping, and, if we can, keep laughing, knowing we'll get wherever it is we are meant to be and learn what we need to know. Ma Kuan Yin will ensure this.

4. KUAN YIN OF COMPLETE LIGHT

This form of Kuan Yin is especially for those who are caught up in punishment by an authority, be it society at large, a political group, a legal or governing body or people in other ruling or powerful positions (the leader of your social clique or of a religious organisation, for example).

The sūtra teaches that the weapon seeking to cause harm to the devotee of Kuan Yin will shatter. The shattered weapon symbolises that harm directed towards you will be obstructed and disempowered. You do not need to defend yourself or attack the other person (or group). This is a protection from even the intention of harm and indicates the method by which the offending party is seeking to harm you will fall apart.

'Political protection' may be literal—and many can benefit from such protection—but it can also be subtler. It might refer to a person engaging in power play, or someone trying to destroy your reputation or dissuade you from taking an action which would inconvenience them, even though it could reveal an important truth. Or perhaps you are feeling bullied or victimised by an administrative process. Excessive red tape, in the shape of seemingly endless forms and confusing processes, may have you stepping back rather than moving forward in pursuit of an important dream. To protect that dream and allow you to move through even the most intimidating obstacles, Kuan Yin provides her protective light.

The Kuan Yin of Complete Light, or Complete Hallow, as she is otherwise called, is completely holy. The presence of a holy person has a palpable effect on all levels of existence. The holy being is connected to divine bliss, wisdom and healing love. Such a being brings peace to our hearts and releases pain, pacifies distress and calms agitation. When the Dalai Lama visits an area, crime rates reportedly drop. However, negative attempts to block him increase. Hence, he has higher personal security than one would expect for an often-laughing monk whose consistent and simple message is, "Be kind." Mahatma Gandhi's devotion to non-violence and justice shifted the political reality of India towards independence and freedom. Yet, because his open-mindedness and open-heartedness were not restricted by religious conventions, he had enemies within both the Hindu and Muslim communities. The resistance one encounters can, at times, be a testament to the power of one's light to create healing and destabilise darkness. With Kuan Yin's protection, we can continue to grow our light with faith that she is our shield and our shelter.

This form of Kuan Yin is depicted seated on a rock, palms together, flames blazing in a circle behind her. Her seat upon the rock means she is spiritually 'above' earthly situations, even those which may appear incapable of transformation. The *mudra* (gesture) of her palms placed together represents peace, devotion and the ability to remain unruffled in the face of apparently insurmountable obstacles. A Buddhist may say this is because she understands the emptiness or spiritual spaciousness beneath all phenomena and therefore cannot be overpowered by worldly appearances. The flames behind her are a symbol of protection, purification, transformation and power.

5. Kuan Yin of Enjoyment and Playfulness

This light-hearted Kuan Yin offers protection, especially to those who have been influenced by extreme negativity and have lost their footing on their path. We've probably all experienced this at one time or another. We may have attained that elusive sense of balance in our lives, and then—*bam!*—the rug is pulled out from beneath us. It may be that we hear mean-spirited gossip about us or become the target of someone's jealousy or negativity. Or perhaps we experience a traumatic event that shakes us to the core.

In the hero's journey, the nemesis often appears in the last moments before victory. This can be a good sign. Father Thomas Keating said evil forces don't worry about most of us, as we aren't making enough spiritual progress to cause them any disturbance. They see us in our muddle, roll over and go back to sleep! So, if you are feeling like negative forces are blocking you, you can at least be flattered that your light is growing strong enough to cause some positive influence in the world! That being said, when you are struggling to regain sure footing on the path of light, it is comforting to know Kuan Yin is there for you.

It may seem strange to pair darkness with such a light-hearted form. In a beautiful teaching about Orange Tara, a particularly vibrant and active emanation of Kuan Yin, she stomps her foot and conquers demonic forces with her laughter. This is the healing power of joyfulness.

I wrote an oracle deck called *Divine Circus*. Some people loved it to bits, and some were attracted to it, but couldn't understand what it is all about. That's the point of it. It is funny and mischievous. I couldn't help but giggle at some of the healing processes that came through for the project because they were incredibly fun as well as deeply healing. And they ignited the sacred rebel within. It takes my *Sacred Rebels Oracle* to a cheekier place. *Divine Circus* uses the power of humour, irreverence and laughter to destabilise negative patterns in our psyche. It is like a court jester who tells the truth in creative ways and helps prevent evil from gaining an upper hand in the kingdom.

The problem with negativity is that it can be so 'sticky' and difficult to release once it gets a grip on our hearts. We can become so intense when we try to change something which is causing us pain that we lose our connection with the joy and laughter that can break it up. Often, we find it easier to fall into a habit of negative thinking than a pattern of positive behaviour. We focus on the one negative thing, rather than the hundred positive things! At such times, Kuan Yin can rescue us with her divine playfulness by reminding us there are joyful ways to overcome even the most intense darkness. Evil is repelled by lightness of spirit like a junk-food addict would run from a lettuce leaf, even when it is the best thing for us all.

6. White-Robed Kuan Yin

Most depictions of Kuan Yin show her in this maternal form. Here, Kuan Yin's white robes symbolise spiritual purity, referring to the inherent nature of spirit, which remains stainless and unchanged, even in the face of many and varied experiences.

When we recognise the purity of our own spirit, we are relieved of tremendous suffering to do with shame and guilt. It is natural to feel healthy shame when we have taken actions which are out of alignment with our integrity or values. It isn't a pleasant feeling, but neither is it a self-destructive emotion. It can simply help us realise the behaviour in question isn't right for us; it's not in harmony with our spirit. We can then take steps to heal the issues that trigger such behaviour. We grow in inner peace, as a result. That healthy shame helped us grow. Healthy shame helps us take responsibility for ourselves and our contribution to the world.

However, if we have been subject to toxic shame, we may not believe it is our behaviour that needs to change, but that we are fundamentally not enough, that we are damaged or inadequate in some way. Then, instead of being an opportunity to grow, any experience which opens us to embarrassment, shame or guilt can reinforce our devalued, denigrated sense of self. This is so very painful! Toxic shaming can cause us to pull back, shut down and refuse the loving invitations life offers us to develop and express our potential.

During my twenties, I sought out a therapist to help me explore, heal and free myself from the childhood patterns I felt were behind the base-level anxiety that seemed to be with me almost constantly. It took years to reach such freedom, but the relief from the underlying stress made the struggle to work through it so worthwhile. The therapist and I had worked together for several years, peeling back layers of unresolved childhood experience and going deep into parts of my psyche I wasn't previously aware of, yet were influencing my life and needed healing. During one session, I was suddenly hit with a feeling I had never consciously experienced before. It was like a phantom dashed in and out of my heart so quickly, I almost missed it. I said to my therapist, "I am feeling something I am finding very hard to express."

There was so much shame coated around this feeling that trying to bring it out from within me and felt like trying to release a lump of hot concrete from my throat. I experienced such powerful resistance that I wondered if I could even physically say the words! My therapist sat patiently, not judging, as I went through an unexpectedly painful inner struggle. Eventually—somehow—I managed to say the words: "I feel like I need you."

It was terrifying to me to express any kind of dependency, especially when it was tinged with a fear of loss. I felt ashamed. I felt I should be able to do everything on my own and be completely self-reliant. I felt any need for anyone else, rather than being a natural and healthy human desire, was a shameful failure on my part. My experience of relationship was based on me being the 'strong one' and 'carrying the load' for myself *and* for my partner. So, I kept choosing men who would rely on me to do that. Behind this, I had a deep fear of being abandoned. Not allowing myself to really need anyone was an attempt to protect myself from feeling further pain.

From my mother's ancestral line, I received the psychological inheritance of being a strong, independent woman, capable of accomplishing whatever I turned my mind towards — and I was grateful for that. I never felt being a woman was an impediment to anything I set out to do. If anything, I felt it was an asset. However, somewhere amongst that helpful conditioning, I had become disconnected from the more vulnerable parts of myself. The suppression of those parts was draining my energy and preventing me from moving forward and learning to identify my needs and meet them, rather than hide from them. In acknowledging those parts, what I became capable of accomplishing increased and I became happier within myself, too.

Kuan Yin helps us release false views of self, including toxic shame. As a healing mother, she helps us reprogram our internal mother-child relationship and develop it in a healthy way. That doesn't turn us into raging infants but, rather, allows us, as mature adults, to feel we are worthy individuals. Such worthiness, when genuine, is not about becoming a greedy, narcissistic person who believes the world owes them something. It is about believing we have something of value within us to be and share with the world.

7. Kuan Yin Seated upon Lotus

In this form, Kuan Yin is in her royal posture, seated upon a lotus, usually with a crown upon her head. Today, we may think of the actions of European monarchs or the excitement of imminent royal weddings when we talk about royalty, but the greater concept of royalty has spiritual relevance, too. It relates to our innate dignity.

Dignity refers to our ability to feel and act with respect, grace and maturity. Sometimes, we find ourselves in situations which are beyond our control. Anyone who has felt dehumanised whilst undergoing an invasive or confronting medical procedure or found themselves feeling like a 'number' rather than a person when dealing with a legal or other administrative matter knows this from experience. Yet, retaining one's dignity is not about avoiding such experiences. I remember my beloved grandmother telling me once that, during a medical examination in which the doctor asked her to remove all her clothing, she did so, but absolutely refused to remove her pearl jewellery. When the doctor asked why, she declared that, if she was wearing her pearls, she didn't feel naked! It was her way of retaining some power, dignity and self-respect through what could easily have been an unduly uncomfortable and undignified encounter.

The approach that worked for my strong-minded grandmother may well work for us if we can find our own 'pearls' to sustain us during difficult experiences. Our pearls are whatever connects us to an inner sense of strength, self-respect, love, compassion, dignity and grace — no matter what is going on in our lives. So, if we are drawn into an emotionally fraught situation—for example, having our luggage opened in public (lingerie and all) at airport security or undergoing a medical exam that has us feeling more like an animal than a person — we can still summon an inner connection to dignity, grace and our 'inner royalty' to sustain us.

A friend of mine was travelling with a small group of women to an ashram in India. They were on public transport for prolonged periods during which they were subjected to some negative attention from the far greater numbers of men on the bus. When the bus stopped for the men to use the toilet facilities, there was no place for the women to go. The men began pointing and laughing at the women, who really were in a bit of trouble. With 'necessity being the mother of invention', as the saying goes, the women rallied. They found extra scarves and pashminas in their bags and, creating a circle, held up the fabric for privacy and began singing (Durga chants, to the badass Hindu goddess of light who conquers all evil, if I remember correctly), whilst each woman took her turn squatting in the centre and relieving herself. Through some creative community effort, they overcame potential humiliation, held on to their dignity, released their bladders and paid homage to the goddess at the same time. What a fabulous example of sacred feminine multitasking!

8. Kuan Yin Gazing upon the Waterfall

Flowing water is a powerful symbol. It has the power to invigorate, cleanse and refresh. Visualising oneself standing underneath a waterfall is powerful. I use it on the *Meditations with Ganesha* album. You can try it right now, if you wish. Imagine you are standing beneath a pure waterfall. As the water flows over you, you are cleansed and rejuvenated. You can also practice this visualisation in the shower, especially if you feel an emotional, psychic or psychological cleanse would be beneficial for you. You might sing some of the mantras we will learn later in this book, too, creating a fun, effective, singing-in-the-shower spiritual practice to refresh your body and soul — and perhaps also entertain your pets (am I the only person who finds cats like to sit in the bathroom when you are bathing?).

In the Chinese art of *feng shui* (Chinese geomancy), flowing water can represent the clearing away of negative energy and an opening to positive energies of abundance. I experienced this during a series of back-to-back, long-haul international flights that had me sitting in Singapore Changi Airport for hours. Energetically overloaded from the radiation of the plane and psychically congested from the thoughts and feelings of the passengers with whom I shared space in the cabin, I wandered about the airport, relieved to be off another long flight, but also feeling in need of refreshment. I went in search of the airport's indoor butterfly sanctuary and on my way found a pool with koi fish and running water. As I plonked myself down on the edge of the water feature, I felt my stress just melt away with that running water. It made the trip to the butterfly sanctuary that much more enjoyable.

The waterfall symbolism asks us to trust in a greater flow of energy moving through us. There is much spiritual grace available to cleanse, heal and uplift us on a daily basis, but the struggle with our repetitive thoughts and negative behaviours can be real. So, what's happening there? Is there something we can do to help alleviate our own suffering? Kuan Yin gazing upon the waterfall asks us to let her step in and not feel we must control everything. The healing available when we stand under a waterfall comes from giving ourselves over to something completely, to being open and willing to be overpowered. This is a sacred surrender. It wouldn't be quite the same if you were only willing to step under that waterfall whilst wearing a wet suit and raincoat and holding an open umbrella above your head. If we approach the sanctuary of spiritual grace through prayer and ask for assistance but then try to exert our own control, that's kind of what we are doing. Going to the waterfall, umbrella in hand.

9. Kuan Yin Medicine Buddha

This joy-giving Kuan Yin provides the medicine to heal our worldly struggles. She appears beside a pond, contemplating the lotuses, one hand on her knee, in deep reflection, considering how to best help us on our journey.

The Universe is a great medicine holder. It knows how to provide all that is required for our potential to be expressed and for our inner promise to unfold into beautiful creativity. Through the mysterious workings of life, we are given all we need to grow, unearth our inner talents, develop the qualities we need—strength, courage, wisdom, grace, compassion and optimism—so we can be all we are divinely destined to be. Sometimes, the medicine is delivered through an unpleasant challenge. That is rather like being fed some foul-tasting liquid on a spoon. Even if it makes you better in the long run, it might be hard to feel inspired by it in the short term. I remember my mother mixing up Chinese herbs on the stove for various ailments throughout my childhood. The intensely pungent smell alone was surely enough to scare illness away!

Fortunately, medicine can also be sweet. Yoga has been such a medicine for me, physically and emotionally. Entering certain relationships—therapeutic relationships, professional relationships and one particular romantic relationship—has also been medicinal, helping me overcome unhelpful and painful childhood patterns and open up to a more fearless and internally secure way of being. Sometimes, those more palatable medicines can heal far more than we imagine possible. Something that begins to heal an emotional tendency, can help us take the steps necessary to change our physical behaviours and psychological habits, too. It's been my experience that there can be solutions right under our noses, but until we open our hearts and minds to the possibility of healing, we just don't see them or know how to implement them. It is like holding the bottle of (not too bad-tasting) medicine, yet not drinking it.

Kuan Yin's graceful intervention can help us recognise what we are holding and encourage us to guzzle that goodness down, so it can take effect. She can help us heal our minds, so we don't become stuck in the fear that we won't find a way through our problems. She can support us in opening our hearts, so we can see the many opportunities for healing which are always before us.

That the medicine Kuan Yin is also known as the joy-giving Kuan Yin suggests a beautiful promise — that the path out of suffering need not entail even more suffering. The expression 'better the devil you know,' erroneously assumes what you don't know must also be a devil. The joyful, medicine-giving Kuan Yin knows happiness can be found without struggle. In opening to her, we can release our fears and negative expectations and find, instead, the joy akin to sunlight breaking through the clouds.

10. KUAN YIN BEARING THE FISH BASKET

This form of Kuan Yin often sits or stands upon a koi fish and holds the fish basket in which the negative energies she conquers will be contained. The fish is a powerful and ancient spiritual symbol, predating Christianity where it has become a symbol for Christ. The fish is considered sacred to the goddess Venus, and was eaten on Fridays, the day dedicated to her, as part of her rituals. Venus' later emanation as Aphrodite rising from the ocean connects her again to the fish. The Greek goddess of the moon, Artemis, had a fish symbol associated with her womb. Fishes were also depicted in the goddess art of the ancient Minoans, which related fish to the feminine creative powers of the womb. The Greek word *delphos* can mean both *womb* and *fish* and the goddess worshipped by the Oracle of Delphi, Themis, was a goddess of divine law, with earlier origins as the fish goddess. Christ is still associated with the fish symbol, and on Good Friday in the Christian tradition, one is advised to eat fish — a nice tie to the original connection of fish with the divine mothering energy.

Kuan Yin, in her fish-basket-bearing form, protects humans specifically from the other-worldly beings of Indian tales known as the *rakshas* and *nagas*. These creatures have the capacity to either harm or help humanity.

Rakshas are demon-like warrior beings with a hunger for the chaos of war. In our world, this consciousness is at work when, for example, an advertising company pays top dollar to slot their marketing in after the lead horror story on the evening newscast. Perhaps they do this because they believe an anxious, despairing person is vulnerable to influence and, therefore, more likely to purchase their product. War-profiteers, arms dealers, drug-dealers and others who generate or encourage pain, despair, fear or self-destructive behaviours for profit, could be said to be possessed or driven by rakshas, thus giving rise to the need for this particular form of Kuan Yin's protection.

Nagas are fascinating beings. They are depicted with coiled serpent tails, and often five serpent heads rising behind a human-like face. Typically, their wings are outstretched behind them, and swaths of silk flow around their strange and elegant form. They are adorned with jewels and wear a crown. Nagas who are benevolent to humanity can hold secret treasure between their hands, representing a blessing which can manifest in numerous ways. But, nagas who are not so kindly disposed towards humans can cause afflictions of imbalance in the water element, which can result in poisoning and cancer, among other diseases. Even otherwise benevolent nagas can become disturbed and disturbing when our water sources are polluted and abused.

Kuan Yin in this form can help us soothe the water spirits of nagas and show us ways to work together with nature's wisdom to heal our water sources, along with the water element in our own bodies. According to Tibetan wisdom this relates to numerous diseases yet to be cured by modern medicine. Her loving grace can help us find a way to befriend the nagas and gain their support in positively influencing those around us.

11. Kuan Yin Virtuous Queen

In Buddhism, Brahma is a heavenly divine being. He is also the creator god in Hinduism. Although Buddhism doesn't embrace the idea of a creator god in quite the same way as Hinduism or Christianity, Buddhists do see Brahma as the celestial ruler of a heavenly kingdom — delightfully said to be the realm of all the flowers and the most beautiful place to seek an afterlife. As the supreme being, Brahma is the source of love and all higher knowledge, including that of our life path and spiritual purpose. It is said that when the Buddha obtained enlightenment it was Brahma who urged him to teach what he had learned to others.

As the virtuous queen, Kuan Yin is Brahma, the supreme being, divine principle of guidance, knowledge, wisdom and instruction and the ultimate creative principle. In this form, she is depicted seated on a rock, a willow branch in her right hand and her left hand resting below her navel, over the creative centre or *Dan Tian* point. The placement of that hand is significant.

I very much enjoyed my acupuncture treatments with a healer in Cronulla, on Sydney's southern beaches, when I lived near there. The practitioner enjoyed them too, because I would describe the flow of energy that I felt moving through my body during treatments which invariably corresponded to the *meridians* (energy pathways) he had studied in China, of which I personally knew nothing. It was affirming for us both. During one session, he was nudging a tiny acupuncture needle into a space beneath my belly. It felt like it was going beyond physical space, into an inner space. Eventually, the tip of the needle hit an energy point, and suddenly I was aware of an egg-like object inside my belly. I asked my practitioner what it was. He responded, "That's Dan Tian."

The energy centre in Traditional Chinese Medicine (TCM) known as Dan Tian is not like the *chakras* we think of as 'energy centres', in the west. Chakras are not holding places so much as intersection points or vortices that help move energy through the body. Dan Tian is an actual container of energy. Like a rechargeable battery, it can be topped up with life-affirming practices, or drained when we are constantly giving out and not taking enough back in. When Dan Tian is filled, we feel vital, present and alive. Our instincts are excellent, and our creativity is heightened. We manifest more easily and recognise the guiding presence of the Divine in our lives more readily. It's easier to meditate, move, or be still, depending on what circumstances require. We feel more grounded and connected to ourselves and the Universe. We are present and capable of taking action on our life path. Dan Tian is also a well of joyful, playful vitality. Kuan Yin's protection of this inner reservoir ensures the maximisation of our creative capabilities and enhances our ability to see and dwell within the beauty of life, just like Brahma, shining in his fields of celestial flowers.

12. KUAN YIN OF THE WATER MOON

Kuan Yin of the Water Moon is known as a *lone Buddha*. Buddhism teaches us we can attain enlightenment by sincere effort, even without a teacher, during times when such teachers are not available. There are certainly realised masters on this planet helping people find their way. Even so, many have not yet consciously connected with a capable teacher and may feel they are without a guiding spiritual friend on this earth.

Perhaps we have a teacher, but they are not always able to assist us, either because of the limits of their skilfulness or our inability to connect with them on the inner level when they are unavailable to us physically. Or, we might consider ourselves 'lone wolves', and, because of past negative experiences, will not allow a teacher into our lives. Even so, as much as those who are open to it, we still require a mentor, friend, guardian and guide who can care for us and ensure we stay true to our path. A teacher never walks our path for us but can be active in our consciousness in such a way that they protect and encourage us to take our own journey with authenticity and grace.

This form of Kuan Yin generates spontaneously-emerging inner awareness. This is the operation of the inner teacher, when there is no outer teacher to guide us. My first spiritual teacher taught me that spirit guides could plant thoughts in one's mind telepathically. So, one day, you'd be asking for help on an issue, and later an amazing solution would occur to you. Whilst you were congratulating yourself on being brilliant—but also wondering why you hadn't seen such an obvious solution in the first place—your spirit guides were happy you'd gotten their message (being enlightened, they didn't give a hoot if they got credit for the idea; they just wanted to help you prosper and succeed).

Like such spirit guides, Kuan Yin of the Water Moon helps you understand the things that you need to know. Numerous times, when I was pondering some question, an understanding of great wisdom came to me and placed the question in a completely different context. Was I suddenly brilliant? I suspect not. My experience was so seamless and gracious it was *almost* impossible to detect exactly where the stream of higher wisdom met my own consciousness — a bit like trying to figure out exactly, when standing at the meeting point of river and ocean, which water drops are river, and which are ocean. However, I have learned to detect Kuan Yin's 'hand' in planting greater awareness in my mind. I experience it as effortless understanding. I just instantly 'get' something I hadn't understood that way before. And it usually happens randomly, when I am walking or meditating and not trying to figure it out. It is a spontaneous, inner-divine reframe, which assists me in resolving problems through a new and effective approach.

When Kuan Yin of the Water Moon comes to you, it may be that you have no teacher or that you've been relying on a teacher to the detriment of your confidence in wisdom to spontaneously emerge in your own heart. Kuan Yin comes in this form to remind us we are not separate from the great wisdom, and if we allow her, she will assist us in finding our way and provide us with teachers who will care for our souls. She will also protect us if our teacher, despite a well-intentioned heart, is limited in their capacity to truly assist us in making progress. It is safe to develop confidence in our own inner knowing. Just as the moon reflects the sun and the water reflects the moon, so, too, is the great light perceptible within us.

13. KUAN YIN OF THE SINGLE LEAF

Seated upon a single lotus petal, one hand on her knee, the other supporting her body, she floats upon the waters. This form of Kuan Yin is dedicated to those in dangerous waters, who are drifting helplessly in floods. We call on her name to reach the safety of shallow waters.

The danger of floods and drowning is both physical and symbolic of spiritual danger. Spiritually, we are drowning in dangerous waters when our emotions or fixed opinions overpower our wisdom. We may be so convinced by the power of what we feel or believe that we act in harmful ways.

I see this in spiritual groups from time to time. Energies in such groups tend to run strong. Invoking higher beings, doing healing rituals and connecting with others in the process—then sharing your vulnerabilities and discussing your journey—tends to dredge up psychic material to be cleared away. This can be very constructive, but it is not always easy to manage. In the process, you may feel triggered by the greater-than-usual energy, and what arises for you can seem real and compelling. Once the material has been expressed, it tends to unravel, liberating itself and leaving you with more peace and clarity than you had before. You may soon realise it was simply a release, a purification of something which no longer applies in your current life — even if it felt real just moments before. That alone can be instructive. It teaches us to rest with our feelings, to allow them some space to play out before we decide how or whether to act upon them. It can also be disconcerting to discover we can believe something to be utterly true only to feel differently about it shortly afterwards. This is a necessary understanding for the development of wisdom.

Kuan Yin can help us develop the capacity to honour and express how we feel in the moment, respecting it as our truth while holding the space for a greater truth to emerge as the initial energy plays itself out and is released. With her help, this happens *before* we decide how or if we need to take further action. For us to access such skilfulness, the waters must first be calmed, so that one can gain a sense of perspective and not act rashly, hurting oneself or others only to regret it later. Allowing emotional pain from the past to direct our actions can create distress. For example, you might break up a healthy relationship due to an emotional reaction based on your childhood history, rather than on what is happening in the present moment with your partner. Or, you might yell at your children in a pique of rage, rather than tapping into how you feel—perhaps fearful for their safety, tired or needing more support—and expressing that in a calm, constructive manner which generates solutions.

Emotionally-driven reactions can all too easily sow seeds of regret. If we are wise enough to recognise our error, then we can attempt to repair the damage as best we can. However, when we don't even recognise our emotionally-driven reactions are just that, and not a higher truth, there is no chance of stemming the tide of negative repercussions. One example of such unconscious emotional overwhelm is the momentum of mass panic, which can build like an emotional 'Mexican wave' through the collective human energy field.

The morning after the 9/11 bombing of the twin towers in New York, a newspaper depicting scenes of the destruction was left on a weights bench at my local gym. I looked at the images without reading the text first (such is the power of images) and assumed I was seeing a report from war-torn Eastern Europe or the Middle East. My sadness transformed into shock, when I realised the scene was New York City. Suddenly, it felt as if the distinction between warring and peaceable nations had been torn apart.

I was holding a meditation class the following evening. The participants turned up looking exhausted, and the energy in the room was fraught with tension, fear, anxiety and grief. These were mostly middle-class Australian women who had no ties with the United States. Yet, the media has made the world a global village these days. And, apart from that, with our developing soul growth, we no longer experience the world so much in 'us and them' terms. We are less able to shut off from what is happening in the world, even if the direct impact isn't in our own back yard.

In that meditation circle, we were processing the collective emotional field of humanity which is affected by global events whether we have the sensitivity to be consciously aware of that or not. If you throw a stone in a pond, the ripples reach beyond the point of impact. For better and worse, we are all connected, emotionally. It is always so, but some of us are more aware, willing and capable of processing it consciously than others. In a world where there is so much peril, the blessing of Kuan Yin lifts us into more manageable emotional waters, whether that means processing what is happening in our personal lives or in the world around us. Through her grace, we can not only manage those potentially disruptive collective waves, but become a positive, calming influence, stemming the tide of fear with the healing qualities of hope, compassion and light.

14. BLUE-NECK KUAN YIN

Here we meet the disease-curing, poison-overcoming Kuan Yin, who takes the name and form of Shiva, one of the most popular and powerful *devas* or gods in Hinduism. I have adored Shiva since I first heard his name, even in his most terrifying aspects, such as Bhairav who teaches us to use fear to grow on the spiritual path. Shiva is a wrathful deity and the destructive face of the Divine. He is the spiritual husband of Kali, the ferocious Black Madonna Hindu Goddess. He is the master of meditation, but if you disturb or distract him, or attempt to curb his will, he has a terrible temper! Nonetheless, he is a protective sanctuary for all sorts of beings, including those who are drawn to his masculine beauty and trust in his tenderness in the face of our devotion and those who, like Shiva, dwell beyond the confines of polite society. This includes thieves and other outcasts.

Shiva is known as the way to *satchitananda*, a Sanskrit word which essentially translates as *truth*, *consciousness* and *bliss*. He is the bringer of a destruction that is constructive at its heart and leads to liberation, rather than breaking things for the sake of it. In principle, wrathful deities appear as more dramatic, intense and powerful versions of the very thing they overcome. This is why Shiva, a manifestation of divine destruction, is so effective at overpowering harmful or sabotaging tendencies in ourselves and in others. He can even help with diseases and poisonous substances. This leads us to the story of how he became known as the Blue-Necked One.

In the creation of the Universe, a juicy piece of gossip began circling amongst the holy beings and demons. It was said there existed a nectar of immortality, a veritable fountain of youth, and whomever got their hands on it—whether good or evil—would command the Universe, gaining ultimate power. As you might imagine, both sides were determined to win the prize. The demons wanted to control the Universe and the holy ones wanted to protect it from such a dire outcome. As it turned out, this nectar was rather hard to come by and this led to the unexpected requirement that both sides work together. It was only with the combined strength of the light and dark that the ocean of consciousness could be sufficiently churned, causing this precious nectar to rise from its hiding place in the depths. Then it was a matter of who would grab it first!

In the process of liberating the healing nectar of life, its opposite (the great poison which could destroy all beings) was also released. Such are nature's checks and balances — night and day and the like. The holy ones and the demons implored Shiva to save them from being annihilated by this poison, saying only he was powerful enough to overcome its destructive nature, which he did by consuming it. And the power of that poison turned his throat blue.

When we are doing the inner work required to liberate our divine essence, we too are churning the ocean of consciousness to release the sacred inner nectar. However, it is not just the soul that is interested in the spiritual power of that precious divine inner radiance. The ego, liking nothing better than to feel more important and powerful than everyone else, will be most keen to lay claim to it. When one taps into that true inner essence, spiritual grace will flow through you. Before you realise it, the ego can sneak in and decide that you must be spiritually superior, and the effects of that grace are your own doing. Such distortion and arrogance push the truth of our essence back into hiding, undoing all the brave inner work that temporarily liberated it. It perpetuates an illusion of spiritual superiority, which reinforces ego thus creating obstacles for ourselves and others that distance us from the spiritual light within. Kuan Yin as Shiva offers much needed protection from distortions of ego which is especially important as we begin to connect with the powerful inner spiritual nature of our true essence.

15. Majestic Kuan Yin of Power

There's an inner-child healing technique which helps us overcome feelings of fear, anxiety and inadequacy when dealing with the numerous challenges arising in our lives. Essentially, the 'adult you' writes a list for the 'inner-child you' which instils confidence, trust and relaxation. What is the content of this 'magical' list? It simply contains everything you have already done that would be awesome from the viewpoint of a child. That could include owning a car, paying your bills on time, having a bank account or a job (and maybe some important or interesting things in that job), or having a great relationship. These things, important as they are, can seem kind of ordinary from an adult's perspective. However, from the perspective of a child, they show you are a capable adult. Your child self might see you having flown around the world twice as being cool, whereas your adult self might think more about claiming frequent flyer miles. Undertaking such an exercise can also help your adult self gain some confidence. It can remind you that you don't have to have everything figured out to be doing a good job of living your life.

As empowered as we can be as individuals, there is something fundamentally nourishing and humbling (in a healthy way) about surrendering into a power far greater than our own — especially when we know the source of that power is benevolent, kind, genuinely interested in us and capable of taking care of us. Life seems so much more exciting (rather than utterly terrifying), when you know you are a beloved child of the Universe. The relief that can come from having a safe place, a sanctuary, a powerful and wise guardian of refuge, is palpable. It can create peace where there was despair and trust where there was once anxiety, uncertainty and fear.

In this majestic form, Kuan Yin is like the Divine pulling out all the stops in the most-spectacular-sunset-over-mountains-you've-ever-seen sort of moment. Those are the moments when you simply cannot comprehend the vastness, magnificence and beauty of nature, of the Universe and of life. Such a loving, intelligent and wise presence makes itself known to your heart, even whilst your mind may not be able to grasp it. These rare moments are meant to scramble your intellect and open your mystical heart to the presence of something that stops the flow of insecurity and distress and simply invites you, in wordless surrender, into greater beauty, power and grace.

There are some hacks for tapping in to this state. Prayer and meditation can be powerful triggers for such awareness, but often it takes time and practice to be able to tune in to such a state at will. So, in the interim, you may want to explore what poet William Wordsworth described as the *numinous*, a feeling of something spiritual and divine. Documentaries on natural phenomena, including the nature of the planets, might work for you, as may a trip to a wildlife park. Time in nature, which is where Wordsworth found his divine connection, can tune you back in to the vital beauty of life and ground your anxiousness, transforming it into presence. In that presence, you can receive Kuan Yin's reminder that she is trustworthy, and she is with you.

16. Long-Life Kuan Yin

One of the last things my beloved grandmother said to me before she passed away was, "Alana, the date of your birth and your death are stamped in your heart. I've had my life. Now, it is time for you to live yours."

In many cultures there is a sense that life and death are prescribed by heavenly forces, whether it be a certain length of time or a certain number of breaths. While Tibetans agree with this, they also believe our allotted lifespan can be cut short by negative influences. Therefore, spiritual protection against such negativities is essential — especially, if we are on a spiritual path and want to make as much progress as possible during this lifetime (something most Tibetans would automatically assume).

When we're young, we may take the idea of a long life for granted. In the West, we tend to think of prolonging life as a medical rather than spiritual matter. In the East, the spiritual is just as important as the medical. Spiritual protection can attract the best medical care, repel confusing misdiagnoses and ameliorate the errors of medical practitioners.

The Tibetan concept of the Universe is colourful. Although it may seem folksy to the more scientifically-skewed, if you know the language and have some basic understanding of the subtle energies which connect and influence all beings on this planet, the sophistication of the Tibetan cosmology begins to reveal itself. So, whether our life force is stolen by hungry ghosts, demons or negative karma—or (in a slightly more Western view) toxic relationship dynamics, unresolved issues from the past, environmental poisons and pathogens or genetic predisposition to disease—spiritual protection of our allotted lifespan is important.

When I first saw my Dzogchen master, it was via a live online broadcast for a spiritual transmission. My heart just opened to him. He was happy, peaceful and had a great sense of humour, combined with a Yoda-esque appearance I couldn't resist. As he sounded the first mantra, a long-held tension in my head melted like ice in the warmth of the sun. When he urged us to relax into our true nature, it felt like the most appealing spiritual invitation I'd ever received. He was also an interesting man, having had many adventures, from cheeky boyhood antics in Tibet to overcoming great challenges as an adult, including a very serious form of cancer. So serious was this cancer, that he was told by medical professionals in Europe he would not live beyond a certain date. Well, that expiration date was decades prior to my first encounter with him. He worked hard throughout his life to overcome the forces of disease which could minimise his lifespan.

Why did he do this? As a highly-realised being, fear of death was not an issue, nor was attachment to that body. In fact, when he did eventually pass away, his energy became even more powerful. However, he fought for his health, living for eighty years, because he was passionate about helping those who relied on him for spiritual guidance and needed to relate to him in a human body in order to obtain teachings. The spiritual responsibility he willingly assumed as a teacher required that he take responsibility for his health to keep his body, seen in Tibetan Buddhism as a precious vehicle, alive and well for as long as possible for the benefit of those who are assisted by his presence on this earth.

Medical experts were astonished at the diseases he overcame during his incarnation. He was a very skilful healer, but he humbly stated, "The human body is very complicated." That an illumined being such as this teacher found sustaining wellbeing tough at times provides reassurance if we are also finding the cultivation of wellbeing to be a challenge, even with all the knowledge that is emerging in the helpful field of integrative and functional modern medicine. It is also an encouragement for those of us working through health challenges whilst treading, for example, the path of healer, guide, parent or teacher, and who want to live long for the benefit of their spiritual path and for those they support.

Apart from the rare precious being who pops out of the womb fully enlightened and ready to go, most of us need to work on ourselves for years, likely decades, to clear the confusion and pain that obscures our awareness of our true nature. Once we begin to 'get' the (spiritual) program—say, some forty, sixty or seventy years into our life— we want as much time as possible to share the treasures we have earned, so others can benefit from our hard-won experience. We don't want to labour our entire lives to find the treasure feast, finally hold a tasty morsel of divine nourishment up to our lips and then drop dead! What a loss to go through all that and then be denied the opportunity to take a bite and maybe even moan with such delight that others are curious to see what the fuss is about and find their way to the sacred table, too! Imagine getting so close and then needing to reincarnate, do another seventy-odd years of prep, just to get pipped at the post again! Better to connect with Kuan Yin and make the most of the beautiful spiritual growth which comes in the latter part of our life journey, so we can make enough progress to pull ourselves, and others, further along the path.

Spiritual intervention can help so much. We don't need to judge illness but, rather, accept the invitation to ask the Divine for assistance in all ways so we can work through it for the greater good.

This form of Kuan Yin is seated behind a rock, resting one hand on her cheek and one upon the rock, with a crown with the Buddha of Infinite Light, Amitabha, upon her head. She protects all beings from negative influences that can shorten our lifespan.

17. Kuan Yin of Many Treasures

In the movie *Indiana Jones and the Last Crusade*, our hero—part professor of archaeology, part adventurous treasure hunter—has found a series of clues, purportedly leading to the resting place of the famed Holy Grail. Following these clues leads him on a journey fraught with peril. At one stage, he repeats the clue meant to help him overcome a challenge. "Only a penitent man shall pass," he says over and over whilst tension builds, and he (and the viewer) feels certain some dreadful moment shall soon be upon him if he doesn't figure out what that clue means! Suddenly, he says, "A penitent man kneels before God. Kneel!" and he drops to his knees just as a weapon swoops through the space where his neck would have otherwise been. He overcomes further tests and secures the Grail, but only for long enough to restore his father's health. The Grail, it seems, is a power too great for human beings to wisely handle, and it falls into a cavernous opening in the earth, not to be found again — at least for the time being.

Sometimes, it may seem that the more precious the treasure the more fraught the journey to obtain it. Perhaps it is worldly wealth one seeks, and the protection needed is to keep one's soul, one's sense of what really matters and one's integrity, intact. Perhaps the journey is taking you to a deeper treasure. Maybe you are seeking to unearth a talent, or the means for a cherished dream to come to life or you are on a journey of self-discovery and spiritual awakening, compelled by an inner desire you do not fully understand.

By its very nature, a quest of any description will lead beyond what we know. In the realms of unknown territory, no matter how much preparation we undertake, elements different from any we have encountered before will arise in ways we simply cannot anticipate. Not having the experience to guide us, we need to wing it, remaining present and open to spontaneous wisdom and blessings to help us.

This specific form of Kuan Yin protects us when we seek treasures in unknown lands. Those lands may be the unprocessed fears of your inner world, when you journey within your own psyche to heal an issue or obtain the great treasure of illumination. The unknown lands could also be the emotional terrain you seek to navigate when meeting your new partner's children for the first time. Those lands could be literal, as when you are travelling to a new place which is very different to any other country you have visited, and you are not certain of matters of safety or cultural mores.

Living with courage and boldness requires confidence. Knowing you have spiritual protection, especially for those moments when one's heart seems to lead one straight into dangerous territory—emotionally or physically or on any level, really—is a great comfort. I have been in situations I would not particularly wish to repeat, but I have always felt a sense of protection and divine assistance. Kuan Yin is our great ally. She helps our adventurous spirit to thrive, so we can explore, learn and grow — even through hair-raising moments.

18. Kuan Yin of the Cave

Caves have provided dwelling places for those who worship the sacred feminine and pursue spiritual enlightenment for thousands of years and across numerous spiritual traditions. The cave-dwelling *yogi* or *spiritual practitioner* has separated themselves from society, unplugging from mainstream consciousness and, instead, seeking the truth within. To find that more truthful, empowered awareness, they may endure great hardship. For those who are going on spiritual retreat (whether in a cave or not), Kuan

Yin in this form ensures protection.

Even if we are not inclined to go on a cave-dwelling spiritual retreat, the desire to withdraw from the mainstream to choose a more authentic, heart-oriented lifestyle is something that many on a spiritual path will experience at some time. The pressure to conform to our loved ones' belief systems, to face their concern that we will step beyond what they have known and their resistance to our change and growth, can create tripping points on our journey. When you feel you are the only person seeing things a certain way, you may fear you are going crazy. You are not, of course. You are simply waking up. But whilst this can be a gentle experience for some, for others it can feel deeply challenging. Kuan Yin's protection, as we step beyond societal values and conditioning, can help us have the courage we need to stay true to our genuine path and spiritual promise.

In the West, we are limited in our understanding of the tremendous gift an enlightened person can bring. Their spiritual work can be the equivalent of switching on a bright light in the darkness to help a massive number of souls find their way. One must understand the power of spiritual energy, and that all are connected and effected by each other (for better or worse), to accept this.

My Dzogchen master tells a story of a mountain-cave-dwelling spiritual practitioner who became so well known in his Tibetan village that many sought him out for guidance and instruction. His fame grew so that even a high-ranking political official decided he wanted to talk with the yogi. The problem was, this practitioner's cave was not easily accessible. High in the cold Himalayas, it was not only hard to reach, but the way was frequented by dangerous wildlife. Such was the yogi's reputation, however, that even the somewhat unfit politician was undeterred in his quest.

Our determined, political heavyweight spent weeks travelling through dangerous terrain and finally reached the outskirts of the yogi's cave. He scrambled up a last rocky cliff face to the clearing before the cave. His quest was about to be fulfilled! He laid eyes upon the yogi, who sat peaceful and naked, in meditation, despite the cold, his hair long, matted and wild. The politician was about to clear his throat to gain the yogi's attention, when he noticed the yogi was not alone. Beside him sat a very large, presumably very wild, mountain lion! Although the fearsome creature was quiet in the yogi's presence, the politician had enough sense to know that could change in an instant, and he beat a hasty retreat back down the mountain. Perhaps his close encounter with the yogi and the mountain lion taught him that sometimes wisdom requires that we change our course.

Just as this yogi was able to reach and teach, even whilst in meditation, so too do we have a far-reaching spiritual capacity within, waiting to be developed. As our light grows stronger through our own spiritual practices, we have an increased capacity to positively influence our world. We might even influence people we never meet. Kuan Yin of the Cave offers us the refuge and protection to take the difficult steps on our spiritual journey which ultimately lead us beyond social conditioning, helping us become free to pursue our authentic spiritual path and, in doing so, benefit many beings.

19. KUAN YIN OF TRANQUILLITY

This form of Kuan Yin provides calm and tranquillity and is especially dedicated to assisting those who are subject to disasters beyond their control. When we have to deal with anything from a natural disaster, to living in a war zone, to the onslaught of a plague, to the collective insanity which may arise after a traumatic event, the balm of peace can flow from her heart to ours.

Something important and helpful happens in that place of inner peace. When the roiling disturbances of the mind begin to settle, we let go of our fears of the future and release negative attachments to disturbances from the past. Instead, we become present in that moment and discover all sorts of resources are available to us. These might include helping hands from those around us or our own inner resources, such as courage, strength, wisdom, patience and determination. We may not have known we had those qualities, or had them to that degree, until that moment.

When we are fully present, we can accept a difficult situation and quiet the painful 'whys' which might otherwise result in unhelpful interpretations of events and, thus, to unnecessary feelings of guilt, shame and blame. While we can wish with all our heart an event hadn't taken place, we can also push up our sleeves and get on with the business of cleaning up the mess, using our particular talents to contribute something constructive to the situation.

Far from making us passive, peacefulness leads us to being less reactive—and, therefore, less likely to do something we regret later—and it empowers us to become more strategic and creative our actions.

Most New Age teachings encourage us not to indulge in victim mentality and, instead, take responsibility for our lives. That is generally good advice. However, we must be careful we don't take it too far and end up using that teaching to excuse an absence of compassion for those who are victims of situations beyond their control. In the case of natural disaster, for example, we need to realise we all contribute at some level to what is happening on this planet, constructively and destructively. When there is a disaster, we are part of the reason nature released her energies in such a way. But taking responsibility is never about apportioning blame to ourselves or others. It is about recognising we have the power to contribute towards a better outcome. We may not be able to do that on our own. We may not even see how our talents could help. But if we are willing to step into a peaceful acceptance of what is, the Universe will inspire us with the steps we can take. I honestly believe each of us has a vital role to play in supporting each other, and that the Universe arranges and expresses itself through us in ways our limited mindsets cannot fathom. All we need to do is open our hearts and participate with trust — even in the face of mystery.

20. Thousand-Armed Kuan Yin

This depiction of Kuan Yin, arrayed with a thousand arms and multiple faces, is one of the most evocative. In this form, she is the ultimate, cosmic, multi-tasking mother, capable of tending to the needs of all beings, simultaneously — particularly those who are castaway at sea. When facing the possibility of drowning, if one calls on her name, they shall not be harmed.

This reminds me of a beautiful story of Mother Mary, venerated as Our Lady of Charity. Two men and a boy were at sea in a small vessel when a storm came upon them. The boy wore a medal of the Virgin Mary. As the storm grew more intense, and they were fearful for their lives, they prayed to her for protection. Suddenly, the storm quietened, and in the light of the now cloudless sky, they saw an object bobbing on the gentle waves. They rowed towards it and picked it up. It was a statue of Mother Mary, with an inscription which read, "I am the Virgin of Charity." They were astonished to find the statue perfectly dry, even though it had been adrift on the sea.

French writer and Nobel Prize winner André Gide is credited with saying, "You cannot discover new oceans unless you have the courage to lose sight of the shore." To take our journeys, we may—literally or symbolically—need to cross many oceans. The ocean is a symbol of the great unknown, of consciousness, fear, our belief systems and the creative potential to birth new life. Mary, who I believe to be an emanation of Kuan Yin, bears the ancient title of *Stella Maris*, or Our Lady, Star of the Sea.

In this form of guardian of seafarers, Kuan Yin is also the guardian of our consciousness, even when our feet are on dry land. Whenever we seek to expand our consciousness, through travel, psychic development, meditation or study, we enter a process of transition, which brings with it a certain vulnerability. In exposing ourselves to fresh ideas, we need to be discerning and allow what is not right for us to pass us by. Through our exploration of new worlds, seeking out what can bring deeper meaning to our lives, we may take some wrong turns and need help extricating ourselves from places we are not meant to be. The icon in the ocean which stays dry symbolises the protective power of Mary and of Kuan Yin of a Thousand Arms. This protection is so *the mud won't stick*, so to speak. If we find ourselves in situations where we are not safe, where we do not belong, or where we could be derailed from our life path (even if it was our genuine intention to make progress which led us into a less-than-ideal situation), we will be rescued by the Divine Mother. We will be able to move on from those experiences without being harmed. This is the beautiful generosity and kindness of her grace.

21. FEARLESS KUAN YIN

How many times have you considered pursuing a certain dream, only to bring the translation of that fantasy into reality to a grinding halt by thinking, *if only I had the money?* I had a crash course in financial fear when I took a leap of faith from my corporate job and began working as a psychic, which is how my career in the metaphysical field began. I didn't have much money at the time. In fact, I had more debt than I ever had — misery loved shopping, as far as I was concerned back then. Overwhelmed by a credit card bill I couldn't easily pay off, I cut up my card and swore never to own one again. It took years to pay off that debt, but I did. And true to my word, I haven't owned a credit card since.

Whilst that helped me feel that I had more financial integrity, which in turn made me feel more in control and relaxed, it also meant I had to rely on the Universe, rather than the bank, to provide what I needed. This meant that every issue I had about being supported rather than abandoned, neglected and left to fend for myself emotionally, reared its very vocal head. The eighteen months that followed my leap of faith was my testing period. However, it wasn't the Universe testing me. I was testing myself! I knew I could trust and just see where things went and on one level, I was doing that. Yet I was also deluged by so much unprocessed fear about not being supported, which expressed itself as financial fear, that getting through each day without feeling emotionally crippled by anxiety was a challenge.

After those first eighteen months as a psychic, I noticed two things: First, I was fed up with the daily emotional onslaught and just wanted to drop it and see what happened when I truly let go. Second, despite my fear, I was managing to pay my bills. I may not have paid off that credit card as fast as I wanted, and occasionally, my bank balance was nearly zero (which triggered some very painful feelings and thoughts), yet it always replenished itself. When I needed money for rent, food and even the occasional new dress, a flurry of clients booked readings. Things were working out.

I was willing to go through those growing pains because I genuinely believed it was the pathway to my higher purpose and therefore, even if it was hard sometimes, I believed the Universe would help me break through the pain and struggle and into a more gracious way of being. As that began to happen, I gained more confidence and became willing to take more risks, creatively and professionally. I began teaching meditation and spiritual growth at a community college, then writing for a New Age magazine, then teaching interstate, then recording and self-publishing meditation CDs, then reaching out for a publisher, both for those CDs and so I could write oracle decks and books. Then I reached for international teaching opportunities, added dance and singing into my workshops and created musical performances to shift consciousness in the hearts of the audience. Soon, I was writing my own healer training programs, too. I just took step after step. Some were emotional risks, others were financial risks, but as my confidence and trust grew, so too did my ability to tune in to my heart and go for it when I felt inspired.

Sometimes we just need to know that if we leap the Universe will catch us. This form of Kuan Yin (known as Kubera in India and Dzambhala in Tibet), is a wealth-giving deity, who provides us with all we need to manifest our spiritual destiny. Our creative output can soar, and our spiritual energy can grow when we are not expending precious time and vital forces worrying about financial matters. We become more productive and are willing to take necessary steps forward when we know the Universe is capable and willing to provide for our financial and material prosperity in such a way that our spiritual path is protected and, thus, all beings can derive benefit.

22. Kuan Yin Adorned in Leaves

In this form as a mountain-dwelling hermit goddess, Kuan Yin is also known as Parnashavari. She is dressed in leaves, protects against contagious disease and offers general healing. Her powers extend not only to curing disease, but to preventing it from occurring in the first place. She is a delightful combination of peaceful and wrathful divine energy who brings peace *and* scares off disease-causing negativity. She is a manifestation of Tara, from the *karma*, or *action*, family of Buddhas, which means she gets the job done swiftly and effectively.

Kuan Yin manifests in this active form to help us figure out what we really want and need. When it comes to the demands of the ego, sometimes *not* getting what you want is a wonderful turn of events. It's not about the Universe being a big old meanie and denying you out of spite or for tough love. This sort of protection is just that — protection. It is the holiday trip you miss, to later learn that a typhoon blew through your destination. It's the relationship which doesn't quite happen, and then either you (the other person or both of you), meet the love(s) of your life. It's the job offer that falls through, which you later see would have taken you down the wrong path. It's a door that closes on a view that, though beguiling, could not bring you what you truly wanted and needed at a deeper level of soul.

Sometimes, we experience the Universe's preventative measures as painful losses, disappointments and shattered dreams. This is not because they *are* negative, but

Yo soy la Virgen de la Caridad

because we interpret them that way. I believe that every time we experience a 'no' from life, it is actually a hidden 'yes' in the form of, "Not that way, there is a better way for you." We can fight it if we choose, but if instead of fighting, we believe a higher plan is at work for our benefit, we may learn to trust that life is fundamentally benevolent and be open to it.

The Universal Mother is our creative energy. She wants for us what we want and need, too. I don't believe life is ever working against us. But when we get into our ego, thinking things will only benefit us if they unfold according to our view, we put ourselves at cross-purposes with life. As life tends to be more creative, imaginative, resourceful and spontaneous than our ego, the best stuff will happen outside of what we know, control and expect.

When this Tara of Prevention manifests in our lives, she is a reminder that whatever isn't working out as we planned is not a bad sign. The Universe is looking out for us, and we need to let go—for a short time or permanently—for a different and more beautiful opportunity to find its way to us.

23. Lapis Lazuli Medicine Mother

Depicted holding a lapis glazed jar of medicinal nectar, this is Kuan Yin in the masculine form of the Medicine Buddha, supreme healer of inner and outer ills. The Medicine Buddha, known in Tibetan Buddhism as the Master of Medicine and the King of Lapis Lazuli Light, is pictured with a skin of dark blue, the colour of the healing lapis lazuli stone. He often holds a precious, rare-blooming plant in one hand, symbolising that the rare cure we need for our ills is in his grasp.

The powerful Medicine Buddha leads those who have suffered—or become lost or estranged from their spiritual path or personal integrity—lovingly back to their genuine life path. The Medicine Buddha offers healing for both the inner being and for the body so one's life can come into harmony with the Universe. In that place of harmony, there is a continual flow of healing and development. This means no matter how much of a mess our lives may have become, there is a clear path on which progress can made into a happier way of being. This is not temporary relief, but rather permanent transformation. It is the curing of a condition, be it physical or spiritual, so the real radiance of one's inner nature can shine through. The Medicine Buddha grants wish fulfilment, provides blessings for healing and wealth and offers protection against danger and violence — as all Kuan Yin's forms do.

From the Buddhist perspective, 'inner sickness' could refer to an attachment that prevents us from loving with courage and faith or perhaps emotions of hatred and anger that block us from seeing that we are all connected. A beautiful vow tells us that, if someone suffered from starvation and committed a crime to obtain food and they call faithfully upon the Medicine Buddha's name, they will be divinely guided to find spiritual connection, receive the best food and eventually lead a happy, tranquil life. Whether we have been starved of love and stolen the affections of someone we would have been better off leaving alone, or starved of fulfilment and allowed our jealousy to steal away happiness for another's success, or starved of financial security and resorted to unethical practices to overcome our sense of lack, the Medicine Buddha promises there is a way forward. If you genuinely wish to put guilt and pain behind you and open to a new life, you will be shown how to obtain it. This will foster harmony in your own world and in the world of those around you.

The special 'extra grace' of the Medicine Buddha is for those who have no-one to turn to or rely upon. They will be blessed with family, with connections and support, love and healing, happiness and grace. If you have been alone, Medicine Buddha will connect you to your tribe. If labouring under misdiagnosis, Medicine Buddha will shine the light of clarity. The Medicine Buddha watches over and protects those who faithfully call upon his name during all transitions, including birth and death. The Medicine Buddha is a luminous, shining, generous being of unending compassion dedicated to the relief of suffering of all beings.

24. Kuan Yin of Salvation

This form of Kuan Yin, as goddess Tara, is the saviour deity. She provides salvation, protection and endless blessings. She has the power to transform hostile intent into mercy. Her form is especially for protection from those with vicious, malicious intentions.

Kuan Yin of Salvation brings the extraordinary life of Peace Pilgrim to mind. This woman gave up her birth name and walked for peace, from one side of North America to the other, for twenty-eight years. She ate when she was given food, and she took shelter when it was offered. It was always offered; she never asked. Radiant with love for the Divine, she spoke of the innate goodness which exists within all people, even if it seems hard to find at times. Buddhists also believe our true nature is goodness, and that the violence of doing harm to the self or other is not a reflection of our real nature but, rather, karmic wounding expressing itself.

Peace Pilgrim tells of a man she encountered when walking alone as she did on her journey. She immediately knew he intended to harm her. She also had the spiritual capacity to see the good in him, not just theoretically or intellectually, but deeply and authentically. She told him what she saw in him. That honestly-spoken truth held such spiritual purity that it freed him from his ill intentions and transformed the nature of their interaction. He followed her for quite some time afterwards, to protect her on her journey.

The distillation of our true nature can take the wind out of our ego's sails, which is helpful when we have set sail on a course that is not going to lead anywhere worthwhile. We may be yet to develop sufficient inner spiritual power to transform malevolence into mercy, such as Peace Pilgrim was able to do, but Tara can accomplish this on our behalf and our connection with her will grant us the protective shield of such power.

We need to build our faith in the goodness of others before we can trust that Tara's power to transform harmful intent into merciful release is even possible. Culturally, socially and in the media, the emphasis is too often placed on negative aspects of human behaviour. However, Peace Pilgrim cautioned, "If you knew the power of a negative thought, you'd never think one again."

There is a story that regularly circulates through social media on a regular basis, typically after a terrible event. In it, a grandfather tells his grandson of two wolves that sit on either side of him, one which is hateful and one which is forgiving. They are at war with each other. When the grandson asks his grandfather which wolf will win, the grandfather's response is, "The one that I feed."

Tara's ability to manifest powerful grace through us really does require that we make some choices. We can become ambassadors for peace if we are willing to open our hearts to her. Sometimes, we want to be mad, but, as the Dalai Lama teaches, although anger might be a common experience, it is not part of our natural state. It is something which is learned, and thus, can be unlearned. Whilst I believe you can learn from your anger and use it to know when you need to set boundaries or transform it into passionate commitment to a higher cause, I don't believe holding on to it is healthy. Learning from anger means you can let it go, having made decisions based on what it taught you. Perhaps it taught you to not be so hard on someone, or to let go of your fear that things won't work out or to let yourself off the hook for having made a very human mistake (and perhaps still have faith that things can work out, anyway). When we call upon Kuan Yin of Salvation in the form of Tara, we can be blessed with a softening of hatred and a freedom from harmful intentions, not only from others, but from within ourselves, too.

25. KUAN YIN OF THE CLAM

The giant clamshell is considered sacred in Tibet. It is one of seven precious objects to be included in a *stupa*, or *shrine*, along with gold, silver, lapis, agate and carnelian. In Christian heraldry, the clam signifies one who has completed a pilgrimage. It is associated with the love goddess Aphrodite, who is famously depicted rising from an open clam shell. The clam is also a symbol for Mother Mary who I believe to be an emanation of Kuan Yin.

Certain clams produce pearls, and some clams live extraordinarily long lives. The oldest discovered (at the time of writing) is more than 500 years old and was dredged up off the coast of Iceland from around 80 metres down in cold waters. The clam's exoskeleton grows as it does, offering it protection from predators. To survive the winter, a clam will bury itself deeper into the mud.

The sacred 'clam medicine' of this form of Kuan Yin can protect those who are seeking the 'pearl beyond price', a treasure which can only be found through courage, determination and skilfulness. She reassures us that whatever struggles we are going through, something truly precious and worthwhile will come from the suffering. Kuan Yin offers protection for such journeys whether they be literal trips across the ocean or symbolic journeys within the self to mine hidden treasures.

In this form, Kuan Yin can confirm your desire to travel to a certain place is a 'soul pilgrimage' meaning your soul is calling you there for experience, growth and learning. I very much enjoy leading retreats in various places around the world. However, I have learned to wait until I am spiritually inspired to do so, because everything runs so much more smoothly as a result — even though the places I am called to are not always the easiest places to travel. When such trips occur, they feel very much like pilgrimages, even if that word had not crossed my mind prior to the journey. Pilgrimages are journeys with spiritual significance. Sometimes you know why you are taking them, and at other times the understanding comes years after the event, when you realise something truly meaningful has unfolded as a result of the journey.

A pilgrimage requires you to hear the call of your heart. In Tibetan and Indian iconography, a blast on a conch shell is often the signifier of a spiritual call to gather, to adventure, to receive. Then, one needs the courage to act upon it. To hear the call requires us not to invalidate what we feel or sense because it is difficult, for example, or challenges us to overcome uncertainties or fears.

To act on the call often involves huge inner upheaval and outer chaos as we uproot ourselves from our 'regular life' and begin the preparations required to commence the journey. Although the journey itself will undoubtedly have its challenges, it is often these first stages which are most confronting. When one is on the journey, there is grace. What felt like a confronting, and yet compelling, challenge can begin to feel akin to our spirit taking flight. There can be freedom, insight, healing and spiritual growth, all rolled into one sacred journey.

Just like the clam can bury itself deeper into the mud for protection, we might also close ourselves off and retreat into what we know when we feel vulnerable or in the face of potential danger. Kuan Yin comes to us with encouragement. Her power can protect us as we open up to what may feel intimidating at first. When a pilgrimage is meant for us, she will help us navigate the journey as we nestle into her grace.

Some say timing is everything. I believe a higher divine timing predicts the perfect moments for our personal stars to align. This may be when you meet a person who will be significant in your life or the moment you find yourself ready to accept and fulfil a certain opportunity. I have tried to push for opportunities and ended up falling flat on my face because my enthusiasm outweighed my skilfulness! At other times, opportunities have opened for me effortlessly and with grace, and because of all that had happened previously, I moved through them with some degree of elegance and capability. Timing makes all the difference.

This does mean we need to develop a more embracing attitude of the oft-maligned quality of *patience*. One way I learned to do that was by seeing our spiritual journeys as car trips. We all have our various destinations. Perhaps the notion of all roads leading to Rome, as my Catholic grandmother used to say, means we are ultimately headed to the same place. Nonetheless, the route we take to get there will be unique for each of us. We are all churning our karma, which means there will be blessings and easy opportunities, along with soul-strengthening challenges, to deal with along the way.

Imagine everyone wants to get to their destination as quickly and joyfully as they can. Of course, we will meet green lights and red lights. We could become frustrated at the red lights. We could assume they mean 'no!' instead of 'hang on, some things need to happen first so the right people and circumstances are ready for you at the right moment.'

If we trust in the grace of the Universe and believe it is not against us—something we constantly need to fight—then we can proceed a little more patiently *and* happily. Some of my students literally groan when I speak about having patience. They think it is a burden to bear, as though their frustrations will last for as long as they must be patient for ... as though those two things go hand in hand. But one can choose to experience patience as a form of letting go, surrender and trust. There is a relief that comes with patience. It is the end of frustration, not the enduring of it. We don't have to go through the exhausting process of continually trying to make something happen that is not within our power or responsibility to manifest. We can, instead, focus on what we *can* do with great enthusiasm and dedication, and leave the rest to the Universe. We can trust in the process and simply take the journey — delays, apparent obstacles, challenges and all.

Kuan Yin of the Six Times refers to the various times throughout the day that Tibetan spiritual practice dedicates to meditation, ceremony, devotion and so forth. She knows the right time for the right thing, and if we trust in her, she will guide us through the green lights, reassure us during the red lights and help us reach our destination at the perfect time.

Maheshvara is a name for Shiva, the wild, enlightened, destructive and protective deity we met earlier on in his 'blue-throated' form of Kuan Yin. Depending on your religious or cultural orientation, Shiva can be known as a divine being, much like the God of Christianity, as an enlightened yogi or as a Buddha in his own right, an emanation of Kuan Yin.

As a form of Kuan Yin, wild Shiva is beautifully relevant to what is happening in our world. According to Hindu philosophy, we are currently in a spiritual dark age. To recognise this, one only has to look at reality TV celebrities, who are worshipped as deities of sorts, and who have extraordinary influence over how many people think, behave and cultivate their values. They may be great people, but they are humans, not divine guardians. Whilst they may provide some inspiration (which could, in certain cases, be a positive thing), they cannot provide spiritual protection for the soul. To unconsciously cast godliness upon that which is not divine never ends well. It is looking for love in all the wrong places, as the expression goes. It distracts us from seeking and experiencing a relationship with a real divine being. We can still admire and be inspired by celebrities who speak to us, if that's our thing, but we need to keep our devotion in perspective and ensure we don't feed glitter to our soul when it hungers for true gold.

To entice us into divine connection and ensure we don't unwittingly starve our souls of what they need, the Divine shows up in myriad forms, paths, religions, deities and practices. Whatever is required to get and keep our wandering attention erupts from the divine mind, so we can seek guidance, love and comfort, support, instruction and happiness from a source that can provide it.

This doesn't mean the pleasures of the world—or even some questionable television—are necessarily bad. The danger comes when we try to make someone into what we want them to be, rather than seeing and accepting who they are. If you have ever tried to do this in a romantic relationship, you know how disastrous that can be. We can grow spiritually by learning how to live well and navigate all parts of our earthly experience. Everything can provide spiritual value, even if it only teaches us discernment. But this world does not provide enough on its own. We need a spiritual connection to relate to the world in such a way that it promotes our spiritual growth, rather than hampering it.

Maheshvara Shiva is a beautiful, fierce, protective but ultimately wild divine masculine energy. I absolutely adore him. Whenever I sing his mantra, I simply melt. For those of us who want to establish a respectful and evolved inner masculine energy to help us cut through nonsense, see clearly and have the courage to do what is necessary to honour our souls, he is a wonderful guardian. Tuning in to the many and varied energies of goddesses can help awaken the sacred feminine in ourselves, in the women in our lives, in our world, and even in those men who are courageous enough to tune in to their feelings and live from the heart. I devoted my book *Crystal Goddesses 888* to that topic. Our connection with the divine masculine can assist the men in our lives and deepen the masculine energy of protection. The divine masculine will help us value our true priorities. When it acts in a woman's psyche, masculine energy will rise up and flourish, empowering her creativity. If she is dedicated to a spiritual path, then her creative output can be for the benefit of all beings. If one has had difficult or degrading connections to male energy, this form of Kuan Yin can help heal those connections, redefine them and liberate those energies into an entirely new way of being in our lives. The true and sacred masculine energy is just as much in need of being understood, recognised and honoured as the sacred feminine. All beings benefit from such healing.

28. Lady Ma Kuan Yin

In the previous form, we saw the Divine manifest as an ultra-masculine form to empower souls in need of such energy. Here, as the Lady Ma Kuan Yin, the Divine Mother manifests in an ultra-feminine form to entice those in need of subtle, beautiful, feminine energy.

The story behind this emanation is that the warriors of a province were all basically 'boys behaving badly.' Interested in hunting and fighting, they didn't give two hoots for spiritual matters. However, the Divine wanted to save others from the warriors' violence, and to save them from their own lack of understanding by helping them grow spiritually. So, Kuan Yin manifested as an exquisitely beautiful woman, whom all the hunters wanted to marry. She set a task, so they could prove themselves worthy of her hand (clearly showing an excellent understanding of male psychology). They had to learn some complicated spiritual texts by heart. The competition was rife! Each man threw himself into mastering the texts, so he could beat the other tribesmen and get the girl. Whilst their motivation may not have been particularly pure, the end result was that the warrior tribe learned about spiritual matters.

When one man won the competition, his wife—our goddess in disguise— immediately died. To add some magic to the apparently tragic, a monk suddenly appeared and asked the tribesman to seek her remains. Intrigued by this holy man, who spontaneously emerged out of nowhere, they did so, but all they found was a golden collarbone! The monk then revealed the beautiful, mysterious woman had not been mortal, but was in fact the goddess Kuan Yin, who had taken form to assist them, and departed once the task was complete. The monk then promptly dematerialised himself! That was enough to seal the spiritual deal, and the tribe became devoutly spiritual, forever more.

In this form, Kuan Yin teaches us that we can sometimes accomplish more by meeting people where they are at and gently evoking change, than by trying to force change upon them. In Taoist wisdom, the more we try to force something to happen, the more resistance we create, and we can end up pushing away what we want to bring closer. If you've ever been in the clinging/commitment-phobic relationship dynamic (where the more unavailable you are, the more a prospective partner pursues you, or the more you cling the more the other seeks distance) you've already experienced what the Taoists are talking about. With divine wisdom there is no pushing, yet everything is accomplished. This is the way of higher intelligence and one of the reasons it's smart to trust the Universe, even when what is happening in your life doesn't make sense to you. The Divine sometimes utilises sacred mischief to help you achieve a necessary breakthrough, but there is always a loving higher purpose at work.

29. PRAYING KUAN YIN

Unlike the ready availability of celebrities to worship, some of us will be fortunate enough to see, hear or perhaps even meet the rare, genuine holy people upon the Earth during our lifetime. There *are* charlatans who claim holiness and use the appearance of enlightenment to seduce others. Rather than being oriented towards service, they charm followers out of their finances or gain a sense of personal power from having devotees.

Plenty of us are still climbing the spiritual mountain, but there are some who are much further ahead and willing to help us reach the next level of our journey. Such further-along-the-path, authentically holy people are advanced enough to be free from the delusion of ego and therefore genuinely dedicated to and highly skilled at helping others break free from their pain, so they can access true spiritual illumination. Like warm-hearted older brothers and sisters or great friends to our souls, such holy ones provide us real comfort and support on the spiritual path.

Such beings are inspirational. They help us feel how the presence of truth, spirit and divine love within the soul can ignite the heart to overcome the challenges of life, with so much joy in their hearts. They show us how humans can be divine (and still cheeky and rebellious and quirky) and give us something real to witness so our divine inner nature can stir in response. They stimulate, inspire and encourage us to keep coming back to what is true so we can realise the path is more fun and empowering than we imagined.

The genuinely holy people I've been lucky enough to read about, connect with online and occasionally meet in person, are all unique. Some are gentle, others are sterner, but they all have kindness and great strength within them. It is the not a strength that comes from fighting battles, but a fortitude of knowing a deeper truth. This knowledge means matters of the world, which can seem so frightening to us mere mortals, do not challenge them in the same way. They see those 'waves' for what they are and are not deluded by them. As a parent who feels compassion for a child frightened by a nightmare, but also sees the nightmare for what it is, they offer us a sense that we don't have to be afraid, that the truth they hold is within us, too. We just need to be willing to look inside ourselves for that truth.

When we feel the spiritual call to go beyond the appearances of life and deeper into the mysteries, these holy ones are there for us. Rather than climbing a literal mountain to seek a meditating yogi (perhaps with a mountain lion next to him), the mountain we need to climb may be our own attachment to habits or to keeping things as they are. We may need to let go of the momentous feeling that *it's okay for them to be at peace, they are holy people, but I'm just an ordinary person! How can I be so spiritually secure and wise? I can't.* Even holy people were rambunctious little monkeys at some point in their spiritual journey. Some of them are still mischief-makers (though with kind intentions behind their actions and helpful outcomes from their antics).

When Kuan Yin comes to us in this form, she is letting us know we have the makings of a holy person within us. This doesn't mean we'll enter a monastic order or quit our day job. We might just continue with our lives, but on an inner journey which brings deeper layers of richness and peace to us and allows us to shine a brighter light in this world. This may require us to develop a loving discipline of yoga, prayer, or meditation or another helpful spiritual practice. The path can be hard at times, but when it's the right time for us to take the step, when we are ready, the benefits on every level are beyond description. This form of Kuan Yin puts us on notice that we are indeed ready for spiritual advancement. If you've been wondering about taking a step forward on your path, or even seeking an authentic teacher, consider this an encouraging sign from the Universal Mother.

30. KUAN YIN OF ONENESS

Storms are fascinating. Water transforms into vapour, which can create clouds, rain or a hurricane! Human beings are similarly fascinating, unpredictable, and complex. Our emotional life is a mystery, at times, especially if we are sensitive, deep, empathic and psychically or psychologically open. We can be powerfully affected by those around us, even those we have never met.

One day, a feeling could wash over us and like water off a duck's back, hardly affect us at all. We may congratulate ourselves on navigating a situation that some years back would have set us off on a journey of rage, despair or fear. Yet, at other times, we may not be able to contain our emotions with such awareness and skilfulness. Perhaps some circumstance or other leads to a feeling that triggers an emotional meltdown. In our triggered state, the feeling begins to gather momentum and, suddenly, instead of just feeling the emotion and working through it, we react rashly, acting in ways which may lead to pain, sadness and regret for all involved.

When we are working on our emotional intelligence and gaining awareness through spiritual practice, there may still be times where we are triggered emotionally and a few tears may gather momentum. Then, perhaps egged on by well-meaning but misguided self-help books or relationship-saboteurs masquerading as friends, the emotional equivalent of a hurricane can suddenly tear through the life you've worked so hard to cultivate. Destructive energies can be as swift as they are powerful. As a lyric from the Stereophonics puts it, "It only takes one match to burn a thousand trees."

This is when Kuan Yin of Oneness, known for her protection from disastrous storms, can help. She is there for those under siege from the frightening power of natural disaster and its potentially devastating consequences. She is also there when we experience the emotional storms arising when factors combine in our lives to create instability and volatility. She can disperse those energies and prevent unnecessary damage.

Seated on a lotus throne atop a floating storm cloud, Kuan Yin reminds us to seek her out because, no matter how terrifying or disastrous a situation may seem to be in our lives, she knows how to quell the storm and help peace, clarity and sanity return. May all beings in need know such grace.

31. VAJRADHARA KUAN YIN

Vajradhara means *the vajra holder*. The *vajra* is a Buddhist symbol for indestructibility, truth, lightning bolts and the *diamond body*, or real inner nature. Vajradhara is the Buddha of secret inner wisdom who holds the essence of all the Buddhas from which purification and wisdom deities, such as the karmic-clearing, white-light radiating deity Vajrasattva, emerge.

The Vajradhara can represent access to the deep understanding that all other meanings or interpretations lead to. On the spiritual path, this can apply to getting beneath the seemingly complex into the truest simplicity. It also applies to numerous everyday situations. When we need to unravel a health problem, if we can get beneath the symptoms and any existing layers of dysfunction, we can gain access to the core issue. If you can deal with the core, the other symptoms will begin to right themselves and you can truly begin to heal. If you had dealt only with the upper layers of dysfunction, you'd only have partial improvement at best. The blessing of the Vajra Holder highlights synchronicities which lead to the right information. You might 'randomly' stumble across a relevant article or a friend might tell you of a new medical treatment they heard about in conversation, and you follow these cosmic clues right to the resolution of the issue.

I learned some helpful things during my years at law school. One of them was that whilst I didn't enjoy it, boredom wouldn't kill me. I also learned to discern between a *red herring*, a seemingly important but irrelevant or distracting piece of information, and what really mattered for finding a solution to a problem.

I knew a man who hated his job (to the point of being depressed every Sunday because Monday was not far off). Having detested every single job I had before embarking upon my much-beloved spiritual vocation, I had compassion for him. However much he tried, he couldn't seem to get another job. He was an open-minded sort of fellow and went to see a psychic, figuring maybe she could give him an insight to help him out. She did, but it wasn't what he expected. She told him he needed to learn to be grateful for his job, even if he didn't want to stay in it forever. He didn't like that advice, at all. He railed against it, but eventually, when nothing changed, he decided to try it. He became grateful for his job, and soon gained two things: peace of mind and an offer of a new job.

The Vajradhara's help does not always unfold as we expect it to. But it will allow the right pieces of the puzzle to emerge and reveal the deeper truth we need to understand. This is helpful, because the truth is the only thing that can set us free.

32. LOTUS-BEARING KUAN YIN

When we hear a child say something so profound and beyond their years, perhaps we cannot help but think they are an old soul. Children are not as socially conditioned—nor as emotionally and spiritually hardened—as many adults. They tend to be more in touch with their naturalness, part of which is wisdom. The spiritual journey can often be about unlearning and delayering the conditioning that suppresses our natural intuition and awareness, so that we can tap back into our wisdom, aliveness and curiosity. When we shed what isn't authentic, we can access the enthusiasm and energy residing in our more childlike 'beginner's mind.' Realising we don't know everything there is to know, allows the flow of imagination and possibility to open us up to grace new ways. We don't overthink, we are interested and interesting and the wisdom we need spontaneously arises from within, whenever we need it.

Connecting with children, perhaps as a parent, healer or teacher, can open our hearts to express selflessness and courage. This beautiful form of Kuan Yin appears as a child, to liberate those in need of such help. This may mean an actual child appears in your life. I have lost count of the times I've heard a parent talk about how their child was a saving grace in their lives. Whether your own or another young person of significance in your life, a child can help you awaken your capacity for unconditional love and grow to understand that the Universe is intimately aware of you, your life journey and working with you and all those in your life to fulfil a certain destiny.

Her assistance in this form could also be more symbolic. Much like a child holds the innate potential to grow and fulfil a unique destiny, Lotus-Bearing Kuan Yin holds the promise that something which has yet to be fully developed will eventually reach its fulfilment. In this form, Kuan Yin stands upon a floating lotus leaf and holds lotuses in both hands. One lotus is open only half way, the other is in full bloom. This is a beautiful symbol of what can be. It is a sign that in due course, beginnings will yield fulfilment, be fruitful and achieve their potential.

It is also a symbol of Kuan Yin's presence in your life. You may not be fully aware of her gentle hand guiding your destiny, but her presence in your heart and your life will unfold and become clear to you. This Kuan Yin lets us know we are going to make progress, that a destiny will be fulfilled, that she is with us, like a birth mother to our true divine nature, helping us manifest and express our full potential.

33. Kuan Yin of Pure Water

A woman sits on a rock, meditating, repeating holy words and occasionally sprinkling water from a simple, rustic bowl that rests in her left hand. A willow branch is held in her right hand. She is focused upon her prayers. From time to time, she dips the willow branch in the water and makes a generous, graceful arc, and the sacred waters, imbued with blessed intention, fall from the branch as it glides through the air. Slowly, evening after evening, people gather to watch. Curious about this mysterious woman, they wait for her to speak. After forty-nine days, she does.

The town had been deeply disrupted by war, and this mysterious woman tells the villagers that the souls of many who died were lost, disturbed and needed assistance to let go of their suffering and find freedom. Buddhism teaches that much takes place for the spirit in the forty-nine days after one leaves the body. It undergoes a series of experiences which can challenge it or inspire it to find a good rebirth or even spiritual enlightenment. Special prayers can help soothe and guide the spirit, bringing healing, protection and peace.

This mysterious willow-waving, water-sprinkling woman is Kuan Yin. She brings us faith, hope and effective protection for our loved ones who have left their bodies and us behind. This can be a great comfort to them and to us, also.

When Leo, my much-loved, fluffy, naughty cat, passed away, I was devastated. He had been my soul-companion and fur-friend for over twelve years. From the moment I adopted him from a cat shelter to the moment of his death, I loved him deeply. Our bond lasted longer than the two romantic relationships I had during his feline lifetime!

I worried for his spirit because I knew he didn't want to die when he did. Some beings embrace death and others resist it for numerous reasons, I suspect fear as the main one. So, during his last moments and after his death, I prayed for him.

The Divine agreed to help and asked me to hold a candlelight vigil for three days. I set up an altar with mementos of Leo, pictures of divine beings I loved, and a small tealight in a glass votive holder. I did this—of all places—in the bathroom, because he had loved to rest on the cool tiles there. It was one of his favourite rooms. Even through the thick, heavy grief consuming my heart, I could still sense his spirit. During the nights of the vigil, Leo was in my dreams, up to various antics. During the day, I felt his anxiousness, but also that his spirit was making progress. Then, about halfway through the final day of the vigil, I suddenly and unexpectedly felt peace wash through me. I knew he had finally let go and crossed the threshold of his fear, making it to the spiritual realms, where he would be happy, safe and free. It was a deeply emotional process. My own grief took rather longer to heal. I suspect, as with most felines, that I was more attached to him, than he to me, but I preferred that. Like every soft touch, I handle my own suffering more readily than that of those I love.

This form of Kuan Yin transformed a battle-scarred land and its battle-weary souls, who were struggling to let go of their pain and reach spiritual freedom in a *Pure Land* which, in Buddhism, is a place of peace and light. She can do the same for us in the face of our own wars, be they legal battles, relationship breakups or fights for our health. If we have lost a loved one from this world, we can ask her to take care of them for us, to guide and console and support them. This, in turn, can bring us peace, which frees us up to process our grief and feel comforted that all is well, even in the face of the loss.

Chapter Four

Our Cosmic Madonna, Mother to All Beings

Getting to know Kuan Yin opened me up to a new appreciation of the Divine Mother. I began to recognise her as an expression of a being that I called the *Cosmic Madonna*, a Universal Mother and spiritual guardian for all beings. Although I wasn't raised Buddhist and am not Chinese, both of which would generally predispose one to be raised with a knowledge of Kuan Yin, she found me anyway. I have the sense she knows who she can benefit and is reaching out to many of us, including those not raised in a cultural or religious tradition that included her. There is something freeing about loving a divine being who is outside your homegrown religious tradition. Perhaps there is less doctrine to obscure the connection, more freedom to discover the deity for yourself, on your own terms.

When I was nine years old, it was time for me to take First Communion. This Catholic ritual gives one permission to receive Holy Communion, said to represent the body of Christ, during mass. I was excited about that. Apparently, as a very young child held in my mother's arms, I would attempt to grab the tiny host from the priest's hand, as he tried to place it on my mother's tongue each Sunday. I would also yell, "Give me that white meat pie!" Not my most elegant moment. So, at nine, I was excited to receive Communion directly. Having this more personal relationship with the Divine made me feel I was growing up spiritually. To be completely honest, I was also excited about designing my own Holy Communion dress, choosing lace and patterns along with my mother and our skilled neighbour-seamstress. My inner fashionista sprouted happily alongside my inner mystic.

When the day came for my First Holy Communion, I wore my dress, sat through endless photographs, received Communion and enjoyed the whole experience immensely. My mother had bought me a gift to honour the occasion. It was a lovely, and likely expensive, gold watch. Although, I recognised it was a nice gift, I was so disappointed! In then-typical Alana fashion (in my defence, I did cultivate more tact as an adult), I didn't hesitate to express that disappointment to my mother. When she enquired why I felt that way, I explained I had wanted religious-themed gifts! I wanted rosary beads like my grandmother's, and a prayer book, and pictures of holy figures. Rather than being appalled at my lack of gratitude, my mother kindly indulged my wish, and soon after presented me with a sweet gift of the religious items I desired. I had begun my love affair with sacred objects and these gifts brought happiness to my heart. I knew I was too obsessed with boys to even contemplate being a nun, but I never doubted or distanced myself from my strong spiritual passion and my family supported that, for which I was grateful.

The Catholic primary school I attended taught religion classes. It was an unusually open-minded school and included teachings on comparative religion, which I found absolutely fascinating. My school friends were from diverse cultural backgrounds, including Hindu, Sikh, Greek Orthodox and Buddhist traditions, as well as Christians who didn't identify with Catholicism, such as Anglicans.

During visits to my friends' homes, I gained exposure to cultures and traditions very different to my own. My family was open-minded and non-judgemental and encouraged me to respect the differences I found between my own upbringing and those of my friends. One of the most beautiful gifts that my family, my mother in particular, gave me was fearless curiosity about, and appreciation for, traditions different to my own. Rather than feeling threatened by religious iconography which was different to the Catholic imagery I grew up with, I was intrigued. The first time I saw a picture of elephant-headed, broken-tusked, round-bellied Ganesha at an Indian friend's house, I was intrigued. It didn't take long for me to fall in love with Ganesha, Buddha, Kali, Shiva and many other expressions of the one divine being — along with my already-beloved Mother Mary, Jesus, Holy Spirit and God. In my heart, there was no spiritual tension, they all just settled comfortably and graciously in there together.

After I entered university to study arts and law, I no longer felt it was appropriate for me to identify as Catholic. Although I never could imagine renouncing my love for the Divine and its forms of Mary and Jesus, I did renounce my religious vows (momentarily confronting a surprisingly intense, previously unconscious fear of going to hell). We must each find our spiritual path, and I knew religion was not going to work for me anymore. Eventually, I found peace and a veritable playground of divine expression for my soul to feast upon and grow. Giving myself permission to become free to love, explore and relate to the Divine without the constraints of religious doctrine was one of the most joyful decisions I ever made. It might not be for everyone, but it suited me.

My love affair with the Divine—including the divine beings recognised in Christianity—only deepened when I no longer identified as a religious person. This doesn't surprise me because I feel that love—whether it be of the human or spiritual variety—blossoms when there is freedom to choose to love without control, demand, guilt, threat or any other manipulation. Others may experience religious doctrine as loving and helpful guidelines for living. For me it was moralism rather than empowerment, so letting it go helped me take personal responsibility for how I chose to live and what I wanted to be and share in this world.

This freedom from religious confines led me into deeper explorations of the Western Occult traditions, which, in turn opened me up to working with energies of nature and exploring *Wicca*, the modern healing craft of witchcraft. I read countless books on witchcraft and felt transported into the realm of my own soul, to a time when the feminine power of magic and healing was respected as a natural and essential part of any thriving community. Having always adored nature and sensed the divine presence speaking to me through the natural world (I still believe trees recognise humans at some level), it was a nourishing journey for me.

My father was a bit nervous about his sweet-natured daughter reading a lot of black-covered, pentagram-encrusted, occult-looking books, but he never tried to stop me. My grandmother watched the ever-growing collection of witchy books I brought into her lounge room to read, instead of my previously beloved fashion magazines (well, they would occasionally still make an appearance). As I read about casting circles and magical correspondences, she watched her 'stories' on television. One day, she asked, "Alana, do you still love Jesus?" I replied, "Of course!" She relaxed and returned to the drama of her soap opera, feeling content there was no spiritual drama going on in my soul.

I was truly fortunate that my family trusted my heart and nature so unconditionally. They weren't afraid of my occult explorations, no matter how weird they may have seemed to the uninitiated. They never teased me about them, either — not even my brothers. Although you'd think a crystal-toting sister would be a prime target for some sibling jibes. Just once, my younger brother offered a hint of a jibe and the very next day, he met the new girlfriend of one of his mates. When she heard we were related, she cried out, "Are you *Alana Fairchild's* brother?" with such respect and awe he was shocked. I don't think he ever saw me in quite the same way again. I found that hilarious.

In my explorations, I also met a woman at a psychic development class who was similarly open-minded, as many people in the New Age are. She used blessed holy water from the sacred Marian site at Lourdes—which her agnostic, gay-activist sister had brought back from France—in her Wiccan healing rituals to bless essential oil and herb blends she intuitively created. This didn't strike me as the least bit odd. It just felt marvellously creative.

However, I was also noticing that many who sought me out for psychic readings and counselling were having very different experiences to mine and those of my open-minded Catholic witch friend. One intense young man was passionate about the nature-based, sacred feminine path of Wicca. His father discovered his writings—his *Book of Shadows*—and his small altar, adorned with items of spiritual healing significance to the young man. Driven by fear, which manifested as anger, his father destroyed them. My heart broke at the thought of this. The young man was devastated and felt severely oppressed by his father. His freedom to express religious devotion in his own way was crushed under the weight of his father's fear and rage. I felt such darkness around that young man, and yet he had a pure and beautiful heart. Eventually, he stopped his practice and no longer came to me for readings. I sincerely hope he eventually found the freedom, authenticity and respect he deserved and resumed his practice in whatever way is most authentic for him, and that his father found true peace, which is not contingent on controlling other people.

Of course, not all witchcraft is about healing. There are darker forms of magical practice, but I never had any interest in pursuing them. Whilst I understand each person has their own path, these practices just seemed disturbed and lacking in genuine spiritual light. With an innate appreciation for karma, I felt practicing in a way that caused harm to another was a bad idea. So, when people asked me to write spells and enchantments to make certain men love them, and so on, I gave them a stern warning about the dangers of such practices and offered to do spells for their personal healing so they could move on, instead. Some took me up on the offer. Others went to find a more obliging witch!

I enjoyed Wicca's beautiful respect for natural feminine cycles and rhythms, and I loved the healing rituals, but I didn't identify it as my religion. I kept what suited my soul growth and moved on in my journey. I became passionate about healing with light and conscious channelling of high-level spiritual guidance. I began developing my own practices and meditation techniques and became rather obsessed with all things New Age including crystals, sound healing, angels and the subtle anatomy of auras and chakras, which I could sometimes see physically. There is a whole world out there—many worlds, in fact—to explore, and my curious, open mind loved the freedom and increasing beauty, grace, love and wisdom I found through those explorations. In a time in which I was dealing with a lot of darkness in my life—including confusion, anxiety and depression—these worlds of light brought me peace and reassurance that everything was somehow going to work out.

Many years on, I had completed my law degree and shifted from explorations of feminine, earth-based religions into the spiritual carnival of crystals, energetic healing, psychics, channels, musicians and healers that comprise the New Age movement. I had learned about different religious paths, including the mystical branch of Christianity and the vibrant, colourful sacred circus of Hinduism, which I fell in love with. Eventually, my studies included Taoism, which felt as natural as breathing to me, along with Tibetan Buddhism. It took decades, and I am still learning — which one could for all their days and still not grasp even the basics of such paths. I didn't seek to be an academic expert, I was just looking for the pieces of the puzzle I intuitively felt I needed to continue progressing on my path and help others in the process, no matter their religious or spiritual inclinations.

This led me into sound healing using energy transmission and mantras. I did that for many years and during a healing session I would sometimes sing little songs that just came to me in the moment, with words of spiritual guidance or a mantra or two, depending on what the soul of the person was calling for. Word got around, and I was invited to sing at a large group event. I had been working very deeply with a beautiful Sanskrit chant to the sacred feminine in her many forms. I shared that with the group.

The next morning, I was meditating when I felt the presence of Mother Mary. I not only saw her but sensed a message from her that I was a channel for her in this lifetime. I wasn't sure whether my mind was playing tricks on me, as it sounded suspiciously like ego-driven nonsense. Who was I to be a channel for such a being? A Hinduism-obsessed former witch and renounced Catholic who loved tarot cards, crystals and chakras and did psychic healing and past life regressions? I seemed to be an unlikely candidate for such a sublime task. However, I did know that my heart was pure, that I loved her, and that she loved me, so I just let the message rest in my heart. If guidance is genuine, something comes of it when the time is right. So, I decided to let time be the judge.

Later that morning, the group facilitator from the evening before contacted me with some feedback about my guest appearance. She told me one of the participants had shared a meaningful experience with her. As I was singing the Indian chant to the divine feminine, this participant saw a column of white light manifest in the centre of the room. In that column of light, she saw a vision of Mother Mary! This synchronicity reinforced something I had forgotten: The Divine will work through willing hearts in mysterious ways. Have you ever been talking to someone who was struggling with an issue, and suddenly, you didn't even know why you were saying what you were saying but it really seemed to help them? I have, and I know many others who have been on both sides of such an experience, too. It is helpful to know the Divine is working through us consciously and with focussed intention. Mary wanted me to know she was with me and, whether I always recognised it, I was one of her undoubtedly numerous channels on this earth. I didn't know why I needed to know that at that time, but I accepted it and waited for further clarity to come when the time was right.

Several years later, I was working with various faces of the divine feminine in my healing sessions and classes, including Saraswati, Lakshmi, Kali and Durga, along with the Egyptian goddesses I first discovered during childhood. I was always a little obsessed with Ancient Egypt. Something in my child's heart stirred at the descriptions of the goddesses, especially the beautiful winged goddess, known as Isis. Flipping through my mother's oversized, lushly illustrated, heavily bound ancient history books, in the cool of the dark, wood-panelled lounge of my childhood home, my imagination ran wild. The cat-headed goddess Bastet, and the lion-headed goddess Sekhmet, seemed fierce and exotic and strange, but also part of my own soul, even though they were so in contrast to my own gentle nature.

Mother Mary still made an appearance from time to time and, eventually, so did a mysterious Oriental goddess named Kuan Yin. I didn't know much about her. I was introduced to her when I found the most extraordinary depictions of her on the internet. I didn't know where these images came from, who created them or their significance. I just loved and craved and felt nourished by these images in a way I couldn't explain. I began collecting them, printing them out and putting them in my hand-written personal-growth journals, along with my drawings and writings, which came through my dreams. I had some of the images printed and framed and I hung them in my healing room, where I saw clients.

Several years after that, I met a Dutch woman at an energetic healing workshop in Sydney. She had moved to Australia, along with her family, for her husband's work. She had a good sense of humour, similar interests to mine and an open mind, and we became friends. When her husband's work led their family back to Holland several years later, she generously invited me to come stay with her and teach workshops in the Netherlands. I agreed, and although it was challenging to be away from my loved ones for nearly two months, I found the work in Holland rewarding. I helped some beautiful people there open their hearts to the sacred feminine. As I saw it, the feminine wanted to be let loose and have fun in Holland. I was happy to be part of that sacred party.

Towards the end of my tour in Holland, I received an email from my publisher. It was early on in our professional relationship, and he had redesigned and republished some meditation CDs I previously self-published. A year or two after publishing the CDs, he somehow came across something I had written. He was surprised. He said he didn't know I could write as well as that and asked if I would like to write something for his publishing house, Blue Angel. I agreed instantly! He sent an email saying that, although he was initially thinking of giving a certain project to a more experienced author, he kept thinking of me for it. He wasn't sure why. He attached a file of artworks and said it was an oracle deck. My heart leapt. I had wanted to write an oracle deck for eleven years but had no idea how to begin. And he was offering me this beautiful opportunity. I felt incredibly grateful and inspired.

Then I read it was an oracle deck dedicated to Kuan Yin. I felt something light up within my heart. I opened the file with the images for the deck and nearly fell off my chair. There were all the images I had been collecting, seemingly randomly, off the internet years earlier! I was stunned. I felt Kuan Yin had known all along that I was going to be writing that deck and had been orchestrating the process. This delightful synchronicity helped me gain a new level of trust in her and in my own destiny. Things would happen when they were meant to happen. When I first wanted to write an oracle deck, my publisher had not even launched Blue Angel. My relationship with him has been pivotal in being able to reach people with my work. I don't believe the depth, innovation and beauty we are able to create together could have happened in any other partnership. It was just meant to be.

Over the years, I have increasingly come to believe the timing for us to meet and work together was predestined. I feel a deep, common soul purpose with him. It's very strong and manifests for me as a reassuring bond between our souls. To have that, I had to wait for the right time. I was about ten years ahead of myself and impatient for things to happen. I didn't know this in advance. I only figured it out in retrospect. Learning to trust in the higher wisdom of divine timing, rather than my own impatience, brought me a lot of peace. It took a while, but eventually, after I realised things would fall into place in ways I could never have orchestrated or predicted, I learned to surrender into the sacred feminine wisdom of divine timing.

I wrote the *Kuan Yin Oracle*, which has reached many people in many languages. What I find interesting is that, when I wrote it, I had no idea if anyone would really get it. I figured maybe there would be a couple of hundred, or maybe a couple of thousand, people in the world who would find it helpful. I wrote it exactly as I heard my spiritual guidance talking to me every day of my life. I shared the messages they shared with me, which I found so helpful. I wanted people to experience the love and beauty the Divine gave to me.

The year after I wrote the *Kuan Yin Oracle*, I was invited back to Holland for another teaching tour. There, I was drawn to the quirky New Age stores around Haarlem and Amsterdam. One store sold glass candles with Mother Mary images affixed to them, as if they'd found their way from the rustic altars of devoted Mexican women all the way to the Netherlands. I also found two stores that sold strange-looking relics from Hindu and Buddhist traditions. Ritual tools have intrigued me since my childhood days attending Catholic mass, with its ringing bells and sacred chalices. It was no wonder I took to the ritual Wiccan knives, chalices, wands and pentacles like a duck to water.

The ritual Nepalese tools I found in those Dutch stores held a powerful magnetic appeal for me. I had yet to understand how to use them in healing rituals, but I felt a sense of connection and inner, guiding desire, as I did when collecting the Kuan Yin images. Without knowing exactly why, I purchased those exotic, mysterious tools, along with a beautiful statue of Green Tara, about whom I knew very little about (other than that I felt an inexplicable bond with her). As I was walking back from one store carrying a heavy bronze ritual stake, known as a *phurba*, in a fabric bag, I felt it 'jumping' in the bag. It was an uncanny and bizarre experience. Eight years later, it was blessed by a lama and identified as a manifestation of Hayagriva, a wrathful deity associated with horses, known in Mahayana Buddhism as an emanation of Kuan Yin. Of course! Every divine statue I have ever bought—and trust me, they have been many and varied—has been revealed to be an emanation of her. When you know how to see her, she really is everywhere.

Eventually, I got the hang of using those tools, trusting the higher consciousness of love and wisdom to guide me. I still use them from time to time. I've had some beautiful, and funny, moments with people's reactions them. One woman told me that when I was using a particular tool and chanting Kali, she felt so electrically charged she opened her eyes to see what on earth I was doing. She got a shock when, instead of seeing me, she saw a wild Kali with arms waving about. Fair enough. We share similar hair. What's impressive is that she closed her eyes and went back into meditation again.

On another occasion, I was chanting the Divine Mother's name and using a ritual tool to clear the space before a workshop. It was in a rented healing space in the Netherlands which had windows without blinds. When you were seated, no-one outside could see you, but when you stood, passers-by could see the upper half of your body. When one of the participants for that day's workshop approached the building early, he saw me with my eyes rolling back in my head, singing loudly, lost in some blissful chant or other, my arms flinging a ritual sword in the air. He was spooked and ran away! Upon further reflection, he decided the energy he felt from me was unconditionally loving, so he returned for the workshop, which he found to be of benefit — and not scary after all.

Spiritual tools—whether unusual ritual tools or crystal wands—can help us focus energy, perform tasks and evoke the energy of divine beings. They are beautiful and powerful to work with. However, they aren't essential to our spiritual path. *The Kuan Yin Transmission*™ healing modality does not require the use of tools, although there is a crystal which can be used in the process if desired. I mention the use of spiritual tools because, if you do the training in *The Kuan Yin Transmission*™ modality with me, you'll probably see me using them at times. You may work with other teachers using spiritual tools, too. It's important you know they are used to evoke certain inner states, rather like an oracle deck, which may be beautiful to behold, but whose real power comes through what happens in your soul when you work with it.

During these times, Mother Mary continued to guide me with her usual subtlety and grace, popping up with marvellous resources to help me in all facets of my life. I loved sharing the grace-filled stories of her presence with others. Whilst many loved her as I did, I found others felt some aversion to or confusion about her because of religious associations. One woman told me that her Catholic friends found her having a copy of the *Mother Mary Oracle* and talking about Mary to be odd because she was not raised Christian. Their limited imaginations had her doubting the veracity of her connection to this divine being for a time. That made me sad. It also made me realise that if Mary can reach many hearts by manifesting as Kuan Yin, she will — and vice versa. Like a school teacher may be both a teacher for her students and a wife to her husband, Mary and Kuan Yin wear different 'hats' to connect with different people. It may be easier for people to open their hearts to Kuan Yin, especially if they are new to her, because they don't carry potentially negative associations with her. She is a clean slate, spiritually speaking. For others, Mary has a strong pull on their hearts and they will not allow anything to get in the way of that.

I began to understand that the Divine Mother would show up in different forms and that there was a hidden spiritual meaning and purpose in that. It may have seemed random, but it was directed by a higher loving spiritual intelligence, who knew what we needed. Sometimes, my heart needed Mary. Sometimes, my heart needed Kuan Yin. Sometimes, it was Tara. It wasn't that I lacked devotion or commitment or loyalty — you only have to look at the body of work I've created to know my commitment and devotion to the beloved Divine Mother is fierce. It was simply a matter of the mind being attracted to, and attracting to it, what could best serve it. Even when I realised these divine beings were one and the same, I still noticed that, depending on the situation and my state of mind, she would show up in different forms. I loved this about the Divine Mother. I even loved it when I visited Nepal and Tibet and Kuan Yin became the Divine Father, Divine Brother and Divine Friend to my soul, my beloved Avalokiteshvara. I adored divine masculine energy and loved the forms of Shiva, especially. To find male energy as part of Kuan Yin's many manifestations was a comfort and delight to me. There were times when I naturally reached for divine masculine sources of light for shelter. And this divine being would be there for me then, too.

One of the Tibetan masters with whom I have studied was invited to research and teach at an Italian university. During his time in Italy, he went to a church. He noted people in devotion, praying to a statue of the Virgin Mary. Matter-of-factly, he thought, *Oh, there's Tara!* With his typical clarity, he recognised the statue of Mary held the same energy and depicted the same being — but wearing more clothing than typically scantily-clad, sky-dancing Tara. He instantly recognised the essence of Mary as the same as that of Tara, who predated Buddhism and was found in many religions, including Buddhism, Hinduism, Celtic spirituality and Himalayan shamanism. And, as it turned out, in Christianity, too.

Tara is known for her swiftness, effectiveness and unconditional love. She will help us, instantly, whenever we ask — not in a couple of weeks or months. Tara comes in numerous forms, which show up as different colours with different mudras, mantras and symbols, although her *bija*, or *seed sound*, is always the same: *Tam* (sounds like *TUM*, as in *tummy* or *tumble*).

I had been working with Tara through mantra and by visualising her beautiful seed syllable in my heart, glowing with light for healing and help for those in need.

Then, one evening, I dreamed of a sacred lake. It was so pure and clean and blessed, I felt it was in a heavenly realm and I was communing in truly sacred space. I was reluctant to leave that dream and begin my day. That morning, I did an internet search with the words 'heavenly lake' which had just popped into my mind. I wanted to see if I could find an image which conjured up something of the magic I experienced in my dream for inclusion in my journal. I felt it would help me remember the experience, which was so special to me. I was shocked to see an image pop up on my computer screen which looked as though a skilful photographer had somehow snapped a photograph directly from my dream. I realised the lake in my dream was a vision of a place that existed on Earth. It was in Tibet, at a very high altitude and not easily accessible. Although I felt intimidated by the prospect, I was deeply inspired and felt I had to visit that lake. I did make it to that beautiful place and brought nearly thirty people from all around the world with me on sacred retreat. It was an incredible experience. I describe the spiritual blessing that took place in the final words of this book. It was that blessing which activated the creation of this project, including this book, the album of mantras and meditations, the card set and the healing modality that all share the name *The Kuan Yin Transmission*™.

In the year and a half that unfolded from the moment of the vision, until the day I visited the holy lake in person, I entered a deep spiritual process of getting to know Tara. I learned, through study and personal experience, about the diverse ways she helps us and the constant, powerful, all-encompassing nature of her being. Tara is the instinct within us that guides us on the spiritual path so we don't become stuck, but continue to grow. She helps us find our way out of difficulties. As the Mother of all Buddhas in Buddhism, she is also the *Theotokos*, the Mother of God (a term used to describe Mary in the Greek Orthodox Church) from a Christian perspective. She births the very nature of being, the highest and truest aspects of existence. She will handle whatever needs to be overcome and eliminate whatever is needed for that to take place. She will amplify and increase that which is loving and wise within us. She is also incredibly kind. She will help us with whatever we need. If we see another being suffering, we can ask, and she will help that being, too.

I had been lying in the sun, listening to an MP3 of one of my Tibetan teachers speaking about Tara. He made me laugh when he said there were times when one couldn't sit and do a long practice imploring Tara for help. If you were about to be in a car accident, or if someone was running straight at you with evil intent, it probably wouldn't work so well to say, "Excuse me, but can you wait a moment please?" and then sit down with your book and bell and perform a ritual and long mantra! He told us that longer, deeper practices can help us develop a stronger relationship with a divine being, so that we can have confidence in the efficacy of a shorter practice when that is all we have time for. He said that, even if we don't really know anything about Tara, if we are led to read or think about her—seeing her statue or picking up this book, for example—then at some time, even in a long-ago past life, we have had a relationship with her, which is developing further in this lifetime. I love that idea and agree with it wholeheartedly. If we have not had much experience with Tara consciously or aren't sure about the whole theory of past-life connection with her, we can still call on her, and she will help. The shortest Tara practice my teacher described was to say this mantra: *Tare!* (sounds like *TAH-RAY!*). It translates as, *Tara, please help!*

I pondered his words as I hurried up the stairs alongside my home to go to a yoga class. As I rushed up the stairs, I noticed a large web with a fly trapped in it. A very large spider hung in wait nearby. I felt a jolt of compassion for the hungry spider, but given his size, he was apparently well fed. As the fly writhed, my heart broke a little in compassion for its suffering. "Tare!" I cried. I worried I would be late for class, but I just couldn't leave the fly there to die in such suffering. So I sought a branch to try and detangle him. I wondered if it would even be possible, as he was very caught in the stickiness of the large web. I grabbed a small branch, but when I went to poke it in the web, I noticed that in the few seconds which had passed the fly had disappeared, leaving only a hole where he had once struggled. I was astonished that in mere seconds he had gone from deeply entangled to free. I felt a spiritual jolt in my heart as a recognition of the mysterious—and, indeed, very swift—workings of Tara.

When the time came to lead the Tibetan retreat I had dedicated to Tara, there were many bureaucratic hoops to jump through and no guarantees that, despite paying for our flights, accommodation, tours and visas that we would be allowed into Tibet. With numerous people depending on me, I had a moment of nervousness. Then I realised, *this is a retreat for Tara!* I needed to trust that if the inspiration for it was authentic—and I believed in my heart my dream vision of the sacred Himalayan lake was a genuine call—then everything would work out. There were quite a few moments when our entry into Tibet seemed uncertain. However, I kept trusting Tara would provide us with what was needed, and that was, of course, what took place.

During our retreat sessions of music, dance, meditation and mantra, we explored the many faces of Tara. I saw her and Isis and Mother Mary as facets of one being. I saw correspondences between Black Tara and the goddess Kali, White Tara and the goddess Saraswati and Yellow Tara and the goddess Lakshmi, although each had their own distinct qualities and emanations, too. Blue Tara can manifest as wrathful protector goddess Ekajati, who guards secret teachings and spiritual treasures. She is also recognised as the star being Sirius (whom I wrote about in *Crystal Stars 11.11*), as is Isis, who is also known as a keeper of secret teachings. It was like discovering every culture in the world has a word for *love*, but thinks their *love* is different because they use different words to express it. In essence, love is love and it is universal.

A story of this oneness of the Divine was recounted by my mantra teacher, Thomas Ashley Farrand. A French traveller was hiking through a remote area of China and, caught in a sudden snowstorm, became separated from his group. Alone, and fearing for his life, he prayed to Mary. Then a Chinese woman appeared before him as a vision in the sky, pointing in a certain direction. Walking in the direction she was pointing, he found a cave, a safe harbour from the dangers of the storm. He slept soundly, finding the cave particularly soft and comfortable. In the morning, he awoke and crept out of the cave, astonished to find it was no longer a soft refuge, but was filled with sharp, jutting rocks. In the light of a new day, with the storm passed, he was able to find the nearest village and there reconnect with his group. Before he could tell them of his experiences, he noticed paintings by some villagers in the marketplace. They were of the woman he had seen in the sky. When he asked the villages who the woman was, they replied, "Kuan Yin."

On a whim, I went to see a film about an Israeli choreographer known as Mr Gaga. His dance style was so vital, so connected to the body, that I felt very inspired. I researched his work online and saw there happened to be a dance retreat in Israel the week after a spiritual retreat I was running in India. The timing felt right, so I booked it on the spot. After an amazing journey celebrating the goddess in India with over thirty beautiful souls from all over the world, I was ready to drop into a country I had yet to visit—which always inspired me—and replenish my soul with conscious dance.

On my way to the retreat in the Negev desert in southern Israel, I visited Nazareth, where I felt the deep spiritual presence of Christ and Mother Mary. I went to the Sea of Galilee, where there was an incredible feeling of peace. I also visited the Basilica of the Annunciation, the church built over the cave, or grotto, where Mary was said to have received the visitation from Archangel Gabriel telling her she would give birth to Jesus. The line of people wanting to have their moment before that little grotto was long and slow moving and all for a few seconds of prayer before the sacred space. I held on to the small icons of Mother Mary I intended to hold up to the grotto for her blessing. One was a gift for my mother, which I felt she would love. The other was an image of Mary with which I have always resonated. In it, she stands upon a crescent moon, and the sun is radiant around her head, blazing with golden light. When it was my moment to step in front of the grotto, tears suddenly welled up, as I was overcome with an unanticipated surge of divine energy. The presence of the Madonna was palpable there. It emanated like a somewhat cool fire concentrated in that one place, reaching for those who were reaching to it. It was an incredibly powerful, visceral experience.

That experience of Mary stayed with me through my time in the desert, where I also sensed the spiritual energy of the desert mystics who had practiced there. I recognised a past life of my own, in which I had been a nomadic trader along the ancient Incense Route which passed through the area. I felt such a sense of expansion that when I returned to my normal life in Australia, I felt like I was trying to push my feet into shoes I had outgrown — a feeling I often need to work through following powerful experiences when travelling.

That blessed icon of Mary rested on an altar in my home, along with an icon of the Black Madonna, another of Mary's forms. She comforted me in my struggles to integrate the freedom and expansiveness I had relished during my journey. One Sunday morning, not long after my return to Sydney, I felt so adrift and unsettled that I yearned to feel closer to her, just as I had in those moments outside her grotto in Israel. It was a soul yearning, like a child needing a hug from her mother. I couldn't 'pop around the corner' to Israel, so I sat with the feeling and asked myself if there was a more practical way to meet my need. Into my head came the thought of Sunday morning high mass at the beautiful St Mary's Cathedral in Sydney, where my own grandmother had been married, more than seventy years prior.

Given that I had not been to church in almost three decades, had renounced religion, been a witch and tarot reader and was now a practicing lightworker and psychic channel, I wasn't quite sure what to make of that impulse! However, I knew Mary loved me unconditionally and didn't give a hoot about such things, so off I went. On my drive into the city, I did waiver a moment. "Is it really you guiding this morning's journey, Mary?" I asked. A dark blue car with the number plate 'MARY 888' pulled in front of me a second later. I began to giggle.

You may wonder why I had a moment of uncertainty and needed a sign from the Madonna. Around that time, my work had been criticised by some evangelical Christians who said it was not holy and not of God. I have loved God since I was a child and never felt that divine being took issue with my spiritual journey. Yet, those who were saying these things were my teachers for a portion of my journey. My experience of Christian mysticism deepened through my time with them. I valued what I learned from them. I felt that they were good people with their own deep spirituality. I loved them and felt that they loved me, too. That they could express such a viewpoint was very upsetting to me. Given our relationship, rather than dismissing their comments as being solely about their own issues and triggered by the clash of my spiritual unconventionality with their religious doctrine, I took pause to consider the merit of their remarks.

It pained me greatly to consider their view that I was leading people away from the very source it was my life purpose to lead them towards. I wanted my work to flow from a pure heart, so it genuinely served the highest loving wisdom and grace. Otherwise, I couldn't see the point of it. I didn't want to be off on some random frolic of my own, even if I was enjoying my journey (which I most certainly was). I needed to know that sharing my unusual path with others would genuinely help them.

Given that my then teachers claimed the Holy Spirit as the source of their insight, I figured I should go straight to the source of the message and ask for clarification. I had always felt a close connection to the Holy Spirit. When my mother was pregnant with me, she became obsessed with a painting in a local framing shop. She walked past the store each day, captivated by the image, yet uncertain if she could afford it. However, she couldn't get the painting out of her mind, so she saved her money for months and the painting seemed to wait for her. When she finally brought it home, it hung in her bedroom. I, too, was fascinated by it. As a young girl, I used to gaze at it, wordlessly moved by its depiction of a white dove descending through a grey, stormy night.

My heart deeply pained, I sat down with the Bible and asked the Holy Spirit for advice. I closed my eyes and opened the Bible to a random page, plonked my finger down on the page, opened my eyes and read the passage to which I pointed. It was a passage from the Book of Psalms, and it urged, "Put your faith in God, not in powerful people."

I felt it was saying, "Don't allow your respect for these people to overcome your faith in the higher workings of the Universe." I had always allowed my heart to direct my course, and I needed to be careful not to let even well-meaning guides derail my unique journey just so it matched their expectations. I still loved these people and respected that their life choices were right for them, but I could not adopt their choices as my own if I was going to honour my heart. Our relationship had reached a crossroads and if I was to continue on my own path, they would no longer be my teachers.

I have never felt comfortable with pressuring someone to adopt certain spiritual beliefs or reject others. I believe this goes against the nature of love, which needs freedom to be expressed. Love cannot be commanded or required. If our religious and/ or spiritual path is not an expression of love, then what exactly is it? This is why I don't like the idea of people praying for someone who they think is off path. Praying for another person can be a beautiful gift. But it needs to be done without agenda, without an intention of what we think should happen. Otherwise, it's not prayer because it violates someone's freewill.

Freewill is a divine gift to be honoured. The moment we try to overcome it, thinking we know best, we are no longer praying, even if we happen to be in church at the time. However, praying that a person finds their true spiritual destiny, that which is intended for them by a loving wisdom beyond our limited capacity for understanding, and that any forces obstructing their true path be overcome by grace — that's a prayer I would welcome for myself and all beings.

In my spiritual guidance session with the Holy Spirit, I asked if there was anything else that I needed to know. A series of numbers popped into my mind. I intuitively understood that the numbers related to a biblical passage, so I looked up the corresponding section of the Bible. Psalm 118.22 read, "The stone the builders rejected became the cornerstone."

The cornerstone is the foundation stone, the reference stone for the entire building. The Bible passage helped me understand that what my former teachers believed I needed to cast aside was actually incredibly important. It was in that moment that I realised the significance of my open-mindedness and open-heartedness, especially when it came to the natural commonality that I felt beneath outwardly different spiritual paths. *Many paths to one light*, as the lyrics of one of my songs (*Love is My Religion*) goes. I had previously assumed that my natural, but apparently unconventional (perhaps even controversial) approach to the Divine was personal to me and not important in the overall scheme of things. However, in this sacred conversation with the Holy Spirit, I saw that having such a heart-space around these matters wasn't just a quirk of my nature to be taken for granted. It was at the foundation of what I was here on this planet to share. I had such traits because I was meant to play some part in helping people feel free in their hearts to love the Divine in the way that resonated most for them.

I felt humbled and grateful for such specific guidance. It helped me feel that, although some of God's children were having problems with me, God and I were good. I was to continue on my path without those teachers, by their choosing actually. I felt sad, abandoned and lonely for a time. I asked the Divine Mother about that and she told me another spiritual community would be important in my journey. I just needed to wait a brief time for that connection to unfold. Not long after that I met my Dzogchen master and began exploring another mystical path. Instead of filling me with doubt, the entire experience strengthened and reinvigorated my sense of purpose with deeper clarity and passion.

With all this still fresh in my heart, I entered St Mary's Cathedral and took my seat. With genuine surprise, I noticed I had unconsciously incorporated the aspects of mass that I loved—such as the sacred rituals, group prayers and uplifting music—into my own work as a non-denominational (or, if anything, New Age) spiritual teacher. As I sat in the cold church, I wrapped myself in a warm pashmina and took it all in. The high ceilings, the abundant artwork and the voices of the priest and choir resonated through the wonderful acoustics of the cathedral. The smell of frankincense drifted through the air, flowers and candles were lit and statues of Mary abounded — more elements I had absorbed into my own work! The cathedral looked like the teaching spaces I created (though admittedly the statues and music were more varied in my sacred spaces). I relaxed into the sumptuousness and sensuality of the experience. My struggle with the patriarchal system of male-only priests performing the mass brought a genuine flash of pain through my heart, but I kept my heart open nonetheless.

Then something unusual took place. I clairvoyantly perceived what was happening through the priest during the preparation of the host for Holy Communion. I sat through countless masses as a child, and although I felt the sacredness, I never actually 'saw' what was going on at a spiritual level. Now, I saw a flash of light and perceived Christ taking form in the host through the presence of the Holy Spirit. Wow! It was an extraordinary phenomenon. I had to clap my hand over my mouth, as I began giggling at the realisation that it wasn't until I became a witch and a psychic that I could finally understand the deeper energetic beauty at the heart of the Catholic mass. This didn't make me want to return Catholicism, but I did cherish the deeper sense of the beauty it could offer. It also reinforced my belief that the Universe has an excellent sense of humour.

I felt nourished by Mary's presence in that cathedral. To remain close to her,

I decided to listen to an audio program by a Christian mystic I had met some years earlier, when I had been invited to sing the opening of one of his workshops. When I pressed *play* on the portion of the program where I had left off, the words, "And now we are going to speak about Mary," were the first blessed sounds I heard. I was intrigued, because I knew Mary was up to something (good). The discussion focused on the woman from the Book of Revelations. Suddenly, I remembered the icon I purchased in Israel. As the program described her iconography, I felt a growing sense of excitement. It was profoundly significant to me that this 'woman clothed in the sun' was the same form of Mary I found so magnetic when I was travelling through Israel. The teacher referred to this woman as the Cosmic Mary, which caused my heart to flutter.

This meant so much to me because I was powerfully drawn to a somewhat obscure Tantric Buddhist practice dedicated to a divine being known as Wozer Chenma in Tibetan or Marici in Sanskrit. She hails from Buddhist and Taoist traditions as the Goddess of the Dawn, and is a bodhisattva, an enlightened being associated with light, specifically, the light which emanates through the sun. Having always loved the sun for its spiritual and physical benefits and feeling concern for the fear-based attitudes that have many people denying themselves the important benefits of solar light, I was delighted to find an enlightened goddess to whom I could dedicate my sun worship. Her iconography has her seated on a lunar disc, clothed in the rays of the sun. I knew, with inner heart certainty, this was the same being.

The Mary in the Book of Revelations *was* the being the Tibetans knew as a form of Tara clothed in the rays of the sun. I just knew she was not only the Cosmic Mary, she was the Cosmic Madonna, an expression of the Universal Mother found in Christianity, Buddhism and Taoism, linking the Middle East with China, India, Nepal and Tibet. I was absolutely fascinated. The name Cosmic Madonna had come to me years earlier, without me knowing exactly what I was meant to do with it. I felt as though I had been given another clue in a divine mystery.

Just before I was due to embark on my retreat to Tibet, I began the Wozer Chenma spiritual practice of mantra and meditation in earnest. It was then I discovered she is especially called upon for travellers. How apt! That is, of course, a protection for which Mother Mary is also known. I needed her. Although my work is based on peacefulness, respect, love, compassion and freedom for all beings to find their destiny, and I have no interest in converting anyone to anything, I knew from experience that my ideas could evoke tremendous resistance in some people. I knew that Kuan Yin/ Tara/Marici/Mary had led me to her at this time because she recognised my need. I continued her practice throughout a two-month tour, across seven time zones and through thirteen flights, during which I remained well and protected. I taught many group practices dedicated to the Goddess Isis and despite the ignorance that has some associating the beautiful face of the Cosmic Madonna known as Isis with a Middle-Eastern terrorist group, I had no issues in my travels. Since one of the venues where I taught had been continually vandalised to the point that they had to remove the name 'Isis' from their long-held business name, this was remarkable.

The significance of the mantra of Wozer Chenma/Marici, which you'll hear on *The Kuan Yin Transmission*™ album in the track dedicated to Mary, felt remarkably apt. Her seed syllable or sacred sound is *Mum* (sounds like *MOOM*), which is the Australian spelling for *mom*. The practice I was learning was channelled by my master's grandmother. I have already mentioned how my own grandmother introduced me to Mary. I loved that I was initiated into her practice via two grandmothers — one from the East, and one from the West. I loved the connection I felt between East and West through the goddess Marici. It felt as though it linked superficially divergent spiritual traditions and united the human heart at a deep level which could not be broken by cultural divisiveness.

The Cosmic Madonna offers a tonic to overcome the human tendency to focus on appearances and lose touch with the nourishing underlying unity. When we discover that underlying unity, we can celebrate and enjoy the differences, without having them create divisiveness or violence. We can take delight in the creative diversity of the Universal Mother, as she births endless resources to meet the needs of all beings. We can allow her to show her many beautiful faces to us with as much diversity as we are willing to embrace. May all beings in need receive her grace.

CHAPTER FIVE

TARA: THE GODDESS
OF GETTING THINGS DONE

TARA IS A LOVING SACRED REBEL. WHEN SOME MONKS TOLD HER that she couldn't become enlightened as easily as if she was a man, she defiantly declared she would take female form until all beings were liberated. She liberated ten thousand beings in the morning of that day and another ten thousand in the evening. Not a bad day's work.

Tara is responsive. She changes from sweet and loving goddess to ferocious warrior in an instant, based on what is going to get the job done. She is one of the most ancient goddesses loved and adored in modern times. Tara is associated with protection, with magnetising all good things into our lives, with abundance, joy and happiness. As well as being a wish-fulfilling jewel, she is considered a saviour for the lost and a nurturing, protective mother for all beings. She manifests as a goddess across cultural boundaries from Tibet to India to South America to North America and Europe. Tara makes her presence felt in Buddhism, Hinduism, Celtic spirituality, Asian and American shamanism and even in Christianity and New Age spirituality. She is the mother goddess of the Celts, the Star Woman of the Cheyenne Indians, Mother Mary and Ishtar of Babylon. Tara's vast reach is part of her spiritual purpose. She will assume as many forms as necessary to meet the needs of all beings. She is Kuan Yin. She is our Divine Mother.

The Sanskrit translation of her name can mean *star* and also *crossing* or *bridge*.

That could mean crossing from life in the body to life in the realm of spirit or crossing from one chapter of our lives into a new one (perhaps after a promotion or when a new relationship asks us to step into more of ourselves or when we outgrow an identity and discover ourselves anew). Tara assists all to cross from the realms of suffering into emotional and psychological freedom. She shows the way and offers protection on our path.

She is also known as the Universal Tree and Mother of All Buddhas. As the Universal Tree, she provides us with strength, safe refuge and an understanding of our place in the greater scheme of life, our sense of life purpose and our path. She teaches us how to ground and connect to the earth for support, so we can grow, reach for the heavens and provide assistance to those around us. Her role of Mother of All Buddhas is akin to Mary's role as Jesus' mother. In this way, she is a symbol of the Universal Mother's capacity to bring out our true nature. This is what sacred feminine energies do for all of humanity. They help birth the soul, the authentic self beneath the social conditioning we received as children and continue to receive as we mature. Under her influence, we figure out who we really are and how to live authentically into that truth. For a New Age person, that may be interpreted as living as one's higher self or soul. For a Christian, it might be learning to be one with Jesus, acting and living with Jesus as a guide and wayshower in the heart. For a practitioner of meditation, it may be realising one is not one's constantly roaming thoughts, nor one's reactions or judgements, but rather a presence which is both part of all things and yet completely free. If we are not particularly religious or spiritual, the sacred feminine could simply help us find a sense of deepest fulfilment and meaning in our lives.

Tara always wants to help us. Even if we keep making mistakes. Even when we may not believe we are worthy of her help. Even if we aren't sure we believe in her at all. She is constantly there for us, reaching out gently and firmly, with loving and capable hands. It can be hard for us to understand such unconditional love, especially if, like most humans, we have learned that love is conditional. Conditional love requires we earn it. Unconditional love is simply given and asks for nothing in return. We may not like the idea that we work hard on our path and yet someone who doesn't appear to have done as much work as we have can 'skip the queue', go straight to Tara and ask for help — and receive it! That wound comes from being required to perform, obey and earn affection, rather than being loved for who you are, no conditions attached. It can hurt to see others receiving if you feel pain that you have been denied such grace. When you realise you can also receive freely, you let go of the wounding. You no longer feel deprived, and you can develop more compassion for all beings. Everyone has bad days and needs a helping hand from the Cosmic Madonna. There's never a competition for her time, attention or affection. They are given in abundance to each of us. The more we open our hearts to her, the more we have and can share with others. In doing so, we can all become 'divine mothers' in this world.

In numerous spiritual traditions, one requires a special initiation to connect with various divine beings — whether we are discussing the sacraments in the Catholic church or the empowerments of the Buddhist tradition. In Buddhism, particularly, there are many prescribed practices for Tara. There are even some rituals and practices known as *termas*, which are secret teachings revealed under extraordinary circumstances to spiritually capable individuals. The Universal Mother is most resourceful and creative when it comes to empowering us to 'get out of our own way' and connect with her wisdom, guiding grace, love and blessings — which are already within us. So, whilst certain initiations of Tara are given, they are not considered necessary to connect with this aspect of the Divine Mother and receive her blessings. She is readily available to all, whether we are advanced practitioners or have no idea whether she is real but are in such a mess we are willing to try anything — including reaching out to a mysterious divine being and asking for her protection and help! When we don't know what we are doing, when we are lost (even if we don't realise how far from our true path we are at the time), when we are feeling vulnerable, when we want to help others but are not sure how to accomplish such a task for the greatest good of all, Tara is ready and waiting for us to simply call her name and ask for her help.

One of her most appealing traits—especially for those of us who lack patience— is that Tara is known for her speed. This means we need to release our expectations about how long a solution will take to manifest and instead practice the mental art of letting go. Rather than imposing our (often negative) expectations, hoping for the best but expecting the worst, we can empower Tara's incredible action in our lives by practicing a different approach. We can ask for her help and then focus on the fact that she instantly has matters under her care. We will know when we have done this, because we will suddenly feel happier and more relaxed. We empower her to empower us.

Tara knows how to play. Modern people can be confused about play, thinking it is either childish and escapist or only to be 'indulged' in after the more serious discipline of hard work. Yet, there is a discipline to cultivating a playful mind that in no way compromises our ability to be highly productive and make valuable contributions to society. Playfulness and humour are essential. They help us develop the flexibility of mind we need to let the Divine *in* to our lives. When we get too caught up in our own ideas, becoming overly serious, Tara is known to stir us up and remind us to play, even playing pranks on us, if needs be.

I felt drawn to live and work in the United States, that it was part of my destiny, although I wasn't sure exactly why, nor how it could happen. When my Canadian partner told me that he had been offered a job in the US, I was stunned. Mostly because his job offer involved him moving to—of all places—Alaska. This was amusing (to my partner) and shocking (to me) because we both knew how much I love and need the sun! Then there were the mosquitoes. I can handle spiders. Growing up in Australia, one learns to deal with such creatures. But mozzies so enormous they were dubbed the state bird of Alaska, well that was another thing, altogether. So, whilst the lure of the northern lights and vast wilderness did appeal, not to mention being with my beloved, essentially, I'd be moving a place where the winters were brutal and long, and I'd have to deal with mosquitoes so large they could pierce human flesh through layers of protective clothing. I won't even go into the discussions I had about guns, bears and moose. Whether I end up visiting or even living in Alaska, I cannot predict, but I do know the process of considering it brought up plenty of issues for me to work through! I would refer to this as 'the Universe having a sense of humour' and an example of the divine prankster (lovingly) at play in my life.

In the Buddhist tradition, Tara manifests in assorted colours, each with their own meaning and purpose. Some have fierce expressions, some are gentle and serene. I was blessed to find a beautiful Green Tara statue, which rests on my bedside altar, and has an expression like the Mona Lisa. She is smiling but mysterious, holding all the secrets of the Universe within her heart. Green Tara is considered the source of all the Taras. The colours that emerge from her may have a pacifying function, creating peace and calm — such as through White Tara who can be compared to Saraswati, from the Hindu tradition, and who perhaps most closely resembles Kuan Yin in her usual form as serene, loving, white-robed mother.

As Yellow Tara, she has an enriching function, increasing our prosperity and abundance. In Hinduism, we would say she is Lakshmi, the loving golden goddess of grace and blessings for spiritual enlightenment and material wealth.

As Red Tara, she is both a subjugating goddess, controlling negative forces, and a magnetising goddess, attracting good things into our world. Sometimes, as Red Tara she is known as Kurukulla, a semi-wrathful, shamanic sorceress deity who predates Buddhism. She conquers negativities and helps us find our true passion and calling in life.

As both Blue and Black Tara (the latter known as Kali, in the Hindu tradition), she becomes a wrathful, demon-conquering goddess who has a zero-tolerance policy for ego interference with your life path. The colours blue and black are used interchangeably in the Tibetan tradition and relate to elimination of negativities, purification and the vastness of space from which the Divine Mother's blessings emerge.

When colours are mixed (for example, red and yellow combine to give rise to Orange Tara) the qualities of enrichment and subjugation combine as well. Orange Tara is a healing form of Tara. She is known to frown and then laugh. She can cure poverty and conquer demons with a stamp of her foot and a cackle.

There are many other forms of Tara, from devotion to the twenty-one forms of Tara practiced in all four Tibetan Buddhist traditions, to lesser known forms of Tara from India, including Light Tan and Dark Tan Taras, Pink Tara and more. Below, I share my experience of the six main forms of Tara (described above), as these are the forms I have learned to work with and find so rewarding.

Green Tara's help is immediate. Swift, fearless and protective, she is unlimited in her ability to assist instantaneously. When she is at work, her power is so absolute and her intervention so complete, it can be as if an issue simply never existed. However, we are required to trust. When we take refuge in her, we allow her to do what she can and wants to do for us. Imagine asking someone for a hug, then refusing to let them hug you. Even though you asked for the hug, can you receive its full benefit? You can receive some benefit in knowing the person is approaching you with open arms and wants to hug you. That's a good start! But the full hug requires you to uncross your arms, drop your defences and let that person comfort, love and be there for you. So, the first step is asking, and the second step is allowing space for a response to happen. Now you understand why, even though it's a remarkably straightforward process to set Tara's intervention in motion in our lives, it's not always easy. If we've had trouble with trust, self-worth, relaxing and flowing, manifestation, protection from negative forces, health issues or any type of judgement, criticism or betrayal, those past issues tend to arise when it's time to open up. This can make letting Tara in something of a challenge for us — at least the first few times. It gets easier with practice. Tara specialises in overcoming fear. When we connect with her, she teaches us how to become liberated from fear and all negativities by taking sanctuary in her.

Green Tara is depicted with her right foot extended, as though she is about to leap up from her lotus throne and into action in the world. She is known as the Buddha Goddess of Enlightened Activity. Good intentions are a start, but, as the expression goes, "The road to hell is paved with good intentions." Good intentions are not enough on their own. Dzogchen master Chogyal Namkhai Norbu Rinpoche once described it this way: When you are sick, a very loving friend may want to help. However, if that friend is not a doctor, then their desire to help is not enough. They also need the skilfulness to be able to help. In that instance, the skilfulness might be medical training.

Enlightened activity is the sort of activity that really does help. 'Skilful means' is less to do with us needing to know the perfect thing to say or do and more about opening up, so a higher, wiser, more compassionate presence can flow through us into the world. Then, our actions come not from our ego, but from inspiration which is beyond our limited human understanding. Although, we can learn to sense, heed and flow with it, nonetheless. The Divine will speak and act through every willing vessel.

A heart-wrenching comment was shared under a music video for *Shake it Out*, by the marvellously talented Florence + The Machine. A man wrote that he had been planning to kill himself, and then he heard that song for the first time. He said it had such an effect on him, he decided not to commit suicide. He lived to share his story. How mysterious and wonderful that this beautiful song found him at the necessary moment. Something within him was willing to listen. That openness was enough for grace to find its way through the willing creative vessel of a skilful musician into the man's mind at the right time.

We may never know how living our authentic life can be a comfort to others. We may never know the extent of our positive influence. But we can know that the blessings of the Universal Mother pour through us when we are living the truth of our nature and not hiding our real selves in fear. If we are struggling to be our real self, or we don't know who that is—even if we identify more with the one who needs help, rather than the one who can help—Tara is there for us, showing us the way, lifting us with her grace and, through that assistance, empowering us to lift others, too.

Green Tara holds her hands in mudras, postures of protection and blessing. When we see her right hand extended down in *varada mudra* or *boon-granting pose*, we can relax, knowing she will give generously to us. When we see her left hand in *abhaya mudra*, or *refuge-giving pose*, we know she is saying, "Come to me. I've got this. You've no need to feel afraid."

Her mantra is *Om Tare Tuttare Ture Soham* (sounds like *OHM TAR-RAY TWO-TAR-RAY TWO-RAY SOH-HUM*.) This mantra calls upon Tara's protection, especially as Green Tara. You can also simply call upon Tara with a simple *Tare* (pronounced *TAR-RAY*).

Green Tara is our go-to Tara when we aren't sure which version of Tara is best suited to meet our needs at the time. She will provide what is needed and work swiftly for our benefit. It is from her that all other Taras emanate. If we call upon her, but White Tara would really be the better help, Green Tara will manifest as White Tara, or whomever we most need at the time. She could come as Jesus, Isis, Mother Mary or a rampaging Black Tara/Kali, ready to rumble. I have known some hardcore devotees on the spiritual path to believe they need tough love and a kick in the pants to get moving, only to find the softness and gentleness of the peaceful mother shows up for them. They don't need more force, they need to learn how to be kinder to themselves because that will get them a lot further.

Since the Divine appears in the way which will help us most, it makes little sense to impose our view of the Divine onto another person. If a one-size-fits-all approach created spiritual enlightenment for all beings, there would be only one approach. It doesn't. Different minds need different paths. Trust helps us attract and accept the best path for ourselves (and allow others to do the same).

Whilst Green Tara is perched, ready to leap into action, White Tara is seated in peaceful meditation posture. Green Tara is known for swift response and White Tara is known for building the divine presence in us slowly. She knows we may need time to adjust to a new reality or learn patience so that later, we will be willing to hand over the reins to a greater guiding inner wisdom (rather than reacting from a place of frustration) when it matters most.

White Tara is known for bestowing healing, protection, peace and blessings. In particular, she has some special roles, such as the Wish-Fulfilling Wheel or Chakra. In that form, she is depicted with a violet or rainbow-coloured aura. As the *Cintachakra*, or Wish-Fulfilling Wheel, White Tara grants wishes that promote progress as if turning the wheel of our destiny. The wish fulfilment quality of White Tara is spiritual magic at its kindest and most generous. It is said to cool that which is hot and warm that which is cold. It can cause rain to fall when there is drought or a spring to appear when one is thirsty. It pacifies out-of-control waters, such as floods or torrential downpours. It is said to emit various coloured lights to heal all possible afflictions of body and mind. It brings fruition to everything the holder desires. White Tara promotes the fulfilment of our desires in such a way that we don't undermine or sabotage ourselves unintentionally, but rather maximise our progress. Like a wheel, she creates swifter movement and easier travel along our path.

In Tarot, the *Wheel of Fortune* card in the Major Arcana depicts significant change, the ending of a cycle and the beginning of a new chapter in one's life. Similarly, White Tara as the Wish-Fulfilling Wheel assists with our dramatic changes, helping them unfold more seamlessly and gracefully. The Chinese philosophy of Taoism teaches that the way forward sometimes appears to go backwards, and the way backwards sometimes appears to go forward. When the Wheel of Destiny turns, we don't always know how things are going to work out. We can, if we choose, believe the Universe is benevolent and always working towards the ultimate spiritual benefit of all beings. In which case, anything and everything that happens in our life can be said to hold an inherent blessing. Sometimes, we will work through an unwanted situation only to discover it made us who we are. It may have taught us to tap into our inner courage and wisdom and realise we are made of stronger stuff than we ever knew. Our attitude and approach to living becomes more fearless as a result and we become open to meet the love of our lives or discover new talents or a sense of higher calling, all because that undesired experience was secretly leading us towards fulfilment all along. The Universe is clever like that.

White Tara provides gentle, long-term purification. Unlike the more rigorous actions of her Black and Blue Tara forms, White Tara accomplishes powerful purification without intensity. She is said to conquer all poisons, removing them and their effects without a trace. In Tibetan understanding, poisons are the basis of all problems in our lives, all afflictions in our mind and body, so White Tara is called upon to heal all ills. Specifically, she is said to protect one's life, nullifying negativities which could shorten it and assisting so that, when the time is right for one's life to end, the circumstances are blessed.

At three places—her crown, throat and heart—rest the sacred syllables of *OM*, *AH*, and *HUM* (in Sanskrit, or *HUNG* in Tibetan). These sacred sounds create light rays for protection from all obstacles, ensuring we are insulated from any harm, evil or other negative interference. The rays of light generated by these sacred sounds protect us from negative activity directed towards us and from inner obstacles created by our own mind and actions, which can cause suffering, illness and confusion. These rays of White Tara's light pacify all negativities, so they disappear completely.

The concept of psychic and emotional vampires has entered mainstream awareness in recent years. Such people are said to consciously or unconsciously feed off the emotional or vital energies of another, without regard for the impact of such actions on the 'host.' Once they have drained a person, they move on. Far from being about give and take in a relationship, psychic vampirism is a parasitic exploitation and is extremely dysfunctional. White Tara's rays of light protect against such actions. If life force has been siphoned off already, she breaks the connection and restores what has been lost. If you sense that you tend to attract more than your fair share of such wounded people into your life, and feel the worse for it, White Tara can protect you and show you a better, healthier, happier and more effective way to deal with such relationship dynamics. Sometimes those raised by emotionally-damaged parents learned not just to support others but to martyr themselves to the unconscious wounding of other people. Learning that loving another does not require you to meet their every need at the expense of your own wellbeing is an important healing gift for such people, one that White Tara willingly provides. If you feel it is your path to be a healer, she guides you to become an empowered healer, rather than one who is used as fuel for other people's egos. If harmful intentions or actions are directed towards you by any being, White Tara's rays of light, formed from these three sacred sounds, eliminate the harmful intentions and their potentially negative effects.

The syllables *Om Ah Hum* represent the three facets of being, from a Buddhist perspective. *Om* stands for the body, *Ah* for speech (which also includes our energy), and *Hum* for the mind. The *Om* transforms the body by purifying all negative actions committed through your body, the *Ah* purifies negative speech (which revitalises and refreshes our subtle energies) and *Hum* purifies negative thoughts or intentions. Reciting these sounds, we not only purify ourselves, but the environment in which we dwell on all levels, from the subtlest spiritual energies to the tangible physical world. Even those who don't feel particularly sensitive to energy often notice how great it feels

to enter a spiritually purified space or to be around a spiritually purified person (which is basically the same thing). Problems and bad moods can melt away, leaving us with a feeling of openness, relaxation and a sense that, somehow, things are going to work out for the best.

The purification process is gentled through the presence of White Tara. Without her softening light pacifying the negativities which can arise, purification can feel quite intense. When thoughts and feelings from the past arise, especially if you have been doing a spiritual practice, such as prayer, meditation, yoga or mindfulness, it can be a sign purification is taking place. This is good. It will result in more clarity and peace within you and around you, eventually. In the interim, however, if you are intensively purifying, you can feel you are being inundated with old issues. You may wonder what is going on, feeling as though you are going backwards even when you were taking steps forwards on your path. With White Tara, those thoughts and feelings evaporate swiftly, without any disturbance to our being.

You can imagine the purification process like this: You have an old piece of clothing filled with associations from the past — some negative, some positive, some neutral. You don't wear the item anymore because it doesn't fit properly. Maybe it has holes in it, your style has changed, or it just doesn't feel like 'you' anymore. However, you are still a bit attached to what it once represented, so you throw it in the back of the wardrobe.

When you are rummaging in the wardrobe for a shirt to wear, that old piece of clothing may get caught on your shirt button and get pulled out along with what you were wanting to wear. You disentangle it from the day's clothing choices and shove it back in the wardrobe. However, it keeps getting pulled out. You cannot seem to shake it. And you won't, until you make peace with whatever is keeping you holding on to that old piece of clothing and discard it, once and for all.

That is purification in its essence. The old attachments keep arising and getting tangled up in moments in which they no longer have a role, until we clear them. When they are released, we have been purified. We no longer get tangled up in what was.

With White Tara, this process becomes more effortless. That old piece of clothing is gone, and we are at peace about it. We don't think of it anymore, don't dream of it, don't worry about whether we should have held on to it longer. We are free. That old piece of clothing is free, too — to find its way to someone else, or to decompose in the trash or whatever needs to happen. Without Tara, we can feel angry and frustrated that the shirt keeps getting dragged out, criticise ourselves for the messy state of our wardrobe and yet feel unable to let go of that old piece of clothing (perhaps it would involve conquering some deeply held shame or fear to do so), and so we maintain the cycle of attachment and judgement which is creating pain and disturbance in our hearts. Tara's purification breaks the cycle, freeing us.

White Tara is an invincible queen of positivity and light. She eliminates bad dreams by healing and protecting us with her rays of light. She is the Seven-Eyed Mother with two eyes beneath her eyebrows, an open third eye in her forehead and an eye in each palm and sole of each foot. She sees all, across all realms. In typical Tara fashion, however, if needs be, White Tara will shed her peaceful demeanour and manifest as a terrifyingly wrathful blue-skinned goddess protector known as *Palden Lhamo*.

White Tara's mantra is an extension of the mantra of Green Tara. It includes requests for health, wisdom and the abundance of blessings in many ways. The mantra is *Om Tare Tuttare Ture Mama Ayur Pune Jnana Putim Kuru Soham* (sounds like *OHM TAR-RAY TWO-TAR-RAY TWO-RAY MAMA EYE-YAH PUN-YAY JAR-NAH PUT-HIM KOO-ROO SO-HUM*).

Her mudras or hand postures are the same as those of Green Tara. The blessing or boon-giving mudra is in her right hand and the refuge mudra is in her left. These let us know she will provide us with all that is needed and desired, and we can seek sanctuary in her grace.

YELLOW TARA

Beautiful, golden Yellow Tara is a goddess of wealth and prosperity. She eliminates poverty and brings good fortune. Her appearance is a positive sign of good things flowing towards us. She helps us overcome limited thinking and heal issues around self-worth, receiving and trust. If we want to receive a blessing that transforms our life, we need to grow our confidence and our trust so that these qualities within our hearts become big enough to allow it to happen.

This gracious Tara dwells in the heart, where the sacred alchemical meeting of our human and divine selves takes place. Her essence is ambrosial liquid prana, which can give life, wash away shame and poverty of spirit, and bring an abundance of blessings both spiritual and material. She helps us tune into divine beauty and radiate that beauty in the world. Often, our connection to Yellow Tara comes out of darkness. We may have experienced the darkness of loss or financial struggle, or our own real beauty may never have been mirrored to us, so we feel we are ugly, unworthy or not enough. We may place so much emphasis on our looks that we devalue the real beauty of who we are as a person. My partner recently gave me this lovely compliment: "You're so gorgeous, and that's only your fifth best quality." One of Yellow Tara's profound wisdom teachings is about restoring our inner dignity and creating a resilient sense of self-worth. This includes overcoming experiences of shame, guilt or judgement from the past, so we are able to embrace the goodness within us and, through that, awaken it in those around us.

Yellow Tara has obvious appeal. She bestows wealth, beauty, success, love and spiritual enlightenment — an amazing combination of blessings. However, I believe our attraction to her comes from a deeper place. I often tell my students that if you want to empower the Divine in your life, you must trust unconditionally. In private readings, people have often told me, "I'll trust the Universe with everything ... except my mortgage." The fear for survival is one which can strike very deep, as I know from my own earlier experiences. As I learned how to trust the Divine, even with my needs for shelter, the results opened my mind and brought deeper peace to my heart. My confidence in the Universe grew exponentially. If the Divine could take care of something I thought was so difficult, I was sure it could manage anything else I was willing to hand over.

Financial fear can be tricky for many people to overcome, even during times of relative wealth. If we connect with a divine being who can heal our biggest fears, then trusting them with the smaller stuff becomes less of a challenge. Which leads us to the deeper purpose of Yellow Tara and what I feel we really crave from her. She awakens a sense of unification of the spiritual and the material, something we need not only for peace, but which opens us to a different and more loving experience of the sacredness and meaning we can find in the world when we are willing to look beneath appearances and seek hidden wisdom.

Life can be tough at times. When we are outgrowing what we know, it can be exciting but, also, intimidating. When we are growing psychologically and emotionally, we may undergo certain testing experiences. Life may push us to let go of fear and become bold enough to fulfil our potential. If we believe the Universe is basically taking care of us, we are more likely to meet our challenges with a sense of optimism and curiosity, rather than shying away from whatever takes us beyond the world we've known. We will realise that trying to control life is like a drop of water trying to control the ocean. We don't need to freak out because we belong to something greater. We are a part of something beautiful. We matter.

I find it intriguing that Yellow Tara shows up when we finally give up *always* needing to be the warrior with the world upon our shoulders, always doing it alone, hyper-independent and driving ourselves forward. Her presence is softening. She teaches us how to be gentle with ourselves and others. If you have been conditioned to believe gentleness is a weakness or indulgence, Yellow Tara can show you it is an extremely effective way to attract what you need and accomplish what your heart desires. She teaches you how to become a powerful presence whilst treading more gently upon the earth.

Yellow Tara, known as Lakshmi in the Hindu tradition, is a preserving rather than destructive presence. Destruction—clearing the way for the new—can be essential to creation. I was very familiar with that more intense approach to spiritual growth in my early years. Then, when I became interested in the golden goddess Lakshmi, I noticed something changed. I began to take better care of things I wished to continue to own — from furniture to clothing to my own body. I gave of my time and attention,

whereas in the past, my fast and furious personality would have rampaged in, torn things apart, cast aside things—with perhaps more enthusiasm and less judiciousness than was called for—and moved on. I was something of a tornado, far more oriented in behaviour to wild, dark Kali than to a gentle, sustaining goddess of abundance. That harder, more dramatic, more intense path was familiar and exciting for a time. Then I realised how hard it is for a human being to live that way constantly. It became wearying for my body, mind and soul. I yearned for peace and stability within myself and my life. I knew I was strong. I had proved I had courage. I was willing to stop needing to prove that to myself again and again. Instead, I sought a different expression for my strength and courage — that of loving myself enough to tread a gentler path and refusing to buy into the Western notion that being powerful required me to be forceful.

Yellow Tara can teach us that we can grow best from a stable foundation of love, respect and care. Like White Tara, she teaches that sometimes the gentler way is the more powerful way. The Tao teaches that only the truly strong are capable of being gentle. This doesn't turn one into a pushover or a doormat. Rather, it suggests we learn not to use a pickaxe when a toothpick will get the job done.

When our connection to Yellow Tara is lost, so too is the connection to our inner light. In the Hindu tradition, her disappearance cast the world into darkness. People became greedy and disinterested in the sacred. The lack of energy directed from humans to the divine realms meant the gods began to lose their power and the *asuras* (demons) increased their control in the minds and hearts of human beings. People began to place more faith in hate and fear than in love and trust. As the inner light became cloaked in negativity, people felt lost and confused and suffering increased.

To reverse this trend, the divine beings began to stir things up. Rather than let the world be consumed by darkness, they put some proverbial spanners in the works. This happens when our ego is happily leading us towards our destruction, whilst we think we are going to get everything we want continuing down that path. The Divine Mother knows otherwise. She knows walking an ego-driven path will keep us from fulfilling a destiny we haven't even grasped yet.

As a girl of six, I fell in love with dance — a love affair that continues to this day. At the time, I yearned to be a ballet dancer. I studied hard and had a natural flair for emotional expression through my body, but despite spending years trying to get my hip sockets to turn out, they just would not do it. Because of my joints, my height and my naturally curvaceous form, I was not divinely designed to be a ballet dancer. When I realised this, I felt as though a cherished dream had died — which is exactly what had happened.

The many gifts and blessings that followed led me into a life far more suitable, which brought me the kind of joy and fulfilment I could not have imagined. Funnily enough, the emotional bliss I sought through devoting myself to the transcendent and expansive experience of dance was granted to me in my later work. I was able to sing and dance as part of my work — in workshops with a hundred other spiritual enthusiasts or on stage as part of my consciousness-raising, electronic-dance-music performance called *Divine Circus*. Although I loved Kali, with her ferocity and dark grace, Lakshmi blessed me with an ease that helped me thrive with a greater sense of balance. My early pain and disappointment gave way to my higher destiny.

When we are going through experiences that thwart our cherished ideas, Yellow Tara's wisdom and generosity is always at play. Peace of mind and boldness of heart require us to detach from what we think *should* happen—or what we *want to* happen—and participate in what *is* happening. This doesn't mean we cannot hold a vision. It is important to the soul's journey to learn to hold a vision and manifest what we desire. But there will be a time when we are willing to let the Universal Mother see for us. Then, we must trust her higher perspective and follow her higher workings, no matter where they lead. The more we understand that the Universe is expressing itself for the fulfilment of all beings, the more we realise that when we let go and allow life to unfold, we will find only benefit. We can have faith that our wishes will be granted. We will need to let go of exactly how and when that takes place.

The mantra for invoking all the Taras is *Om Tare Tuttare Ture Soham* (sounds like *OHM TAR-RAY TWO-TAR-RAY TWO-RAY SO-HUM*). There is also a specific mantra for Yellow Tara, which is a derivation of the White Tara mantra focusing on increasing, wealth-giving and enriching. It is *Om Tare Tuttare Ture Pushtim Kuru Om Swaha* (sounds like *OHM TAR-RAY TWO-TAR-RAY TWO-RAY PUSH-TIM KOO-ROO OHM SWAH-HA*).

The mudras or hand positions of Yellow Tara can be the same as Green Tara. She is also often shown holding a lotus flower but can be depicted holding a treasure vase. Yellow Tara is also known as wealth goddess Vasudhara, a consort of wrathful wealth protector Dzhambala (a form of Avalokiteshvara/Kuan Yin). In this form she holds a conch, a symbol for the Divine calling to our essence and giving us guidance and blessings to fulfil our destiny. Along with the treasure vase, Yellow Dzambhala holds one of the more fabulous Tibetan spirit animals — a jewel-disgorging mongoose. The mongoose is capable of hunting down a snake, so this special mongoose is a symbol of Yellow Dzambhala's control of potentially poisonous energies, whilst she spews forth precious gems to support our life journey.

Red Tara is associated with passion, magnetic attraction and subduing negative forces. In Nepal, she is recognised as the Wish-Fulfilling Tara. She magnetises all good things into our lives. Red Tara can evoke courage, wisdom, strength and great bliss. She is the aspect of our true nature that is open and exploring and simply refuses to be put down, blocked or stopped.

In her peaceful form, Red Tara is an attractor. She teaches us to use our desires and passions to move along the spiritual path and work towards what we want in such a way that there is benefit for all beings. She teaches us how to be in loving harmony with the Universe, so that as we manifest our desires, the benefits reach beyond us. Rather than pursuing our ego-driven goals, no matter the cost to anyone else, Red Tara helps us realise there is no win when another suffers at the expense of our actions. She shows how we can obtain fulfilment without harming one another and in such a way that the wins benefit others, too.

At Avalon beach one summer, I noticed a woman wearing a dress I liked a lot. I recognised the designer and style and felt it would suit me. However, it was an older style, long since unavailable in stores. Although it would be a rare find, I just had the feeling I could find it. Of course, when I have those intuitive moments, strange things happen. When I went home that afternoon, I easily found it online and purchased it. Surprisingly, despite the satisfaction I felt in the ease of manifestation, I never wore the dress. The colour wasn't quite right on my skin tone, and the cut wasn't quite right on me, after all. I have a policy that life is too short to dress in a way that makes you feel frumpy. So, I knew I needed to let it go. Sometimes I clean out my wardrobe by giving away items to charity or, sometimes, when the mood takes me, I sell them on eBay.

If I wait for Spirit to tell me to sell something on eBay, it always sells very quickly and there's usually some funny series of events involved in the process. The nudge came from Spirit to list this dress, so I did. Someone purchased it within about twenty minutes of the listing going up.

However, after the purchase came a pleading email from another person, begging me to cancel the sale, offering to pay me more money, because she had been trying to buy this dress for a long time. She had seen it online three times and missed out each time. I felt for her, but I replied that it wasn't about the money. It just didn't feel right to cancel the sale, even though I really was moved by the emotional tone of her email. It popped into my head that she would get her dress, anyway. So, I told her that. She didn't believe me, but thanked me, and that was that.

A few minutes later, I received an email from the buyer thanking me so much for the dress. She wanted to purchase it for a friend of hers who had been trying to buy this dress but kept missing out. She was so excited she could surprise her friend with the dress she had coveted. I started to giggle. I emailed the buyer back and found out that, yes, the poor woman who had contacted me begging for the dress was going to be the recipient, after all. I soon had another round of emails from both women thanking me and saying how happy they were to have fulfilled a wish.

I loved that experience. It was delightful that all three of us obtained what we wanted. I sold the dress to a loving home, the woman who wanted the dress received it and the friend who wanted to help her did so. It was a triple fulfilment. It felt a lot like the handiwork of Red Tara, from her art of effortless manifestation, to her beautiful capacity to bring fulfilment to all simultaneously.

Red Tara teaches discriminating awareness, which helps us sense the difference between our ego and genuine spiritual inspiration. This makes it a lot easier to live in harmony with the Universe and recognise genuine divine guidance which, in turn, reduces confusion and suffering and helps us move through challenges with more equanimity and wisdom.

Red Tara increases our enjoyment, bliss and courageous willingness to embrace life. When we are connected to her, we feel our path is unobstructed and the energies of divine bliss and healing can flow to us and from us freely. Meditation upon Red Tara removes obstacles, whilst attracting the best opportunities. One does need to be a little careful with such magnetic power, however. When I taught a Red Tara session for my retreat group of women, the attentiveness of (fortunately for us, respectful and lovely) men spiked all day! Her allure is hard to resist!

If we focus on having compassion and wisdom, and on asking that our needs and desires be fulfilled in such a way that all beings obtain the most spiritual benefit (we don't have to know how that can happen, the Divine Mother knows), then we can ask for what we want and need, let go, and trust in what flows in—and out—of our lives as a consequence.

In her semi-wrathful state, Red Tara becomes Kurukulla, destroyer of opposing forces, subduer of negativity and harmfulness, swift heroine and protector. Kurukulla is a fascinating being. Typically depicted with little fangs, a pretty face and a stunning headdress, she dances, scantily clad, with a flower-covered bow drawn, her arrow ready to fire at any moment. The story of how the flowers came to decorate Kurukulla's bow and arrow involves another deity, Shiva, whom we met earlier. Shiva was meditating in the forest, one of his favourite things to do. The Hindu god of love and lust known as Kama, decided he was going to play a trick on Shiva, causing him to fall passionately in love. Shiva—with his perfect clarity—sensed what the mischievous Kama had planned. His shocking temper roused at the thought of his meditation being disturbed, and he promptly zapped hapless Kama with one electrifying shot of energy from his third eye. Kama exploded into an impressive array of beautiful blossoms, which came to adorn Kurukulla's weapon of choice. Kurukulla has the enchanting power of Kama. She is a sorceress, a love goddess and a magnetic manifestation goddess. She is our capacity to

transform the selfish desires which feed our ego (and fail to create genuine fulfilment, joy or satisfaction) into higher passion which can nourish our hearts and bring us genuine delight and happiness.

Kurukulla has four arms, two upon her bow and arrow, and two holding the hook and noose which symbolise how she binds the lower will to the higher or, in other words, how she helps us learn to fall in love with our soul path rather than our ego obsessions. The hook and noose symbolise her ability to keep us on the path, whatever that may be for us. We may have a fabulous idea, but if it's just not on point for our life purpose at that time, we'll need to let it go — perhaps for a time, perhaps permanently. You can be sure that for each project I've created (and there's a fair number of creations), at least ten other ideas had to be laid aside! Kurukulla helps us choose what has real spiritual substance from our various options. Given that the number of opportunities for us increases through her presence, it is helpful that her discerning wisdom grows within us, too.

Kurukulla grants commanding presence and the ability to attract others and influence people. She is known as the Tara who increases power. She is an enchantress, attracting people to the path through her magnetic charisma. This vibrant, ruby-red sorceress can help us amplify our own magnetic power in such a way that people are drawn to us for the goodness we shine. We can then give to others more freely, and the more we give, the more we can receive from the Cosmic Madonna in a positive spiral of flowing abundance. It is so much more joyful than the ego-driven ways of trying to take from others to fill a void within.

As tends to be the way with religious traditions imposed upon native shamanic traditions, Kurukulla predated Buddhism as an independent goddess in her own right before she was absorbed into the form of Red Tara. A shamanic goddess of witchcraft, her positive nature was distilled through Buddhist practices. A certain number of repetitions of her mantra was said to bring various beings under one's control — from cattle and earth spirits, to kings, politicians and other spiritual practitioners. The idea is not to create power-obsessed egomaniacs running the world (one might suggest we've experienced more than enough of that). With Kurukulla, we have the chance to actually help people. She helps us charm, attract and love those who can benefit from her wisdom, courage and light. Buddhism teaches us that very few beings are truly capable of helping others. Even if our intentions are good, there can be so much confusion and suffering in our own lives that our capacity to assist others is restricted. With Kurukulla's power, we can heal our own lives and bring the negative energies which afflict humanity under the control of the Divine Mother's spiritual light. We can become effective healers and helpers, even when we are working on our own issues.

If our desires lead us into unhealthy places—perhaps through addictions or obsessions—Red Tara, especially in the form of Kurukulla, can help us. She can heal all afflictions with the multi-coloured lights which emanate from her crown. With her bow and arrow, she helps us overcome false ideas and get back to the clear, focused direction of our path. Ultimately, this keeps us safe, protected and brings us happiness and fulfilment.

Some stories of Kama say he was burnt to ash by Shiva's angry gaze and some, that he exploded into flowers. Both versions are part of Kurukulla's secret symbolism. The ashes refer to her ability to eliminate all negative influence, so that we can rise anew — like a Phoenix. Ash is sacred in Indian spirituality. It can be a vehicle of blessing. Kurukulla brings us fearlessly into the endings of various cycles and the letting go of old behaviours or self-identities. She frees us from bondage of any kind and opens us to rebirth, to blossoming.

As Kurukulla dances in her ring of flames, smiling but fierce, with multiple lights shining from her ruby-red body, she is the manifestation of bliss, courage and energy. We can visualise her seed syllable *Hrih* at our hearts and repeat her mantra, feeling its warmth, love and openness: *Om Kurukulle Hrih Soham* (sounds like *OHM COO-ROO-COO-LAY HREE SO-HUM*).

As the more peaceful, magnetic form of Red Tara, the mantra *Om Tare Tam Swaha* (sounds like *OHM TAR-RAY TUM SWAH-HA*) can be said or sung whilst we imagine a beautiful shining Red Tara is in our hearts, seated in meditation posture, right foot extended, ready to leap into action. In her right hand, she holds a long-life treasure vat of healing nectar, and in her left hand, resting before her heart, she holds a red lotus between her thumb and ring finger.

While chanting this mantra, imagine all your magnetic, vital goodness growing so powerful it overflows and endless light radiates from the Red Tara in your heart, helping all beings in need. Tara, in any of her forms, is a beautiful deity to work with in such a *tonglen* meditation (a Buddhist teaching centring around the receiving and sending of light). *Tonglen* is a Tibetan word which translates as *letting go* (*tong*) and *accepting* (*len*), and this meditation technique is a light-healing practice that anyone can do. It has the capacity to transform negative energies into positive energy. In the practice of tonglen taught to me by my Dzogchen master, we receive then give the divine light, healing and wisdom that flows to us. To aid that process we can visualise, imagine or feel we are receiving, then shine that beautiful divine presence from the heart to any and all beings in need. It is simple, and it feels amazing.

The more you truly allow yourself to receive, with compassion for your own needs and struggles, the more you open to becoming a vehicle of Tara. When we receive true divine grace, we want to share it. It naturally radiates out of us and heals others.

In the TV sitcom *Seinfeld,* the character George Costanza struggles through his life. Everything that could go wrong, does. His is not the most gracious or apparently blessed existence. He is negative and complains a lot, and then one day he decides to do things differently. He is going to be Opposite George, doing the opposite of whatever he would usually do, think or say. The result is extraordinary. His life quickly becomes filled with opportunities and joy. He becomes incredibly successful. He gets everything he wanted. Opposite George is a hit! However, George isn't quite sure about this success and happiness. He misses his old ways of negativity and grouchiness. He decides he'd rather be miserable as old George than happy as Opposite George.

Whilst this is hilarious and ridiculous, there is a grain of wisdom in it. The struggle George has is not with being someone else, but with letting go of his ego attachment to the pain and suffering associated with whom he thinks he is. This struggle is real for most of us at some time. We become accustomed to our ideas about who we think we are and what we think life is about. To let that go can take us into unfamiliar waters of peace. Giving up the struggle allows us to use our energies in more constructive ways such as helping others by practicing light-giving ways of living, from meditation to yoga to remembering to laugh so hard that you snort, as often as possible.

When we practice tonglen, especially when visualising the healing lights from Red Tara, the change we feel can be instant. Getting used to vibrating at a higher frequency is a journey, but far from being some airy-fairy notion, it has far-reaching practical effects. It leads us to change our lifestyles — from food to exercise to health care to the types of thoughts we cultivate and the ways we treat other people. We become less reactive and more forgiving. Life has its challenging moments, but the rough edges are softened and much of what we once struggled to accept becomes easier.

With Red Tara's presence, especially as kick-ass Kurukulla, attachments are loosened, karmic clearing takes place and blessings flow generously. We feel gratitude, freedom, love and a sense of playfulness. We are willing to move forward more fearlessly in our lives, with boldness and joy. We do things we never would have believed we would have the courage to do, and we do so with happiness in our hearts. She gives the precious gift of the freedom to express our authentic nature, unbound from suffering and obstacle. *Om Tare Tam Swaha!*

ORANGE TARA

Orange Tara laughs away the darkness in our lives. She is a free-spirited, wandering Tara, connected with the in-between times and phases in our lives. That could be childbirth, death or any other major transition that involves changing cycles or new opportunities. She safeguards us when we are vulnerable, so we can boldly live our path.

Orange Tara is a goddess of liberation. She is connected to freedom of body and of mind. She is said to free prisoners from their shackles, which could be the physical restraint of the body or psychological restraints. She conquers all prisons and forms of control — external and internal. She purifies and eliminates poverty and any kind of oppression. Oppression is rife in the modern world. Whether we are asylum seekers or political prisoners, trapped in wars or religious oppression—or even if consider ourselves to be free—the spirit of oppression lurks in shadows, capable of stifling our willingness to take heartfelt chances and express ourselves without fear.

Oppressive energies can arise from our own minds and from external negativities which seek to undermine our spiritual progress, steal our hope and optimism and trap us in doubt. In Tantric Buddhism, lack of confidence is considered one of the most significant issues to overcome on the spiritual path. Without a healthy sense of confidence, it is easy to become lost in confusion and suffering. Because life is so uncertain, we need to find certainty within our hearts. When our confidence wavers or we don't know which way to turn, Orange Tara is our bright light and guardian goddess. If we feel trapped in a situation, invoking Orange Tara will help us find our way out.

Known as the mountain-dwelling mendicant, Orange Tara represents the wisdom and power of the monastic way of life, even for those of us who are not monks or nuns. We don't have to take vows of renunciation to connect with Orange Tara. She can teach us how to dedicate ourselves wholeheartedly to our higher purpose. Like a monk who accepts only what is offered, Orange Tara can help us learn how to receive. Growing up in the Western world, where the revolting expression 'it's a dog eat dog world' was familiar to me, I never really understood the difference between taking and receiving. I thought if I wanted something, I had to go out and get it for myself. It was a grasping, stressful, power-oriented way to live. When I began to work as a spiritual healer, I learned differently. It was a relief to my heart, even whilst my mind struggled to trust the notions of surrender and grace which are so antithetical to the philosophies I grew up believing.

A teaching I received in a dream helped me understand. In the dream, I was walking at the edge of a beautiful ocean. There was a stunning lyrebird nearby. A lyrebird is an extraordinary, ground-dwelling Australian bird which mimics the sounds around it, faithfully reflecting what it hears in a rich and ornate song. This can include anything from a complicated birdcall to the sound of the camera shutter releasing, when someone takes a picture of the lyrebird with its beautiful wispy, tail feathers curling above its head.

In my dream, the ocean drew back. Resting at the dry base of the ocean was a perfect lyrebird feather. It was right at my feet. When I reached down to pick it up, the lyrebird nearby stepped forward and gripped my grasping fingers with its beak. It didn't hurt me, but I did realise it was a warning. I surrendered my intention to obtain the feather and the ocean gently rose up again, reclaiming the feather. And that was the end of my dream.

I was puzzled by this dream. I reflected on its meaning for some time, before I realised it was an important—and, for me, life changing—wisdom teaching. It was about the difference between taking something—even if it was right there in front of

me—rather than receiving it at the right time, and only then if it was meant to be. I needed to trust in what was meant for me and when it was meant for me. That dream marked the beginning of a maturation process. I learned to embrace patience, whilst still working hard, but with less attachment to how things unfolded and with more trust in the higher workings of the Universe, rather than my own plans.

Orange Tara, as the mendicant, or beggar, is not a symbol of poverty. Her medicine overcomes the poverty-consciousness at the base of all grasping behaviour. A mendicant doesn't even ask for food. She announces her presence with the rattling of rings on a staff. If someone wants to give to her, they will. If not, she moves on. She is receptive and present, trusting and flowing in the grace that comes to her, without trying to manipulate others or circumstances to get what she wants. This is probably the exact opposite of everything most modern people have been taught is necessary for success and happiness. Yet, I found the success and happiness I sought for myself and others only began to flow when I learned to trust in my capacity to receive and the Universal Mother's desire to deliver!

Orange Tara is also a patron goddess for healers. Her tools are protective amulets and medicines. It is said, when one truly opens to her, she will cut out the cause of even the most dangerous affliction at the root, nullifying it completely. She is depicted holding a treasure vase filled with the divine nectar of bliss and a lotus. Her left eye is the full moon, and clear nectar flows from it, curing the effects of all diseases and negativities. Her right eye is the solar eye, a blazing sun with rays that burn through all evil, including negative interference.

In Eastern spiritual traditions, the solar and lunar energies are the masculine and feminine energy channels that connect with the central channel that runs up through the spine. I have experienced that channel in meditation. Within the spinal cord, I felt a spacious tube, with lava lamp-like bubbles of bliss moving through it. It was sublime ecstasy, to be so immersed in that inner subtle world of the spinal channel. It was so subtle, luminous and powerful. Tibetan Tantric Buddhists believe the true nature of self is hidden in the deeper subtle layers of the body. Orange Tara can purify, balance and empower the solar and lunar channels in our bodies. This helps us access the inner worlds of bliss, light, love and spaciousness that are our true nature and can be experienced when we begin to venture into the deeper realms of our physical bodies. For those who wish to experience the true self as a counterpoint and relief from the fearful workings of the mind, Orange Tara is a gateway to grace, beauty and increasing levels of spiritual realisation in a feminine, embodied way.

I experience Orange Tara as the source of emanation of two of my favourite Egyptian goddesses. The first is the lion-headed warrior goddess of the sun, Sekhmet. The other is Bastet, the cat-headed goddess of birth, dance, joy, celebration and the moon, also known as Bast. Both Sekhmet and Bastet are protective, healing goddesses and patron goddesses for healers, just like Orange Tara.

Sekhmet, whom I believe emanates from Orange Tara's right solar eye, is known as She Before Whom Evil Trembles. She is an absolute badass, destroying anything that would block truth, light and freedom. She uses the fiery destructive power of the sun to manifest higher justice. She loves Ma'at, the goddess of divine justice from ancient Egypt.

Bastet, whom I experience as an emanation from Tara's left lunar eye, is a goddess of protection in darkness. She sees in the dark like a cat. She watches over births of all kinds and promotes celebration, joy, dance and pleasure. She is the guardian of ointments, potions, perfumes and all sacred healing substances, like the nectar which pours from Orange Tara's left eye.

These goddesses together provide us with an opportunity to tap into an experience of the sacred feminine energy that is wild, fearless, protective and not afraid to call bullshit for what it is, on the one hand, and blissful, ecstatic, sensual, pleasure that leads to healing and joy, on the other. These wild goddesses have incredibly empowering vital energies that can assist you in connecting with your own unique expression of sacred feminine energy. I believe sacred feminine energy, with its ability to create, nurture and protect, is essential for the wellbeing of our planet and every individual upon this earth, no matter our biology or gender.

If you'd like to learn more about these Egyptian goddesses and how to connect with them, I have included a chapter on each, along with their associated crystal and healing processes, in the book *Crystal Goddesses 888*. They are also featured in the *Crystal Mandala Oracle*, where each has her own oracle card, crystal correspondence, mandala, healing process and message. I created a meditation CD titled, *Meditations with Lion-Headed Deities*, which features an in-depth meditation journey with Sekhmet if you wish to journey deeper with her.

Orange Tara's mantra is one of my favourites, and with a little practice, you can say it in a hypnotic, meditative rhythm. It is *Om Tare Tuttare Ture Nama Tare Namo Hara Hung Hara Swaha* (sounds like *OHM TAR-RAY TWO-TAR-RAY TWO-RAY NUMB-AH TAR-RAY NUMB-OH HAH-RAH HOONG HAH-RAH SWA-HAH*). It drives away darkness and connects us to Orange Tara's freedom-giving light.

Blue Tara is a fierce manifestation of Tara. She is associated with the transmutation of anger. Tantric wisdom from both Hindu and Buddhist traditions tells us we do not need to fight against potentially negative energies such as anger. Rather, we can transform them through wisdom and appropriate spiritual practices. Anger can work like a poison in the body, stealing joy and equanimity, eroding trust in relationships and leading to obsession and negative repercussions for all, especially the angered person. However, with spiritual skilfulness, that same anger can be transformed into clarity. Moments of intense emotion can obscure our vision, but if we use the energies in a mature rather than reactive way, they can penetrate delusion, so we see things with far greater clarity. Sometimes, a single moment of clarity is so powerful that life-changing decisions are made, and long-term negative attitudes fall away permanently. Anger can be a powerful force, for better or worse, depending on how we learn to handle it.

Blue Tara manifests in various forms, one of which is Ekajati, a ferocious and protective form of the Divine Mother. Ekajati is a principle protector of the ancient and mysterious Dzogchen spiritual practice, which filters into Buddhism, Hinduism and Himalayan shamanic practices and is said to predate all of them. It focuses on the most direct path to enlightenment. The connection between Ekajati and Dzogchen (as the most direct path to enlightenment) provides a clue to her role in all of our lives, not just those of us who are drawn to Dzogchen. As a goddess who moves us on to the most direct path, we can trust that her interventions are ultimately going to bring us the most bliss and progress — even if it feels like ripping off the proverbial Band-Aid at the time.

Ekajati is the protector of the path and the destroyer of obstacles on the path. As I have mentioned, sometimes we think we know what our path should be. Personally, I had many ideas about what I wanted to be doing, how I wanted to be doing it and when I thought it should happen. You may be relieved and/or amused to know none of it unfolded the way I wanted. Eventually, I was grateful for this because everything that *did* happen was perfect and helped me grow in ways which suggested the Universe knew who I really was and what I really needed far better than I did.

If we are graced with a visitation from Ekajati, it is an extraordinary grace. If we receive such a blessing, she may well mess up our plans and appear as a threat to everything we have held dear! Whether we sense her presence consciously or not, the effect is obvious. We feel pushed to face our deepest aversions and fears, to become free from impediments and fulfil our spiritual destiny. That doesn't sound like much fun and it can, for a time, seem like a nightmare.

I once encountered an emanation of the wrathful Divine Mother during a romantic relationship in which I had become very stuck. Although I loved the man in question, the relationship was unhealthy, to put it mildly, and the nature of the dysfunction made it essential that I end it. However, it literally took me years to work through the emotional journey required to end it, and then even more years to process the psychological mess that had been generated through the relationship. It was a devastating time for me on emotional and physical levels. Yet, severing that attachment, although very painful, was absolutely necessary. Because of it, I was able to let go of my past patterns and find my way into the loving arms of my true inner nature (and, after that, into the beautiful, muscular, loving arms of a truly special man).

None of that arduous, painful, essential, profoundly liberating and (eventually) joy-creating process could have happened without some intense spiritual intervention. I knew that at the time (well, I didn't know how wonderful the outcome would be, but I guessed it would be something along those lines). That knowledge did not make the process much easier to endure. But the loving grace of the fierce Mother helped me stay the course through the years required to sort myself out.

When we have a destiny to meet, Blue Tara will manifest if we need a (loving) kick in the pants to get to the right place at the right time. This is one reason she hovers around lazy or confused practitioners, making sure they pull themselves together and make the appropriate dedication to their path. She's rather like the menacing Zen master prowling behind his meditating students, waiting to pounce upon those who lose focus and fall asleep with a deft whack of his cane. Quite a way to bring one back into the moment!

Ekajati, like Green Tara, is known for her swiftness. She does not meander, nor does she gently coddle one along the path. She is deliberate and aims for maximum progress in minimum time. She appears when we are ready, which may be rather different to when we *think* we are ready. I remember reading an interview with Barbra Streisand, the incredibly talented vocalist. It was interesting to hear she always got nervous before a performance and found sitting, rather than standing, more calming to her. What really resonated from that interview, which I must have read over a decade ago, was that even though she was obviously capable of sharing her tremendous gifts with the world, she didn't always feel like she was. There may be dissonance between our sense of timing and our actual readiness. We can be a touch too enthusiastic or lacking in confidence. Our timing may not coincide with the Divine Mother's higher timing for us. This doesn't have to be negative. It can reinforce patience and confidence, so we are responsive to what is offered and accepting of our journey, without torturing ourselves with unhelpful expectations or comparisons to anyone else or to an ideal in our own minds.

Ekajati is depicted as single-eyed, with a single braid and, often, a single breast. These all symbolise her powerful, non-dual, unwavering focus. Her skin may be a deep midnight or sapphire blue, and she can hold a crystal vajra (lightning bolt) dagger to cut through opposition and represent her supreme strength. Her mantra contains two special syllables that protect us and perform her helpful 'severing' function. The first

syllable, *Bhim* (sounds like *BEAM*), helps to pierce the layers of confusion and delusion, and the second syllable, *Vhrim* (sounds like *VHREEM*), cuts through obstacles and destructive forces. Her simple mantra is *Om Bhim Tare Vhrim Swaha* (sounds like *OHM BEAM TAR-RAY VRHEEM SWA-HAH*).

Naked but for a cloud and a tiger skin—a symbol of the *mahasiddhas*, or great yogis with supernatural powers—Ekajati represents the fearless, direct path to enlightenment and all the benefits that accompany it, including the power to help others make spiritual progress. Her nakedness symbolises her wildness, her raw, untamed nature — which we also possess, beneath our layers of mental conditioning. Our spiritual capacity rapidly develops under her influence.

Some spiritual practitioners worry about becoming obsessed with power. It's easy enough to do, and arrogance, with a sense of superiority at being 'more evolved' than others (even if you want to help those others), is rarely far behind. Then, as if we were sliding down the snake in the game of *Snakes and Ladders*, the gains we made become tainted, and we need to clean ourselves up before we can make further progress.

The greatest healers I have encountered—and I've met many, from a variety of modalities and traditions over the last forty years—are those who combine skilfulness with an absence of ego. They do not personalise or lay claim to what results for those who encounter them. I have the sense some don't know the extent of what they do for others, nor do they have much sense of the extraordinary which can manifest through their presence. They just show up for whatever calling they have and accomplish it according to their inner sense of direction and guidance. In doing so, without any pride, the spiritual protection of thousands upon thousands of people (perhaps millions upon millions, in certain cases), rests comfortably within the spaciousness of their inner being. It is truly a beautiful thing to behold.

This doesn't mean that one can only obtain spiritual *siddhis*, or powers, through selflessness and spiritual advancement. One can do practices to develop powers to meet one's own ego-driven agenda. My mantra teacher, Thomas Ashley Farrand, shared a room with one such man at a spiritual retreat. They, and two other participants, had three pieces of bread to share between the four of them. In his arrogance, this attendee claimed more than his share, as though the others were less important. Despite his deficit in compassion and generosity, he had abundant discipline and a strong power drive. With these characteristics, he had developed the extraordinary ability of manifesting lingam (Shiva stones) from the Narmada River in the palm of his hands — even when standing in a classroom at the retreat. During one demonstration, my teacher saw the stone in the man's hand was still dripping with river water. Despite his skills at meditation and materialisation, this man lacked true spiritual development, which would have been marked by compassion and wisdom. He ignored the warnings he was given while he was meditating near a river that was due to flood, and eventually drowned in that flooding. One can only pray that he is blessed with the sweetness of the

Divine Mother in future lifetimes, so his abilities may be put to more helpful uses in the world. No doubt, she has a marvellous plan for him in the works.

Ekajati is known as the protector and guardian of the secret or higher teachings, the inner-mind treasures which, if they were to come into unready hands, could result in terrible outcomes for all. She is an occult priestess in that sense, revealing the blessings to those who are ready to receive them. She teaches us to hold our tongue and not give information to others that may overwhelm or discourage them. She also helps us realise when we are ready to shed our once-cherished viewpoints and travel deeper into the spiritual wisdom we may access this lifetime.

Blue Tara, as Ekajati, is known as the Mistress of the Blue Protector Wolves, the Dogs and Hounds of Heaven. Her canine totems are her messengers and her assistants in the protection of all beings. She is linked to Sirius, the Dog Star (or Wolf Star, in China) and, of course, the name *Tara* translates as *Star Mother*. With a throng of demonesses to do her bidding, and often a pack of a hundred she-wolves at her side, Ekajati is an unstoppable liberating force. She is linked—through the medicine of dogs, wrathfulness, protection and the crone or wise-old-woman aspect of the sacred feminine—to Hecate, the Greek goddess of crossroads whose three-headed hound, Cerberus, guards the gates of hell. Hecate and Ekajati are initiators, opening the way into fearlessness by processing the darker, previously hidden, aspects of self.

When we are blessed with a vision of Blue Tara, especially in her wrathful form of Ekajati—with that single eye staring deep into our hearts—you can be sure a false vision or limiting point of view is going to give way to something new. Your own inner eye will open to see yourself and your life in a more truthful and vitalising way. Her presence is the Universe signalling, *it is time.*

BLACK TARA

Black and blue can be used interchangeably in the Tibetan theory of colour, so there are some qualities Black and Blue Tara share. Both can be referred to as Ugra Tara, have a wrathful nature and are associated with enlightened divine destruction. This means that the Divine expresses itself ferociously when there is no other means to obtain a desired higher purpose.

As an expression of the Hindu goddess Kali, Black Tara has her own unique qualities. Associated with the use of power in service to wisdom, Black Tara subdues harmful spirits and malignant beings, as well as negative intentions. She is particularly helpful for situations where there is a need to overcome ill-intentioned magic, spells or curses. For some, those things are very real. For others, they seem like silliness. Having experienced my fair share of such things through my line of work, I believe they are a

form of occult bullying.

The Swedish company IKEA conducted an experiment to bring awareness to the effects of bullying. Two nearly identical houseplants were placed in a school and given the same amount of sunlight, water and fertiliser for one month. Kids were asked to record their voices. One taped loop was played to each house plant constantly for thirty days. One plant received encouragement and loving words, while the other received negative words. The 'bullied' plant wilted considerably. Whilst this will not surprise any gardener who knows plants respond well to positive emotional energy (and sometimes particular types of music), it also helps us understand that the thoughts and words which are directed towards us have a profound effect on our—or any being's—ability to thrive.

I've always tended to stand apart from the crowd. Combined with my mostly gentle nature, this meant that I experienced what it was like to be bullied as a school girl. I wish I could have reassured that girl she didn't have a thing to worry about, that everything would work out in her favour later, but at the time, it was a struggle to deal with the mean-spiritedness. I was genuinely confused as to why those people were behaving in such a way and that added to my struggle. I later came to feel compassion for people who had learned—likely through how they were treated themselves—to try to dominate others. I also learned quite a lot about setting boundaries. However, that all took some time. And some Kali! Black Tara, as Kali, is known for her ability to thwart negative intentions and block psychic attacks, whether they be expressed through online trolling or through other dysfunctional and aggressive social interactions, such as bullying.

She is known as the Invincible One, who crushes the forces of others. She can render our intentions and ambitions invincible, which means nothing can derail us from our path. When we are in connection with Black Tara, we sense that our spiritual fulfilment is inevitable. You may not know how or when, but you know it will happen. This generates boldness. How would you act if you knew you couldn't fail? Would you take steps you would otherwise have procrastinated over or avoided out of fear of failure, uncertainty or a lack of confidence in yourself or the Universe? That sense of inevitability is the shining vajra of Black Tara. She impregnates your intentions into the karmic fabric of the Universe, which your soul recognises, and so then can move forward with faith.

Often depicted with the fangs of a tiger to represent her ferocious, insatiable appetite for the demons of the mind, her aura is said to be fiery and smoky, representing her ability to transform energies through the purification of fire (because, as the expression goes, where there's smoke, there's fire). Her great void-like nature, endless blackness and spaciousness, can absorb all negativities and ward off evil. She is the guardian to whom we can offer anything — even what appears to be the most enormous struggles or issues. She can devour them effortlessly. So, whether she is removing spells or the negative effects on our self-esteem from bullies in the workplace or at school, mean girls at the gym or jealous trolls on social media, we have a double blessing when we call on Black Tara. She will nullify negativity in our lives and, because we have called on the presence of the Divine Mother, we will also be helping those beings who are so trapped in suffering that their only relief is to try and cause pain to others (which, if you think about it, must be a living hell for their hearts).

Tibetan teachings describe her power to affect the physical world as her making the world quake by striking the mountains and islands with the palms of her hands and stamping her foot to make structures tremble. With her glare, the unshakeable and unbreakable diamond light of the vajra emanates from her eyes and shatters forms. This refers to her ability to cause genuine change in our lives. Remember, wrathful deities show up when there are no other (gentler) means to accomplish what needs to take place. They are the divine faces of last resort, the extreme measures of sacred intervention. So, it may not be the subtlest of effects they evoke in our lives. The shattering of natural forms can refer to our karma, the natural consequences of our actions being demolished. Our karma may have created mountains for us to climb, rather than a clear and easy path ahead. Or, perhaps we have become an 'island' of sorts (which can happen if we withdraw from others to protect ourselves from painful feelings), which has separated us from nourishing resources. One strike of Black Tara's hand, and the barriers between us and others can crumble. We then have the choice to accept the hands that are finally able to reach for us, and perhaps take the chance to reach out to others, too. Great peace can flow from such activity.

A mantra for Black Tara is *Om Tare Tuttare Ture Tray Phay Soham* (sounds like *OHM TAR-RAY TWO-TAR-RAY TWO-RAY TRAY PAY SO-HUM*). This mantra empowers Black Tara's action in our lives. If you'd like to experience more of Black Tara as Kali, I have written a chapter to Kali (as well as a chapter devoted to Tara) in the book *Crystal Goddesses 888*. Both goddess forms also have their own mandala, associated crystal and healing process included in the *Crystal Mandala Oracle*.

This dark mother of grace is a fierce emanation of the great Kuan Yin, yet when we remember that her source is pure love, we can melt into her like a child, without holding anything back, and feel we are loved unconditionally. Our desire for her opens us up to her blessings. It is the desire to be freed from suffering and pain, from mental anguish, from repeated stories of broken hearts or victimisation or failure you have tortured yourself with. It is the desire to be freed from your history and discover your own uniqueness and perfect fulfilment. This desire fuels your heart and mind to open to her grace, to put yourself at her mercy, under her protection and trust unconditionally in her wisdom and love for you.

We can even pray to her when we see other beings—humans, animals, spirits—struggling and in pain. We can become fierce in our devotion to her, knowing she can absorb all that pain and provide a clear path to freedom and relief. This wrathful mother is there for us when the bonds of attachment, fear, doubt and suffering have become too strong for us to break. Through her, we can shift into the bliss of surrender that comes only when one has truly allowed her to take the suffering and transform us through the process. In the darkness of Black Tara's endless spaciousness and grace, there is room to rest, expand and become a more authentic and vibrant expression of truth.

After encountering the wrathful deity, peace comes. Relaxation and relief follow swiftly. Everything that once was, has shifted and become free. As *Prajnaparamita,* the beautiful expression of supreme wisdom, Tara manifests herself for the needs of all beings. She is always spacious and luminous, dispels suffering and opens us up, through her bright mantras, into light and awakening that takes us beyond limitations into her eternal heart.

This is summed up in the *Heart Sūtra* as *Gate Gate Paragate Parasamgate Bodhi Swaha* (sounds like GAH-TAY GAH-TAY PAR-AH-GAH-TAY PAR-AH-SUM-GAH-TAY BO-DEE SWAH-HAH) which means, *awakening that has gone beyond, beyond, completely to another shore, beyond.* Tara is our method and our means, transporting us beyond suffering, into bliss. May all beings recognise that they are nurtured in her heart.

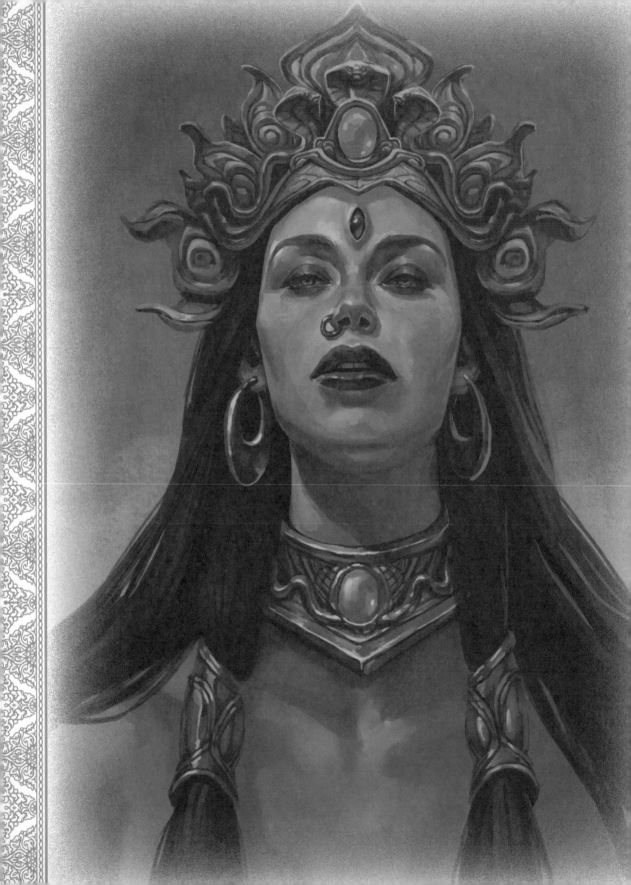

CHAPTER SIX

KALI: ENTERING THE COSMIC VOID

I OFTEN WEAR A SILVER PENDANT WITH EITHER A CARVING OF DURGA or a carving of Bhairav, a fierce form of Shiva. Both pendants are intimately connected to Kali. Durga is known as the source from which Kali arose, and Shiva, as Kali's consort, her other half. Some devotees of Kali believe that *she* is the source from which all else emerges, including Durga and Shiva. As I experience her as the cosmic void, this sits well with me.

I wore those pendants, particularly the one of Shiva, almost constantly during my most recent travels to India. The people there were very drawn to them. They would approach me, asking if that was Kali depicted in the medal that rested over my heart, and they responded with a mixture of awe and fear when I explained it was connected to her. In the West, a near-death experience is probably the closest thing we could undergo that would compare to the experience of Kali in one who has been raised with an understanding of her nature, as tends to be the case in India.

Kali is depicted in various postures and forms — something we perhaps now recognise as a hallmark of the Universal Mother. Her skin is typically jet black, and she has a red protruding tongue, white teeth and wild hair. She is the Black Madonna of India — raw, real, unapologetic divine feminine power. She is considered anti-establishment to put it politely, a 'cosmic bulldozer' might be more apt. She acts unpredictably and those who try to control rather than respect her, will have a tough time handling her initiations. She is the force of nature and the goddess of sacred revolution. When we connect with Kali, we can be sure of two things. Something radically different needs to be born and something we have outgrown (or need to promptly outgrow) will need to die to fuel the new life that is emerging. From one perspective she is chaotic, and yet, from a higher perspective, she is a principle of divine order. She consistently attunes and rebalances our souls, so we are moving in harmony with the greater cycles of the Universe. When her wild grace moves through our lives, we will never be the same again.

Kali homes in on our deepest fears, vulnerabilities and attachments with laser-like precision and destructive intent. Unlike the ego-driven version of that ability, we are not diminished, but empowered when Kali strikes. When we are on the receiving end of one of her loving rampages, Kali's radical intervention can feel a lot like destruction, but it is a positive thing, a reconstruction, that is taking place. Kali can be a goddess of extremity, but only when strictly necessary. When things are difficult in our lives, we have not been abandoned by the Divine. We are amid an obscured, wild grace which is protecting us and pushing us to grow.

Kali has more moderate and gentle forms, as well as ferocious forms. But no matter which form she takes in our lives—which has a lot to do with how we respond to her invitation/edict to evolve—she is there because of our need for profound change and healing.

Kali is not usually a goddess of gentle steps and half measures. She sees the task clearly and does whatever is needed to accomplish it. In contrast, Kuan Yin may manifest herself akin to, say, a master craftsman, subtly chiselling away at the marble until, almost magically, imperceptibly, a beautiful form is revealed, the transformation rendered so skilfully and subtly we almost don't know how it happened. With Kali, she'd more likely approach the task with a hammer and a chainsaw.

There is something about an experience of Kali's initiation that teaches us to trust unconditionally, even when we are going through great pain. We learn to tell the difference between the pain of repeating ego-driven patterns and the pain of stepping into the unfamiliar, yet freeing, path of personal and spiritual growth. The latter helps us grow through our pain more swiftly and with greater awareness, breaking its hold over our life choices. With Kali in our hearts, we really do learn how to acknowledge our fears and become stronger than them.

The first meditation retreat I attended as a young woman was not easy for me. I struggled, physically and mentally, with the long hours of sitting in stillness. The experience was undoubtedly more difficult because I dived in without enough preparation for the practice through a regular discipline at home. The importance of small, regular steps, consistency, structure and discipline was something I only embraced a little later in my life. In my early twenties, I was more likely to be the fool rushing in where angels fear to tread, as the saying goes.

So, with an abundance of courage and an absence of preparation, I found myself in a situation for which I was not equipped. Towards the final days of the retreat, I had a vision in meditation. It wasn't a pretty vision, by any means. It was a vision of me lopping off my own head. It startled me into an intuitive understanding. I had spiritual talents and could help people, no doubt, but I also needed to deal with my own ego (symbolised by my head) and learn how to be at peace whilst being in my body, to tune to a deeper inner wisdom and to stop intellectualising everything.

Sometime later, I learned there is a self-decapitated form of Kali that advanced practitioners work with (who else would dare?). Her name is Chinnamasta, and she is a ferocious, wrathful goddess brandishing a sword, blood spurting from her neck, a garland of skulls around her neck—you get the picture, no doubt. It can be hard for those of us outside of Hinduism to understand the deeper meaning of confronting images such as Kali as Chinnamasta. There's an outer (*exoteric*) and inner (*esoteric*) level of understanding in all spiritual teachings. Which level we access depends on our capacity at the time. We may start off on the outer level and move inward to the deeper mysteries through devotion.

Chinnamasta's exoteric teaching might tell us that if we don't stop being a nasty person and terrorising others with our moods, the Divine Mother will terrorise us! It's an imperfect teaching, but for some people at certain stages on their path, it may be helpful. When one can penetrate the imagery for deeper teaching, great bliss may arise by connecting with Chinnamasta as she teaches us many occult arts, including the ability to drop beyond ego into the depths of being.

The potential for confusion over the meaning of religious images and practices is not limited to those of India, Nepal or Tibet. Numerous branches of Christianity believe in the transubstantiation of the Eucharist. This means the offering of wine and the host (the small, wafer-like pieces of 'bread') are not symbolic of the blood and body of Christ but are spiritually transformed during the mass into the actual body and blood of Christ. Having grown up Catholic, I can tell you no-one ran around the church screaming, "But this makes us cannibals and vampires!" We just accepted this was a mysterious offering born of the great love of Jesus.

Whilst connecting with Kali doesn't necessarily mean we will need to encounter her most ferocious forms—such as the self-beheading goddess—it is reassuring to know we don't need to fear her. In fact, our willingness to open to Kali as a child does to an unconditionally loving mother brings out her gentler side. Instead of trying to resist or avoid what she wants to show us, and thereby incurring her wrath until our ego finally submits, we can become curious and willing even if there is pain, at first. When we trust her, she can work for our benefit more easily because we aren't pushing her away or trying to ignore her. We realise that her chainsaw, or sword or other intimidating spiritual weapon of choice, was never going to harm us or anyone else. It was only ever going to free us from the attachment which was holding us back.

A student recently asked me if that meant she would lose her most cherished personal relationships, so I feel it is wise to explain that severing attachment allows for more loving and deep connections to others. Relationships will not necessarily end through Kali's intervention. They will become more fearless and loving.

We need this more extreme divine goddess when we are having trouble being with our pain sufficiently enough to be able to move through it to find healing. I find there is a process to meeting my inner pain and freeing the wisdom trapped within it. I understand it is not going to go away until I do so and that motivates me. But I have noticed I will live with something until a certain moment—you could call that moment 'Kali'—when the pain becomes unbearable and I just know that the time is upon me to deal with it. We could sum it up in the elegant words of Anaïs Nin: "and the day came when the risk to remain tight in the bud was more painful than the risk it took to blossom." In that moment, the pain breaks through our aversion and avoidance, and healing can begin.

Kali manifests in our lives when we need her unique grace, when we need her vast, empty, void-like nature to hold space for us. Her inner spaciousness is endless. No matter how much emotional or psychological suffering arises for us, no matter how huge a challenge may seem, she is always greater. She will always be able to hold space for our transformation. When we learn how to lean into her, it is incredible how something so painful it may have run (and ruined) our lives for forty years can rise, be witnessed in her space and then dissolve into her openness. Space, despite its amorphous nature, is a container. Without enough space, there is clutter, suffocation and a sense that life is closing in on us. Kali is an antidote, a provider of spaciousness. She teaches us how to make room for what needs to happen in our lives. In the mysterious practice of Dzogchen, space is considered our spiritual ground, our resting place. Earth is important—without it we'd not be able to pull things together—but it is the space that exists within our bodies and our spirit which is our real home, our true nature and the place from which we can gain energy and nourishment.

Holding space is an invisible and yet very real action. Kali holds enough space for the entire Universe. She can manage the space you and I need for healing. I can instantly tell if a person presenting a workshop or event can hold enough space for me or not. I know because of what does or does not happen in my process as I participate. If things really move for me, it is because I instinctively feel safe and held—and I can gain insights beyond those I could gain in holding myself. We do need to hold ourselves— it's part of being an adult. But there will be times when we need someone else to hold space for us, so we can break down, be vulnerable, let things fall apart so they can come back together in a new way, with new understanding.

Someone holding such space would listen and say, "Okay, I am here with you. Let's explore this." And they would communicate this in a way that invokes calm confidence in being with how you feel and trusting you'll find your way through it.

In such space, answers tend to arise because spaciousness is our true nature and our true nature is wisdom. In short, space always precedes grace. To give an example of someone who is definitely *not* holding space, imagine going to a counsellor, describing your problem and having them freak out. They may scream, "Oh my god! There is no possible solution!" You'd probably think they were lacking some of fundamental counselling skills, and you'd be right. The absence of space would make everything seem so much worse.

The capacity to hold space applies in subtler everyday situations, too. For instance, when someone stomps into our life in a foul mood, does our happiness tumble into misery in five seconds flat? This can indicate there is insufficient space around us, something empaths or other sensitive people can struggle with. They have plenty of space for others—maybe sensing the inner workings of someone's emotional life thousands of miles and an ocean away—but not enough personal space to be able to witness another with compassion while maintaining a healthy natural spaciousness for their own being, too. Thus, they can unwittingly be dragged into a drama that doesn't belong to them. There's a world of difference between recognising someone is in crisis and collapsing into the crisis right along with them. Which is going to happen depends on how much space is held (or not).

Insufficient spaciousness can make someone so self-absorbed and closed off that a bomb could be going off in the heart of their beloved, and they have no idea whatsoever. That can be painful for both parties, especially those who feel invisible in the metaphorically closed eyes of their partner. In such instances, there is not enough space to recognise and receive from the beloved, nor is there enough space to empty out one's own inner content and therefore grow. This doesn't mean the person doesn't care. They may care very much but be unskilful in expressing that care, which isn't great for the health of a relationship.

As a healer, for example, if you are working beyond your limits, adjusting to a new role or trying to fulfil too many roles at once, you may struggle to remain present and embodied. You might be distracted, trying to remember all the things you must do, perhaps trying to control things you cannot control. In such cases, you will not be able to hold space, even though you are a very caring and compassionate human facilitating a healing session to the best of your ability.

If you are reading this and thinking you could benefit from strengthening the space element in your life, likely you'll need a therapist, mentor or teacher with enough skill and presence to be there for you. If they are there for you, you'll learn what it is like to be properly held (rather than abandoned or suffocated) and, from that experience, begin to intuitively practice that for yourself and, eventually, others. If the stretch your spirit is asking you to take in terms of growth is radical enough, you'll likely need Kali, too. She is the celestial queen of space, grace and alchemy.

When there is enough space in our lives, enough Kali, we feel that we have room to breathe, no matter how busy we get. If more issues or dramas arise and our sense of space can expand (perhaps by working with Kali), we won't become overwhelmed. We will be able to rest in that space and allow solutions to present themselves according to a higher wisdom and divine timing. The moment we feel claustrophobic or overloaded, you can guarantee there is insufficient space for us to feel confident, relaxed and capable of dealing with more than one matter at a time. If our lives feel crazy, cluttered, filled to capacity (or breaking point) with demands and drama, there is a deficiency of space.

It's all relative, really. You may have much more spaciousness in your being than the average human, yet if you want to open yourself up to manifest a particularly ambitious spiritual destiny, you may need to grow your inner space. That was the case when I began the first year of my online training program called *Soul Guidance and Sacred Mentoring*™. It's a year-long course for self-healing and professional training to become a healer. A lot happens in that year. My team and I witness personal transformations and professional breakthroughs which are quite beyond what I had imagined could occur, especially in a course conducted online.

The enrolments were about quadruple what I expected, and I can tell you, the first three months of the first year of training had me wondering if I was going to be able to handle what was required to hold space for a group of that size. As I tried to adjust to the increased psychic load, it suddenly felt I had over a hundred people move into my home! For weeks, I felt flattened under the substantial weight of all the emotional, psychological, psychic and subtle energies these beautiful souls were releasing into the spiritual container I was holding. It was appropriate they do so. That was the reason so much transformation could happen during the training year. But my goodness, I needed to step up my energy-management skills to handle it.

Fortunately, I was already well-versed in the spiritual reality of Kali, and she blessed me with the grace I needed to go through a series of spiritual growth spurts to accomplish what I needed for the benefit of the trainees. The next year, there was a fresh intake of trainees, along with a newly-formed graduate community of practitioners, and I had to grow again. This continued each year, and I continued to grow along with the SGSM™ community.

If you feel in your heart something is meant to happen, and yet nothing appears to be happening, there are no opportunities or no 'way through' then Kali can assist. Such circumstances can be a question of divine timing, and Kali is divine timing at play — devouring and rebirthing according to a celestial schedule. However, those 'stuck' situations can also be an indication of insufficient space. Our creative dreams are rather like those fish—Bala sharks—which grow to the size of the tank. If we keep our internal space small, walled off by fear or doubt, there will be limits on what can happen. It may be *meant* to happen, but we need to do our part, too. It's no use being called to meet your destiny in India, for example, if you never get on a plane. We need enough inner space to give ourselves permission to grow. When we learn how to open up and create space, working through our issues, emptying out ego-driven notions and resting instead in the possibilities and unknowingness of the cosmic void with trust, things happen.

Kali is scantily clad, symbolising freedom from conditioning, including socially accepted stereotypes of good behaviour and feminine submissiveness. Those who have the courage to seek the truth beyond social conditioning and ego constructs love Kali for her wildness, her refusal to bow down to anything and her unfailing divine love. For those of us who are grappling with the limitations that social and mind conditioning place on us, who want to live in a more authentic, even unconventional way, Kali is our guardian.

She protects us from those who envy our freedom but don't want to take responsibility to live in such a way themselves. I dated a man like that, once. He begrudged the freedom I had to live as I chose, without acknowledging the courage and responsibility it required. He envied me but didn't want to take the risk to leave the corporate world he found so frustrating. That's fine. Perhaps it was not his path. But no-one would benefit from me being negatively impacted by his attitude, nor from him denying his own power to choose how he lived.

Kali was with me constantly during that relationship. It was a time in my life when negativity prevailed. That most of it arose out of my romantic relationship, where one is most open and vulnerable, made it even more difficult to process. I needed Kali, and I prayed to her often. At one stage during my heartbroken, tearful pleas for her assistance in helping me leave a man I loved but who wasn't any good for me, I had a vision. I saw her devouring the relationship as though she was munching on a meal. It hurt to see that taking place, but I also trusted her.

The ego wounds to be overcome ran so deep I needed her extreme grace to help me get out of the relationship and recover emotionally and psychologically in my own space. It took years to unravel the pain that enabled me to enter, and remain for so long in, a relationship so obviously not good for me. It required me to enter my own shadow. Rather than blaming my ex-partner, who behaved as he did due to his own ego wounding, I had to figure out my own wound-driven behaviour.

Eventually, it dawned on me that I was unconsciously re-enacting the pain I had around my relationship with my father. Like my ex, he loved me, but was unable to develop an emotionally intimate relationship with me that let me know I was valued and mattered to him. I realised I had unconsciously played out the same error my mother had made in choosing a partner who was incompatible to her. It took some time to work through that, and to begin to claim my own romantic destiny, rather than repeat childhood wounding or parental mistakes.

Finally, I found a new freedom to love and be loved without the toxic interference of past experiences undermining it. For that to happen, I needed space to search inside of myself and process what I discovered. I also needed to apply what I was discovering in a relationship with a new man. It was not easy, but it brought me great happiness. Being held in Kali's heart got me through the darkest moments. Mother Mary and Kuan Yin were always there, too, and when things began to lighten up for me, those gentler forms of the Universal Mother came to the forefront in my spiritual devotions. However, I always knew Kali would be there for me if I needed her. She is precious to my heart.

Kali is the bridge between life and death. This relates, as well, to phases of our lives which must end so new life can be fertilised. She is shamanic, in that sense, the guide between the worlds of creation and the positive use of destructive energy. This is the difference between sacred revolution, which leads to evolution, and the bloody warfare of ego that pits mind and body and heart and soul against each other and doesn't teach us a damn thing except what it is like to feel unending pain. Kali can end that war by withdrawing the life force—symbolised by my vision of her feasting on my relationship—which would otherwise sustain a painful cycle. If you prune a plant with skill, it will bloom again and again. If you let it reach full potential without cutting it back each season, it won't bloom as well over the long term. If you over-prune it, you can end up killing it. Kali knows how to traverse these distinctions with wisdom and grace.

Another of Kali's wrathful forms—one of my favourites, because of her aptly evocative-sounding name—is Smashana Kali. She dwells in the cremation grounds, a hint that her realm is that of death, decay and taboo. Kali is known as a tantric goddess. In the West, we tend to misunderstand that term. Tantrism, in the context of Kali, is about being able to embrace, rather than run from, what is hidden in the shadows. Those shadows might be within our own psyche, or they might be the projected fears of society that make it difficult to understand, let alone experience, what it is to live as a spiritually free individual. In Tibet, developing the capacity for awareness in the face of death is a life(times)long spiritual pursuit. To be able to hold one's spiritual centre in the face of our greatest aversions (and even our greatest desires) can assist one in breaking cycles of suffering and opening to such spaciousness that the Universal Mother will be able to freely utilise us as if we are one of her many arms at work in this world.

We may not feel comfortable when we are becoming more spiritually spacious — at least at first. Imagine you've been living in a five-room house your entire life, and then suddenly, you're in a hundred-bedroom, three-wing mansion. Exciting? Probably. A bit scary at night when you don't quite know all the new sounds and spaces, yet? Probably. Maybe things exist in those new rooms we aren't so sure are acceptable. We may discover we are not who we thought we were. Whilst that can give us permission to live a different and more authentic life, it may not be an easy transition for us or those around us. Yet it will ultimately benefit all. That's part of Kali's blessing. She unbinds us from external and self-imposed shackles. Then we realise freedom can be equal parts exhilaration and challenge, equal parts death and rebirth.

I was teaching a workshop in Europe when one of the participants caught my attention. I was struck by the image that she was a head sitting atop a body covered

by concrete. I felt a thick, impenetrable layer of emotional weight. I sensed her being inexorably pulled down, as though an inevitable descent into psychic quicksand was going to steal her life away. She sat there quite happily anticipating the day ahead, but as I allowed myself to perceive what was happening in her soul, I felt a growing sense of disturbance and alarm.

During the day, I switched on some music and began singing mantras to Kali. Participants were either singing along, dancing, meditating, doing yoga or witnessing the typical spectacle of my classes for the first time with widened eyes. As I became engrossed in the mantra, a strong and powerful feeling came over me. This happens fairly regularly, with various forms of the Divine Mother suddenly channelling through my body. It is then that the really interesting stuff happens! In this workshop, I was literally moved by the magnetic power I knew to be Kali. I felt my body move so I stood in front of the woman. I felt my arm motion to two of my helpers in the workshop to assist me. I heard myself ask one to hold my arm to balance me, so I didn't fall over, and asking the other to help the now astonished woman to lay face down on the ground and rest her head on my feet, not something I would typically ask someone to do!

The moment her forehead touched the top of my feet, my head tipped back, my eyes rolled back, and a powerful surge of spiritual electricity flowed through my body. I was thankful someone was holding me upright! Then, what I can only describe as a clunking sound erupted as the mechanics of the chakras in my feet changed direction. Instead of taking energy in from the earth, they began pumping it out. I could hear, feel and see the change. It felt like switching gears. The woman held on to my feet and wept. I swayed in an ecstatic trance, singing Kali mantras, and the energy poured like a burst water main out of my feet into the woman's soul. Then, just as abruptly as it started, it stopped. I realised the woman had received whatever the Universal Mother had decided she needed. I felt completely fine. The helpers guided the dazed woman back into her seat, and we all 'resumed normal activities.'

What emerged for that woman in the three days following the event was a mixture of hell and heaven. The inflow of energy had shattered the concrete block of stuck emotion that was threatening to take her life — literally. I later found out that she had been plagued by depression and suicidal thoughts for a long time before she showed up for that workshop. For days following that intense Kali blessing, what had shattered began to move out of her system. She felt terrible! Far worse than before she came to the workshop. Of course, that was the case. Her experience was like a detox where one feels awful when the process is working, and toxins are released, but afterwards one feels revitalised, bouncing about like a frolicking spring lamb in fresh green fields of plenty.

There may be ways to slow down the detox process, but for whatever reason, this woman needed an emergency intervention. This was likely due to the extent of her suffering, even if she was able to hide it behind a smile most of the time. She contacted me the day after the workshop and was not happy! I explained what took place, told her to hang in there and that I would see her again, immediately if she wished, but if she could wait for three days, she would feel very different. She contacted me again after three days, delighted with how she felt. Her husband had been worried about her for a long time and not known what to do. One trip to a hippie workshop, and she had returned home the woman he married. They were both ecstatic. Kali's blessing isn't delicate, but it certainly is divine.

When we are stuck, whether we know it or not, Kali knows. I have fallen into the trap of believing certain issues were so persistent I would have to learn how to live with them—like bad tenants in my soul house—and just do my best, regardless. It was Kali's intervention that pushed me until those unavoidable struggles gave up their residency within. If someone is really in a tight spot, they may need something stronger than a soft word to help them out of it. Kali isn't cruel in any way. She loves us. Her unexpected interruptions may come in the form of a shocking insight or a sudden realisation, which may not be so welcome at the time, yet later is recognised as a grace of divine disruption. She breaks patterns we couldn't break on our own. Sometimes, we love our patterns and self-chosen cages because they are familiar. Kali's waist in her terrible form is often encircled with a girdle of severed human arms. This can represent her capacity to overcome our activities which would otherwise simply continue to create suffering in our lives and the world.

Smashana Kali is best adored by those with a brave spirit. She is depicted with her left foot forward and her sword raised in her right hand. This is symbolic of her wrathful nature and her tendency to lead us into lesser known pathways to confront our fears and become wise. The dead of night, during a waning moon, is the time for her worship. That lunar phase symbolises the times in our lives when we are most in darkness, most uncertain, when there are endings, and we are yet to sense the beginnings which shall emerge from them. To remain confident and committed to our path during such times really does require the courage of a heroic heart.

The beautiful name of one of her benign forms is Dakshina Kali. *Dakshina* is a Sanskrit word that translates as *giving a gift to a guru as a respectful exchange for a teaching or blessing*. The true guru can be expressed through a person, but is essentially spiritual consciousness, a universal intelligence of protection and evolution. We can use the same definition for the Divine Mother. As the Indian expression goes, "the mother is the first guru." It's my experience that the Universal Mother is the Universal Guru, the first and primary expression of love, protection and evolution. When Indian guru Sri Anandamayi Ma said her body was not anyone's guru, she meant the real nature of the guru has nothing to do with personality worship. No matter how charismatic a guru, teacher, leader or mentor, it is your development through that relationship which holds spiritual value. The outer form of the teacher is never a replacement for direct inner connection with the Universal Mother. It is a method or catalyst through which that takes place.

If it is our soul path to enter a relationship with a guru in human form it can be a source of great learning and spiritual progress. A genuine guru can connect you to a spiritual lineage that nourishes your soul and empowers your life path. But someone may call themselves a guru, or have many devotees, and still may not be the teacher who best awakens grace within your heart. When selecting any kind of spiritual guide or teacher, listening to one's heart is essential.

If we are lucky enough to find a human guide who radiates spiritual consciousness in such a way that they help us grow in wisdom and clarity, then the true guru is at work in the souls of all involved. You may never meet that person 'in the flesh' and yet feel they are there for you on a deeper level, a source of light and wisdom you can turn to for spiritual nourishment. These are the wise guides and spiritual guardians that incarnate on Earth to help keep humanity moving forward.

Our best gift to the benevolent, guru-goddess-mother principle in our teachers and our own hearts is our willingness to embrace our life journey, to show courage and commitment to becoming a more conscious human. Think of how proud you would be, how affirmed as a parent or teacher, if your child or student demonstrated the highest ideals you had instilled in them. Perhaps they were kind when they could have been cruel or were brave when they could have played the victim. What greater gift could there be? Dakshina Kali enters our lives, so we can best give back to the Universal Heart that loves us so completely. The delight and light that radiates in our souls as we take our authentic life journey lights the way for other souls, who may be lost in darkness, to find their way home.

Kali's iconography often pictures her standing atop her masculine counterpart, Shiva. This is very different to common depictions of feminine deities, who stand either side-by-side their male counterpart or sit at their feet in a gesture of respect. This symbolises that Kali is the feminine principle in the dominant position. It isn't about emasculation or otherwise disrespecting male energy. It is about understanding there are times when, for a solution to manifest, the feminine principle must be honoured above all else.

The feminine principle is expressed in the wisdom of Mother Nature. Nature is a gospel of sacred feminine wisdom. She knows how to grow things from seedlings into full bloom, whether a plant or a human soul. Nature is a wisdom teaching of the improbable made possible. For example, consider the life cycle of a butterfly or an oak tree, or how the most devastating winter or destructive bushfire gives rise to an abundance of new life.

Honouring the sacred feminine is essential for our spiritual protection. For example, technology can be incredibly helpful and healing. It also holds an inherent danger in that it is not subject to the natural limits of cycles such as night and day. We may prefer the bright light of day, but without night to replenish, we will severely restrict the number of days we have available to enjoy! There is no natural 'night time' for technology. It is only switched off if we consciously choose to do so (or unconsciously lose the phone charger or forget to pay the electricity bill). Anyone who has battled with themselves or their child to 'step away from the computer' and go meditate or sleep, will know that, unless we cultivate enough willpower, our bodies and minds can suffer from overexposure to electronic devices and the content they generate (even if that content is good, too much is not). If we aren't in touch with sacred feminine wisdom, we won't be able to honour the needs of our bodies and minds for rest and repair. If our devices are always on, always strapped to our side or near our heads when we sleep, there is a price to be paid.

When honoured, the body knows how to heal and deal with the stresses of life, even modern life. Our challenge is to remain connected to the body, tuning in to its signals. Sacred feminine wisdom grounds us. It creates limits and boundaries, which are essential for creativity and thriving. You can jump on social media any time of the day or night and something will be happening. The sacred feminine keeps us wise, reminding us that just because you can, doesn't mean you should.

Switching off our devices and sleeping in a dark room without alarm clocks, phones and televisions (to the degree this is possible for you) supports this unplugging process. The more sensitive you are, the more important this becomes. We don't need to panic about the toxicity and potential stressors in our environment, but we do need to take wise action. In 'unplugging' from an otherwise constant flow of information and radiation, we give ourselves a chance to digest, process and integrate. Then we can grow, evolve and create.

As we drop into this more organic way of being, we more easily sense our intuitive instincts. Rather than living according to social rules about what you are supposed to do or not do at a certain age (so unimaginative!), we listen to our intuitive instincts, which are nudges from our soul. Those nudges relate to timing and let us know when to wait, when to acquire more information, when to leap and when to step away. I was recently asked how to tell the difference between procrastination and the intuition to wait, and conversely, between the ego trying to push things to happen and our intuition telling us to take a leap of faith. The man who asked me the question liked to surf, so I asked him to imagine he was sitting on his board, waiting for a wave in his favourite spot out on the ocean. How did he know when to wait and when to paddle? He answered that he just knew. He didn't overthink it and therefore didn't worry about it. When the movement of the ocean was felt, he moved with it. He was more in touch with his intuitive instincts than he realised.

There are times on the path when only a leap of faith is going to get you to the next level of experience. Feminine wisdom is the instinct which leads to astonishing migrations, adaptations and evolutionary mutations which just *work*. She knows what is needed for a creature to thrive and when it's time to let go of what has been so a new form can emerge. The only way we can sense these intuitive instincts is through feeling them in the body. When people worry that they aren't intuitive, it's rarely a question of having intuition. It's that they don't trust their bodies and override their own good sense with overthinking. Like the surfer sensing the movement of the ocean, we are resting upon an ocean of wisdom. When we connect to our bodies, we can learn to sense its movements, and if we are feeling wise and trusting, move with that greater flow.

The story that leads to Kali standing astride her husband begins with Durga, the undefeated warrior goddess of light and protection, who was about to lose a battle with a ferocious demon. Not having any of that, she birthed furious Kali from her third eye. Kali defeated the demon in an instant and in a frenzy of bloodlust almost destroyed the world. The only thing that could stop her was her beloved husband throwing himself on the ground. As she stepped upon him in all her wildness, she suddenly realised she needed to restrain herself and poked out her tongue.

The reason for her protruding tongue is a mystery. It is sometimes said she pokes her tongue out in shame. However, that has never resonated with me. I cannot imagine Kali would be subject to such an emotion, as she is divine will itself, and therefore acts flawlessly (even if, from our perspective, she seems overly enthusiastic in her intensity at times).

As I pondered the deeper meaning of this posture, I imagined myself as Kali in a frenzy and then stuck out my tongue out as I stopped the momentum of my destructive onslaught. (As an aside I do all sorts of things when I write: goddess roleplay, spontaneous singing and having regular 'sidebar' conversations with my spirit guides). Anyway, what I noticed in my Kali roleplay was that, when I stuck out my tongue, I felt like a wild creature! Which made me think how animals stick out their tongues to cool themselves. I felt it expressed Kali cooling her spiritual passions.

Sometimes, if we have a strong desire to see someone become happy, we might feel frustrated if they continue acting in ways that sabotage their healing journey. We might even become angry with them. We might say things to wake them up, but maybe break our bond with them in the process. It may be a necessary loss, but it may be a misjudgement. Calming ourselves and letting them take their journey as they choose may do more for all concerned. I felt Kali's tongue was an invitation for us to trust that, although she can be ferocious, she knows when to cool it, so to speak. She balances her ferocity with wisdom and compassion. She will push us, but not too far.

The tongue is an organ for discerning flavours and taking in food, masticating it readying it for digestion and elimination. Thus, Kali's protruding tongue is a symbol of her enlightened activity. With it, she teaches us to discern and digest our experiences, learn from them and release what is no longer needed.

I also feel the mystery and debate around the meaning of her tongue reflects her incomprehensible nature. When Kali wreaks her sacred havoc in our lives, rising up in the form of a crisis or unavoidable 'no' or some other kick in the pants that gets us moving in the right direction (or stops us moving in the wrong direction), it doesn't necessarily make sense to us at the time. We often simply don't know why things are happening the way they are. All we can do is choose whether we are going to lean into the Divine Mother and participate with trust.

The very first class I ever taught was on spiritual growth at a community college in Sydney. The course went for a number of weeks and, at the end of it, one of the participants was so moved she gave me a bunch of flowers. I was surprised and delighted. In the years which followed, she floated in and out of various classes and workshops I ran. During one of these, she shared her experience of Kali in a meditation. It was intense, violent and, I have to say, a little sadistic. I knew that whilst her experience of Kali was likely to be authentic, her interpretation had crept in and distorted it. I want to mention this because, between the apparently well intentioned 'tough love' people of this world and our own unresolved inner violence, we can put things on Kali that are not of Kali at all.

Inner violence is not reserved for those who self-harm or abuse others verbally, emotionally or physically. Inner violence is based on hatred and can exist within us without us being aware of it. I see it taking over the otherwise healthy activities of a lot of people, turning them into forms of self-harm. Excessive exercise and dieting come to mind as relatively common examples. More subtle is the negative self-talk which, if chronicled in a journal and read out loud to a group of friends, might make them consider staging an emergency psychiatric intervention! That negative self-talk is likely to be the same for most people on this planet. That doesn't make it acceptable, it just makes it common.

I mention this because it is important to recognise the difference between the pains of genuine personal and spiritual growth and abusing oneself. Beating yourself up, enduring great pain without appropriate support (from a therapist, a spiritual advisor, a friend) and without a sense that it is a birthing pang of the soul leading you somewhere constructive and life-affirming, is self-abuse. That is not Kali. When you are in that state, reach for help. Don't let yourself drown in suffering out of some distorted perception that the Universe is asking you to go through it for some higher purpose.

I have seen people put up with and even enact terrible things based on the confused notion that such suffering was 'divinely required.' Religious wars and any act of terror or violence carried out in the name of a holy being are examples of this error. The Divine Mother, even as Kali, would *never* mandate any means to an end. She understands the process and the outcome cannot be separated. If you feel there is an inspired ideal you are reaching for, and it requires a violation of your integrity, heart or spirit to obtain it, step back. Let the Divine show you how to attain what you seek in harmony with your inner nature or give you another ideal to pursue.

Kali's radical intervention brings us peace, healing and comfort. She may rattle our cage, which feels terrifying, but once the door is open and we are shoved through,

we realise it was a good and kind, if not particularly comfortable, action. If it was easy to get there without such rumbling, she wouldn't have needed to intervene on our behalf. Once we are there, however, the view is clear and beautiful.

An auspicious and ever-so-slightly less wild form of Kali is known as Bhadrakali or Wish-Fulfilling Kali. In Sanskrit, the word *Bhadra* translates as *gentle*. She is the granter of boons and the fulfilment of desires. She bestows peace and happiness. Her word and wish cannot be broken, and so her will to fulfil our hearts overcomes even our ego ideas about how things should happen (which rarely amounts to anything more than us getting in the way of the Universe helping us). If we can relax and soften into Kali's wild and unpredictable ways, trusting the gentle and loving nature within her heart, we will be able to get out of our own way (and therefore overcome the greatest obstacle we likely will ever face).

I recently found a wish-fulfilling mantra on YouTube and was reading through the comments below. I could do this with a box of popcorn, it can be so entertaining. A number of people who viewed the video expressed their wishes. I was deeply moved to see how many comments were from pure-hearted people who wanted happiness for their children or wellness for a sick relative. I was so genuinely touched my heart spontaneously opened, and I began praying for them to the Universal Mother, that she may help them in all ways.

Out of the many comments I scrolled through, there were only a couple which came from a confused rather than pure place. One person wanted to be a rock star. A woman who responded quite bluntly, said, "If it's in your destiny you can have it. If it is not, no matter how hard you wish for it, it's not going to happen." She sounded so authoritative and informed that I pondered what she said. I felt there was a grain of truth to it, but that she'd not really hit the mark. I thought how my own sense of things differed and I realised that I truly do believe every human wish will find karmic fulfilment.

The problematic nature of the desire to be a pop star is that the person was telling the Universe how they wanted their wish fulfilled. They confused the essence of what they wanted with the form they wanted it to arrive in. What was that person really wishing for beneath the form of pop stardom? Maybe admiration, respect, creative fulfilment, fabulousness, being seen, mattering to others, touching people with her voice so that her words had positive, powerful effect. All these things and more could be fulfilled in countless ways, which may or may not involve her being a pop star. It's kind of like saying that I'd like to marry a movie star. That is an outer shell of what I really want. The inner truth is that I'd like a deep relationship with a man with the traits I ascribe to that movie star. If I asked for her help, Kali would show me what I needed to heal and how I needed to grow for that to happen. She helps us develop the vibrational frequency to become what we seek and attract it into our experience.

The process by which we become capable of new and more positive experiences usually takes us into our shadow, our disowned unconscious self. That is the realm of Kali. The nature of the shadow is that we project it before we can own it. In certain situations, some people find it too difficult to withdraw the projection and claim their own experience. In such instances, they will continue to blame another, whilst seeing themselves as blameless. In this instance, there is no chance for healing or growth by gentle means. Their incapacity for growth may evoke Kali's great compassion, which will show itself in her offering challenge after challenge to break through their defences, so they can be freed from their own self-imprisonment in hate, judgement, fear and blame.

To work consciously with our own shadow takes courage, but Kali can help us unravel some of our greatest projected pains. The shape of our world can transform before our eyes when we do so. A simple way to begin such inner work is to notice when we feel aversion to what we perceive in another. If something evokes judgement or repulsion, it can be a good idea to do some self-reflecting about what might be coming up for you.

A friend of mine had an interesting experience with a person on social media who scrolled through her Facebook page as often as she could and wrote "MURDERER!" on every post. She did this because she found out my friend was not vegan. In attacking my friend, rather than accepting the pain of her own experience, this person acted with violence, aggression and disrespect. She was embodying the very forces she was dedicating her life to try and eradicate.

Sometimes when pain is too much, all we can do is project it out and see it in the world. We see the bully, and we want to bully them to stop bullying. If you've ever felt infuriated by the state of the world, you'll understand that reaction. You may also see that it doesn't accomplish what you want. Replacing one dictator with another doesn't end tyranny, even if the replacement agrees with your politics and brakes for animals.

The point is not to stop the projection. It's going to happen sometimes, even when we are doing our best to be conscious. The question is whether we can summon the courage to go beyond judgement and into self-reflection. Sometimes, people think shifting from projecting the shadow into self-reflection means if we hate a bully, we must be a bully, too. That is not correct. Self-reflection takes you deeper into why you feel that hate, for example. Maybe you feel a childlike sense of helplessness, which becomes fear and anger. Working through those very understandable feelings (perhaps with a mentor, therapist or spiritual advisor) can help you come to a place where you can approach the situation with empowerment. Maybe your sense of helplessness can turn into trust of the Divine Mother. As you take sanctuary in her, suddenly, you are energised to do something creative and constructive. In processing what you felt, you took a terrible situation and made it fuel something positive. You were able to respond, rather than react. You grew spiritually. Everyone and everything benefit when you grow spiritually.

Kali will assist us in choosing presence instead of aversion, we'll be able to face ourselves and, with her grace, learn to trust and respect the real nature within that wants to thrive — even if that means embracing uncomfortable spaces while we figure things out. In her spiritual form of the mother void, of the unknown, of emptiness and endless potential, we have an opportunity to encounter our own unknown self, our own shadow. She pushes us to go willingly into the blackness, being present, with trust, with what arises. In that state of presence, she will reveal skilful methods for dealing with whatever is within us and around us. Given the degree of darkness operating in the world—violence, hate, judgement, fear, greed, confusion and despair—becoming more aware of our own darkness, which is a prerequisite to dealing effectively with the darkness of others, is essential.

I have created a meditation CD called *Black Madonna Meditations*, which includes the Kali Mantra. That mantra is *Om Krim Kaliyey Namaha* (sounds like *OHM CREAM KAH-LEE-YAY NAM-AH-HAH)*. It basically means, *Welcome to empowered Kali. I bow in respect*. If you want to learn more about Kali, the oracle I have dedicated to her, which includes some of the art featured in this book, will be available through Blue Angel Publishing. I have also written about her in *Crystal Goddesses 888*, which includes her own healing processes. There is also a chapter in that book and an album of meditations dedicated to Durga and her mantra is on my meditation album called *Inner Power.*

May your experience of Kali teach you that she can be trusted, that you need never be hostage to fear and that you are loved.

Chapter Seven

Mother Mary: Our Madonna of Everyday Miracles

Divine beings may seem to exist on a higher spiritual plane from us mere mortals, and in some ways they do. But, as Mother Mary, the Universal Mother bridges the distance between the heavenly and earthly realms. Her feet have walked the earth and she continues to make her connection to humanity felt through her various apparitions.

I was recently speaking with a woman who loves Mother Mary—and many other divine beings— and prays to her regularly for help. She spoke movingly of her experience with Mary. She could sense her presence, and most poignantly, she could feel Mary was crying and feeling her pain along with her. This is one of the hallmarks of the Madonna, and why I feel so many people from so many cultures love her so much. She is truly a loving mother — understanding, kind and unable to distance herself from the suffering of her children.

Although she's a gentle light to Kali's raging fire, Mary still expects us to have courage and to be all that we are. She never panders to ego. I have felt comforted by her during the challenges I have gone through in my life, but never felt she was intervening in such a way that I was prevented from growing through the experience. She didn't remove the challenges but empowered me to move through them. Although sometimes her grace was so powerful it was effortless, and it was like there was no challenge at all.

If you have an experience of a loving mother, opening to Mary is not likely to be so difficult —unless you have unresolved issues with the religious traditions which lay claim to her. If you have such issues, this may be a good opportunity to clear them (if you wish). If not, be assured she will manifest in another form that you can more readily trust. If you do choose to explore a connection to Mary, she may help you rise above any mother issues you have due to childhood experience. She can help you let go of hate or fear around wounded religious figures or restrictive religious doctrines you have encountered in this or other lifetimes.

Opening to Mary may feel like a leap if you are working to heal such matters. That can be a good sign. The greater the trust required, the greater the transformation taking place. If you have not had a healthy mothering experience, you may not be used to unconditional love and instead expect to be judged or found unworthy. You may not be familiar with the ways of the Universal Mother and her resourcefulness and therefore fail to ask for help in matters which seem either too trivial or too severe. Mary can help you overcome such pains if you open to her.

Mary wants to help us in all matters. Learning to rest in the grace of the sacred feminine opens us to her solutions in anything from finances, finding a home, our love life or any daily concern, in ways often so unexpected and left field as to be considered miraculous. When we aren't expending energy on worry, guess what happens? We have more energy to direct to our spiritual path to help ourselves and all beings. That benefits all. That supports the Universal Mother's purpose.

Many people love Mary, whether or not they have a religious background which connects them to her. One of the healers in our spiritual community adores Mary. She is not religious, but one of the most devoted women that I know. She was questioned by some of her Catholic friends about her connection to Mary and Jesus, as though there was something suspicious about it. That is sad and unnecessary. I remember reading comments on a YouTube video of a Kuan Yin mantra. In one post, a woman said she wanted to love God but was afraid of the Christian God and found Kuan Yin gentle and approachable. Another person may not agree with her, but what matters to the Divine Mother is how each person feels. Is this not exactly why so many forms of the Divine exist? If you want to reach out to Mary, I invite you to do so. Get to know her for yourself, without religious or other opinions getting in the way of your personal relationship with her.

From just after the death of Jesus in around 40 CE to the present day, people of varied cultures, living in many different places on our globe, have reported visions of Mary. Marian apparitions are not always considered authentic. Given that some claimed to see a saint in a cinnamon bun, a little caution is wise. Nonetheless, over forty Marian apparitions are considered legitimate. A common theme that consistently comes through these varied experiences is that Mary is aware of what is happening on this planet and cares very deeply. Not only that, but she has the power to assist us and can create extraordinary outcomes to protect and nurture us on our life path.

Miraculous healings have occurred for those calling upon her, and in my own life, Mary has been a consistent and protective presence.

Mary leaves a divine 'calling card' when she is at work in my life. I know of others, who are also open to her grace in their lives, to have similar experiences. It took me a little while to recognise her signature. Her signature in your life may be different, but for me her calling card is an unexpected gift of roses. It is her sign to me that she is present, connected and either approves of what I am doing or is going to help me out of a scrape I have gotten into. She always finds a way to get a rose to me or to have her name appear — on the numberplate of a car in front of me, on the cover of *National Geographic* magazine or on the nametag of the person who upgrades my seat on a flight. The moment she 'pops up' in my awareness, I recognise that she is helping me with something I may have been inadvertently worrying about.

I had been single for many years, wondering if it was possible for someone as quirky and unconventional as myself to find a partner who could love and accept me just as I was — maybe someone quirky and unconventional in his own way. After nearly a year on a dating app (where it felt like I spent more time educating men who behaved as boys about how to treat a woman with respect, rather than being passionately pursued by a wonderful man) my hope for a mature, loving, wild relationship seemed a little unrealistic. In a pique of frustration, I stopped using the app.

A few days later, I went to collect some hemmed yoga pants from my dressmaker. She disappeared into the back room for several minutes, then emerged with my pants and a small bouquet of roses! I was charmed and surprised. I thanked her and asked if there was a reason for the gift. She replied, "Not really, maybe because it's Saturday."

As I walked back to my car with my yoga pants draped over my arm, I gazed at the combination of red, yellow and pink roses in the bouquet. It occurred to me that the bouquet represented the perfect combination of qualities for a marvellous romantic relationship: red for passion, yellow for friendship and pink for unconditional love. Suddenly, I stopped in my tracks, recognising Mary's presence. She was with me and she was telling me not to worry about the state of my love life.

That afternoon I decided to give the dating app one more try. A profile of a handsome, slightly eccentric man showed up, with a request that we connect. Intrigued, but also a little cautious, I accepted the match. We texted back and forth for some weeks. His intelligence, humour and open-mindedness, along with his values of compassion and kindness, made him difficult to resist. His blue eyes sealed the deal and I agreed to meet him for a date. As I walked into the bar for our first date, he stood up to greet me, and before we even spoke, I felt a psychic collision as our souls connected. Well, I'd certainly never experienced anything like that before! I can happily report that he (and Mother Mary and my dressmaker) restored my temporarily-wavering faith in men and romance, bringing much peace and happiness to my heart.

Mary's signs and apparitions are messages from her to us. Her apparitions are

powerful, both in the actual vision and the circumstances that lead to it. The stories of her appearances from hundreds of years ago still hold power for us. Even though the world has changed in many ways in the two thousand years since Mary walked the earth, the fundamental problems humans encounter have not. The struggles of people in the modern era are not so different to those from the past. So, we can likely relate to the fears of the men who were lost at sea in the story of *Our Lady of Charity*, (which I shared in Chapter Three in the 20th of the 33 forms of Kuan Yin), even if we've never set foot on a boat. We all feel a need for protection when the world around us seems out of control and we cannot find a safe harbour.

One of her most well-known apparitions is as Our Lady of Guadalupe. On 9 December 1531, in Mexico, an indigenous man named Juan Diego went out for one of his daily walks. On that ordinary walk, something extraordinary happened. As he reached the hill of Tepeyac (now part of Mexico City), he saw a vision of a most beautiful woman. She spoke to him, identified herself as the Mother of God and requested he have a shrine erected on that exact spot. That spot had been a temple dedicated to the Aztec mother goddess Tonantzin, before it was destroyed by the Spanish colonisers. Tonantzin was celebrated particularly on the winter solstice, which in 1531 fell on December 9, the date of the Marian apparition.

Although Juan Diego had faith and a good heart, he didn't have any notable spiritual power and certainly no political power. Uncertain how an everyday man was going to convince powerful religious officials to build a shrine to the Virgin Mary on Tepeyac Hill, he nonetheless journeyed to the palace of the bishop and requested a meeting. Treated with suspicion, he was told to wait—for some hours—but eventually a meeting took place. Juan Diego described his vision of Mary and what she had requested. The bishop said he would consider it and sent Juan Diego on his way.

No matter how gentle Mary may appear, however, she is also persistent. The original 'iron fist in velvet glove', so to speak. So, when Juan Diego returned from the meeting with the bishop with a 'maybe', Mary was waiting for him. When he implored her to find someone more important or powerful to do her work, she told him straight, "I have chosen you." This part of the story is important. Have you ever felt inspired by an ideal, and then held yourself back, feeling that in some way you weren't 'enough' to pursue it? I have had numerous visions and encounters with divine beings over the years, and in many of those, my first response was doubt, because why on earth would such an illumined being chose to work through me? Eventually, I learned to have a little faith in their wisdom and my own capabilities, and to realise that even though I wasn't perfect, I could still be helpful. Instead of doubting, I would accept more readily and determine to just do my best and get on with it. Which is what Juan Diego ended up doing.

So, when Mary asked again, Juan Diego returned to the bishop, who told Juan Diego he needed a sign before he would agree to build a shrine. Mary appeared to

Juan Diego a third time and told him to have faith, that she had asked him to do this for her, and she would provide him with all he needed to accomplish the task. This is important, too. There's an expression that the proof of the pudding is in the tasting. We can apply this to the healing quality that exists within genuinely inspired creations and also to the notion that when the Universal Mother wants us to do something, she provides us with the means to accomplish it. It may take some spiritual muscle on our part, but she will more than cover the distance between our human efforts and final success. So, Mary asked Juan Diego to trust her. Her exact words were said to be, "Am I not here, I who am your mother?"

When it came time for Juan Diego to go see the bishop again, his uncle fell violently ill. He was near to death and Juan Diego felt that he couldn't leave his side to take the journey to the bishop. He did venture out to find a priest to read his uncle prayers for his passing. Instead, he saw the Madonna again. She implored him not to worry, saying she had healed his uncle in that instant and he was to go to the top of the hill to gather the flowers that were blooming there. Juan Diego ascended the hill, which should have been barren in the December cold, and found a bush of roses in full bloom. He gathered them into his cloak (known as a *tilma*) and returned to the lady. She arranged them in his cloak and sent him on his way to the bishop, assuring him the bishop would have his sign.

When in audience with the bishop, who again requested proof of what Juan Diego claimed, Juan Diego opened his tilma as instructed by the Madonna. The flowers tumbled to the floor, and an image of the Madonna, exactly as Juan Diego had seen and described her, was emblazoned within Juan Diego's cape. The bishop was astonished! He instantly agreed to build the chapel. When Juan Diego returned home, his uncle was not only fully recovered but spoke of a vision of a beautiful woman who said she had sent his nephew with a picture of herself to the bishop and that she was to be known as Santa Maria de Guadalupe.

The tilma of Juan Diego still exists. The portion containing the image of Mary is framed and hanging in a church in Mexico behind bulletproof glass. The tilma has been tested numerous times, and the findings support the aura of the extraordinary surrounding the image, which has not degraded despite its age and absence of varnish. In fact, pieces of the tilma image have been enhanced over the years by artists adding additional flourishes. The gold used to embellish the image has flaked off, and the silver embellishing the moon has discoloured, whilst the original image remains in perfect condition. Painting on fabric with water-soluble pigment and no primer was an artistic technique in use at the time of the apparition, yet work created in that way is known to be fragile and subject to degradation. Images created by such means would typically degrade in fifteen years. That the tilma image has maintained perfect integrity for nearly five hundred years is inexplicable by scientific methods, particularly as it was displayed without any protection for the first 115 years. Personally, I would say so much energy from the Divine is in that image that it is protected from degradation. In this, it is a little like the body of Hindu saint Yogananda whose body did not show any visible signs of decay even twenty days after his death.

When a bomb was hidden in a basket of flowers under the tilma in 1921, the explosion damaged the basilica. The force of it bent a brass crucifix next to the tilma and reduced the marble altar beneath it to rubble. But, the image itself was unaffected, and despite considerable damage to the basilica, no-one was hurt.

Those who have examined the tilma image using modern technology, which shows detail previously not seen, point out the absence of brushstrokes, saying portions of the image appear to have simply 'manifested' as one piece. A Nobel-prize winning biochemist analysed the pigment and found it has no known source — it is neither animal, vegetable or mineral. As there were no synthetic dyes invented until over three hundred years later, the pigment itself is inexplicable (unless you are mystically-inclined). An ophthalmologist enlarged an image of the eyes of the Madonna 2500x and found reflections, just as would occur in a human eye, with the imprint of what that eye had seen in the retina. In the reflection, he identified fourteen figures who were present at the unveiling of the tilma. The constellation in the image has been studied and is said to be a perfect representation of the night sky at the date of the final apparition, on 12 December 1531.

Recently, I facilitated a series of events in the United States. It was my first time sharing my work in person in the US and, given that I had wanted to do so for some time, it was important to me that it went well and accomplish whatever higher purpose it was meant to. After the first event, with a long tour ahead of me, a participant came up to me. She had driven some distance to reach the event. She presented me with a very wilted rose! I was absolutely delighted. She apologised, saying she didn't even know why she brought it, because after the long drive it would not be fresh. But as she was reversing out of her drive, she couldn't shake the idea that she needed to present me with a rose. I explained this held great personal meaning for me and thanked her for listening to her intuition and presenting me with a gift that meant so much. I don't know if she really recognised the depth of what she had done for me, but I felt confident to move ahead with the tour and trusted it was unfolding according to a higher plan, under Mary's grace.

At the last workshop of the tour, something unusual happened. Rather than being sold out, as every other appearance had been, even crammed to capacity with last-minute people turning up, there were so few attendees I considered cancelling the event. However, it just didn't feel right to do so. On the morning of the event, I booked an Uber to the workshop venue. As the driver pulled up, I hopped in the back seat and noticed he had a picture of Mary tucked away on his dashboard. It was in a position where it could only be seen by him and a passenger sitting in the exact spot I was in. I felt a tingle of spiritual electricity. I knew Mary was with me.

Entering the venue for that workshop was interesting. Although the women running the event for me were lovely, I felt strange, like I wasn't welcome, that there was a resistance to me doing the work I wanted to do. In short, it felt blocked. I wondered what was going on. Throughout the day, I heard stories of intensely negative energies being directed towards that store of late. I also learned the building itself had a dark history. I realised I was feeling the effect of negative energies trying to get me out of there because they didn't want that store—with its dedicated staff of healers bringing light and comfort to the local people—to thrive. I realised Mary wanted to protect the store and its healers from being blocked in accomplishing their work. Although the numbers were small, the attendees were loving souls with their own wisdom and the work we did together went very deep. Some had flown interstate, some came from outside the United States, making considerable effort to be there. The work really needed to happen that day, and as I began to understand the situation more clearly, I was relieved I had listened to my heart and gone ahead with it.

Late in the afternoon, one of the participants and I were standing outside the workshop room during a short break. My business manager stood next to us as we chatted. I complimented the woman on her jacket. Suddenly, she opened it to reveal an image of the Madonna of Guadalupe sewn into the inside of it! I just stared for a moment. She told me her father had lovingly sewn it into the jacket to keep Mary next to her heart. I asked, "Did he know the story of Guadalupe, that the way Mary confirmed her presence to those who doubted was when Juan Diego opened his tilma and an image of her was seen?"

Apparently, he didn't. The spiritual tingles we all felt were strong enough to cause my manager to declare, "I just felt chills flowing through me!" I laughed with delight.

You may wonder how you know something is a sign. It's not about what occurs—whether it's the butterfly that lands on your nose or a certain song coming on the radio at a key moment—it's what you feel intuitively, instinctively, instantly before thought kicks in to analysis and interpretation mode which indicates a spiritual communication has taken place.

In that moment, I knew Mary was communicating with all of us. Only the other two people involved in that sacred moment know what she wanted to say to them. For me, she was letting me know I was following her guidance, reminding me she was more powerful than any doubts I may have, and I should stay true to her and my own heart always. She would always have my back, so to speak, and as I trusted her, she could work through me more readily. Even if the circumstances don't seem encouraging, you never know how much your presence matters and how much spiritual grace is flowing into the situation through your simply being there with an open heart.

When we are helping each other, being there for each other, the Universal Mother's presence in the world grows for the benefit of all beings. I felt I was being 'pushed out' of that venue for the exact reason Mary wanted me there. A consciousness with an agenda opposing that of the Divine Mother was trying to dominate the place and she simply wasn't having it.

The image of Guadalupe speaks at a deep level of reinstatement when the feminine has been desecrated. It speaks of her power to rise, even in those who do not consider themselves to be powerbrokers in this world. That she chose an everyday person, one of the more marginalised members of society, to influence a person with great power, was purposeful. She could have simply appeared to the bishop. But there was a deeper healing and meaning in the story unfolding in the way it did. We can take to heart that healing and meaning when we feel we don't have a voice, that we lack the capacity to bring light to the world, that we cannot be as influential as those in powerful positions who seem not to have wisdom in their hearts. Mother Mary lets us know her purpose will be accomplished. The mountains of obstacles we perceive are no match for her creativity and resourcefulness. And her playful sense of humour.

In Paris, France, during the summer of 1830, a young nun by the name of Catherine was awakened during the night by a voice calling her to the chapel. In the chapel, she heard Mary speak to her, telling her she had a special mission and that she would be challenged and contradicted, but would have the grace to do what was necessary. Just over four months later, on 27 November 1830, Catherine received a vision of Mary in her evening meditation. Mary appeared within an oval frame, dazzling rays of light shining from her hands. Twelve stars surrounded her, and a prayer asking for protection for those who sought Mary was inscribed around the oval frame. Catherine heard the Madonna request these images be shared with her superiors, so they could be made into a medal, which would bring grace to any who wore it, especially if worn around the neck.

That the blessing is further empowered when around the throat speaks (no pun intended) of one of Mary's distinct protections. She is dedicated to those sharing their voices, their messages of love and guidance, who are fulfilling the sacred task of translating inner experiences of divine wisdom, beauty, compassion and light into expressions through which others may gain benefit. These may include a dedication to education or birthing a work of art or music or being a voice for the protection of children, animals, the environment, asylum seekers and any marginalised or abused beings. Sky blue is often associated with Mary and is also the colour associated with the throat chakra. When the throat chakra is protected and functioning well, we can move between different realities to gain artistic inspiration and access spiritual guidance. We can also manage complex tasks, set priorities and organise information, all helpful for accomplishing our sacred work. If you feel overwhelmed, uncertain how to prioritise tasks so you can take the practical steps necessary to bring your heart visions to life, Mary's blessings are particularly relevant. They are not limited to that purpose, but certainly can transform and overcome such issues.

Mary's physical life on Earth involved her handling situations which are relevant to us now. Christian teachings tell us Mary's pregnancy with Jesus was an immaculate, or spiritual, conception. Whether you believe that to be literal or symbolic, the takeaway is that our spiritual journey can ask us to bear witness to truths others may not be able to believe or respect.

Remaining true to yourself in the face of possible rejection, abuse or, in Mary's day, the risk of being put to death for being unmarried and pregnant, takes tremendous courage. Anyone who has felt the pressure to abandon or hide their spiritual beliefs for fear of harm, social ridicule or isolation can take comfort in Mary's strength and loving grace. If you feel you have to hide parts of yourself others cannot understand, she can be your source of comfort, can support you in finding the strength within to be yourself without fear and attract those faithful to you who can love you for who you are and accept you without criticism, just as Mary's husband Joseph and her relative Elizabeth were able to do for her during her pregnancy.

Mary witnessed the gruesome death of a beloved child. I've worked with many who have lost a child. Their grief is deep and shocking. Those who have experienced such loss often speak of a sense of violation of natural order — that the elders should pass away first. The loss of a child can be a terrible ordeal to endure. Who could understand and empathise more than Mary? She saw her own son willingly allow hatred, ignorance, violence and fear—the worst traits of ego—to steal his life and denigrate his beautiful heart with malice, cruelty, mockery and venom. There was a stone statue of Mary holding the dead body of Jesus in her arms in one of the churches I attended during my childhood. Even as a little girl, I was overcome with sadness looking at it.

If we experience tremendous grief in our lives, due the death of a child or another reason, Mary is there for us. She has suffered much, and through that suffering developed compassion. Those who have suffered, and developed compassion, can hold the suffering of others effectively. They can be a place of comfort and restoration for them. As I write this paragraph, which I didn't know I was going to write until the words poured through me, my heart is pounding with her presence and grace. I know in the depth of my being that her reaching to us is real. Her capacity to be with us, to help us feel seen and grow stronger through our experiences without becoming lost in bitterness, fear or doubt, is truly divine. I know there are people who need to hear this message direct from her. She is speaking to them through these words, right now.

For reasons that are not completely clear, some statues of Mary have blackened faces. Some say these statues were blackened by the soot of many devotional candles, whilst others believe they were purposefully created to reflect the skin colours of those who loved her. For example, Guadalupe is typically depicted with a darker complexion. I believe no matter what the superficial reason may be, these Black Madonnas fill a legitimate hunger in the human soul for a nourishing archetypal presence of an earthy, dark-skinned mother (often with child in her arms) who connects us to the powerful, ancient mother who is with her people, not somehow dwelling separately in realms

of light. Think of the respect we have for someone who doesn't just talk about things but pushes up their sleeves and joins others to get things done. There is something about the Black Madonna that centres around her capacity to sustain us during times of oppression, suffering and fear. She is there in the fire, right along with us.

The cult of the Black Madonna thrives, even though there is no specific religious doctrine to support its existence. It exists because it is needed. The Universal Mother manifests herself according to the need of the heart, not based on what human intellect says is possible or appropriate. There are around 500 Black Madonna shrines around the world, from America to Asia to Europe and the Middle East. Undoubtedly, there are literally millions in people's homes around the world.

There is something compelling about the Black Madonna. There is mystery and wildness when one contemplates her. She is the patron goddess and protector of the people. She seeks and guards the parts within each of us that are denied, cast aside, misunderstood, rejected or feared. She is the liberating saint of the human shadow. She is practical and down to earth. She works alongside us – sweating with the strain of exertion, messy, bloodied, broken-hearted and powerful, as she more than pulls her weight. She carries the suffering of the world with her efforts and simultaneously shows us that we have the power, strength, dignity, uniqueness and courage we need to stand apart, stand up and stand for what really matters.

We can encounter the Black Madonna in a dream, a vision, an oracle deck, a human being, in this book or whenever we are deeply moved by a primal, protective maternal force. She is always with us, but often we don't want to hear what she has to say because, although she loves us unconditionally, the Black Madonna is a truth speaker. Sometimes, the truth hurts ... but as the saying goes, it is also the truth which will set you free. The Black Madonna empowers us to find our courage. If something is required of us to complete a task, even if it seems intimidating and has us quaking in our boots, we understand that we are enough of a divine badass to shake and shimmy and strut our soul stuff, anyway. And, she's with us every sassy step of the way. She is liberating in that sense, too. With her help, we do not allow others' opinions to derail us from our path and purpose.

Marion Woodman, a marvellous Jungian analyst and true daughter of the Black Madonna, tells of a beautiful series of dreams she had where a big, black goddess came and said, "Marion, where are your pearls?" Marion realised she had lost them and went looking to retrieve them. She found her pearls, only to have another dream of the Black Mother asking, "Where are your pearls, Marion? What have you done with your pearls?" Just before leaving her with those probing questions, she turned to Marion and quipped, "Don't forget to floss!" and then departed.

The 'pearls' the Black Madonna knows we need to treasure and protect are the wisdoms which come from our struggles. Suffering is the threshold through which we can enter the temple of the Black Madonna. We may only find ourselves interested in her when we are pushed to a place of great pain. In that suffering, a new level of devotion and willingness to trust can open for us, and her capacity to be at cause in our lives increases because we let her in. We become willing to value our pearls—our wisdom, our insight, our intuition—and act on them because we've learned from experience that, when we don't, much misery occurs. The practicality and humour in the comment about flossing has important meaning. That we take care of our bodies is important to the Black Madonna. As an expression of the Universal Mother, she is the wisdom of our bodies. She knows they are precious vehicles on our spiritual path. She wants us to love and work with them and 'clean out' what could cause damage to them on a regular basis, both symbolically and literally.

The Black Madonna appeared to me in a dream during a prolonged period of struggle, when I was trying to get my work off the ground. I dreamed of a fabulous African super-model-type woman wearing a tiny white dress and thick-soled, incredibly practical black shoes. She stomped along a catwalk in a darkened underground club, grabbed my hand and dragged me along with her, until I got my own saunter happening. Then she leapt off the catwalk in her practical shoes and proceeded up a winding staircase, where she found a bunch of papers I had written. She stomped all over them with her big black boots until they were in tatters, then marched up the rest of the stairs until she was out of sight.

I awoke from that dream rather disturbed! I realised my forthcoming liberation was going to be uncomfortable, at best. The dream helped me realise that I needed to ground myself more and let the heights take care of themselves. The period of integration following that dream was long and at times painful, but it was also a profoundly freeing, beautiful journey out of my head and into the powerful, creative realm of the sacred feminine. I had to give up my painstaking plans and learn how to dive headfirst into uncertainty. I hated it. Until I didn't. Eventually, I learned how to rest in that place and allow things to happen. The more I did, the more detached I became, and the more things unfolded in my life on all levels. It was not always easy. I needed Mary a lot, and the Black Madonna was etched in my heart as an ally and a kick-ass, truth-revealing soul coach whom I relied upon as I learned to deal with my tendency to try to take control. It was a slow and painful death for that part of me, and it still resurrects itself from time to time, but I trust her more than I trust that old habit. She taught me how to dwell in the dark terrain of uncertainty without anxiety or fear sending me scrambling back to control things. This learning was necessary for the health of my soul.

We have already considered the role of Mary in empowering those who may not feel completely confident, especially when they have a large task to accomplish and feel others will try to block it. If you are one of those precious souls whose life purpose includes embodying and sharing those loving and aware ways of being which threaten fear-based systems, you can be sure that, no matter how marvellous you are, or how talented, or how meaningful and necessary your purpose, without grace assisting you,

you're not going to get very far.

Human effort alone can accomplish a lot. The human spirit is an incredibly powerful, beautiful thing. But when it comes to being a light in this world, if you're doing your job properly, you'll be challenged by forces that require more *oomph* to overcome than human effort alone can muster. This is where our divine connection can make or break our spiritual success. We need human effort, but we also need spiritual grace. The combination of the two creates the magic of manifestation. We do not have to look outside ourselves for that divine connection and the grace it bestows. We may relate to Mary as a Divine Mother, but we could also relate to her as a light of spiritual grace within our own heart, which simply needs to be awakened through faith. Work with what works for you.

In the case of Catherine and her vision, despite initial scepticism from her superiors, they agreed to create the medals. Two years later, the miraculous medal of Mary was cast, and almost two hundred years on, millions of miraculous medals are worn throughout the world.

Before I was granted my Black Madonna dream, before my publisher set up his publishing house, I had an idea for what I thought would be my first book. I was extremely excited, as I felt it was part of my life purpose to write, teach and help lots of people heal and awaken. I felt very inspired. Once I completed my book proposal, I took a chance and sent it to a publisher I thought I wanted to publish my book. I still remember how exhilarated I felt at the prospect of stepping more fully into my life purpose.

Some weeks later, I opened my mailbox and, with a sinking heart, recognised my own handwriting on the stamped, self-addressed envelope I knew contained my book proposal — and a rejection letter. I was further disheartened when I read the letter. The date was wrong, and my name was spelled incorrectly. I felt disappointed, heartbroken and invisible. I doubted they'd even read the outline, although the company said they were receiving unsolicited manuscripts.

In painful confusion, I went out for a walk to clear my head. The inner western suburb where I lived at the time hosted a fair number of pubs, whose litter was scattered on the streets. As I walked along the sidewalk of a busy road, I mentally 'poured my heart out' to the Universe. I felt so uncertain and insecure. I took a few more steps, then noticed a shining object on the sidewalk. My mind decided it was most likely a metal screw top from a beer bottle reflecting the sunlight, but my heart leapt in my chest nonetheless. I leaned down. It was a silver medal bound to a small scroll with pale purple and green ribbons. Curious, I picked it up, slid the scroll from the ribbons and unrolled it. In large blue font, it read, "Fear not, child. God has a purpose for you." I was astonished. I gazed at the silver medal and noticed it had Mother Mary upon it. It was a miraculous medal. I wanted to cry with gratitude at the unexpected sweetness and powerful reassurance of it.

That sign fed my soul with determination and faith for the years it would take for my vision to gain traction, and it helped protect my sensitive heart from the disappointments and frustrations which could have turned me away from my purpose. It helped me find courage to work through long periods when I had no external indication that I would fulfil what I envisioned.

Not long after, I decided to publish my manuscript as an e-book on my website and keep believing in what my heart dreamed of creating, even if I couldn't really see how I was going to get from where I was at that time to where I wanted to be.

It was that e-book that my soon-to-be publisher read without me knowing, many years later. That was what inspired him to offer me the project of the *Kuan Yin Oracle*. That deck, written nearly eleven years after the miraculous medal found its way to me, set my work in motion. I understood divine timing was at work and still is. I tend to see what needs to happen and want it to occur immediately. If someone had told me I would need to wait for thirty years for what I wanted, I might not have been too happy about it! Then again, I may have just relaxed. But the lessons in unconditional trust and patience I received—which came through not knowing if or when what I wanted would manifest—have given me a capacity for equanimity that I, with my fiery nature, would not have otherwise had. That, in turn, has helped me continue to do the work required for things to come together in my professional and personal life.

I have written about Mary in *Crystal Masters 333,* and created an oracle deck dedicated to her titled, *The Mother Mary Oracle*. I have also created two meditation albums, *Mother Mary Meditations* dedicated to Mary and *Holy Sisters Meditations*, which features Mary and Kuan Yin working together for your spiritual growth and personal healing. I don't write about her in a religious sense so much as in a spiritual sense, as a guide and friend, because that is how I experience her. I also have a song dedicated to her on *The Kuan Yin Transmission*™ album of mantras, which you may like to hear. My intention with the mantra and prayer which form the lyrics is to create a field of her protective, guiding grace around all who hear it.

Some years ago, I attended several workshops run by a local spiritual school. I felt that I could learn some valuable teachings, but I also held deep doubts about whether I really belonged there. I also worried that my ego was pushing me away from something out of fear or some other issue of my own. I was second guessing and confusing myself by analysing rather than trusting my intuition.

The clarity I needed began to break through during one particular seminar. During the lunch break, I went for a walk away from the group. I wanted to tune in to my own heart and make sense of what I was feeling. As I wandered about the unfamiliar grounds, I noticed a white magnolia tree. I love magnolias. They are beautiful, and the scent is luscious. My heart happily led me towards that tree, and I unexpectedly felt an overwhelming presence of Mary. A few seconds later, I was close enough to the tree to realise that nestled behind it, hidden from view unless you were quite close, was a tiny grotto dedicated to the Madonna with a statue of her inside. I suddenly understood why she wanted her shrines in this world. They are entry points through which she can emanate her presence and reach people's hearts. I plonked myself down nearby to gaze at the grotto. My thoughts drifted towards my uncertainty about my involvement in the spiritual organisation teaching the workshop. Suddenly, I heard her voice. "I have sent Michael to protect you," she said.

I silently thanked her but didn't really understand what the message meant. I reluctantly left that hallowed spot and returned to the workshop space, only to see a twelve-foot high image of Archangel Michael projected on to a massive screen which had been erected during the break. He literally stood between me and the teacher. I was shocked. I stood open-mouthed, gaping at the image. Then the image was removed—it had nothing to do with the content of the course—and the teaching resumed. I knew I needed to end my involvement with the group and trust my intuitions were not ego. I needed to stop doubting myself and trust that, although that spiritual group may be helpful to others, I was not going to thrive there. I needed to leave, and I did.

The Catholic prayers to Mother Mary are lovely. The Hail Mary prayer comes to mind as an example. Her prayers generally do have some religious references. If you don't abide by Catholic beliefs, you may find them difficult to use as devotional prayers. That's fine and no impediment to devotion to Mary. You can use her prayers, regardless of whether you are Catholic. However, if you do not feel comfortable with the words, and would rather use a prayer less grounded in Christian doctrine, I would offer you the beautiful Tibetan mantra dedicated to the Goddess of the Dawn. She is a form of Tara, manifesting in the rays of the sun, known as Marici in Sanskrit or Wozer Chenma in Tibetan. In Chapter Four, I outlined the connection I found between Mary and this goddess of the rays of the sun who is worshipped in Taoist and Buddhist China, Tibet and India. I've come to know her as an Eastern emanation of the Western form of Mary.

There are some who would no doubt find that assertion, and my work in general, to be controversial (and that's putting it nicely). However, devotion to Mary has not arisen from the strict doctrinal teachings of the church, not even the Catholic church, where I feel her presence is more fully acknowledged than in other branches of Christianity. It has arisen, and continues to arise, from the hearts of everyday people. It may be that the father considers himself the head of the tribe and the rules he sets to be law, but as the mother (aptly named Maria) tells her daughter in the movie *My Big Fat Greek Wedding*, "The man is the head, but the woman is the neck, and she can turn the head any way she wants."

It's a delight to share the Catholic Hail Mary prayer and the Tibetan Wozer Chenma mantra with you now, so you can pray and connect to her with your own devotional chanting or singing. You can also hear my lyrical interpretation of her prayers and the mantras I was taught by my Tibetan master on the companion album, *The Kuan Yin Transmission™ – Music, Mantra & Meditation with the Universal Mother*.

HAIL MARY PRAYER

Hail Mary, Full of Grace,
The Lord is with Thee.
Blessed are thou among women,
And blessed is the fruit of thy womb, Jesus.
Holy Mary, Mother of God,
Pray for us sinners now,
And at the hour of death.
Amen

THE WOZER CHENMA MANTRA

Om Maritse Mum Swaha

(sounds like *OHM MAR-IT-SAY MOOM SWAH-HAH).*

Open your mind and heart to Mary's intervention, protection and guidance by allowing and expecting, her presence to be very real and to manifest in practical matters in your life. You may adore her as Mary, as I do, or be excited and enriched by her various faces, as I am also.

Whatever suits you at this point on your journey is as it is meant to be and may unfold, grow and evolve in surprising ways as you do.

May your path be held in her light and grace, as the Cosmic Madonna shows herself in your life in whatever form your heart can acknowledge and receive.

Chapter Eight

Goddess Isis: The Divinely Defiant Art of Refusing to be Overcome

I HAD BEEN DATING A WONDERFUL MAN FOR ABOUT A YEAR. HE was going through an extremely tough time and, although I experienced true delight when I was with him, certain situations in his life limited the amount of time we spent together. This tapped into my pain around my father being absent in my life, following my parent's divorce. As I further opened my heart in our relationship, the pain lodged in my heart from childhood opened, too. It was excruciating at times. I was astonished at how deep such pain could go, even after years of inner work.

However, it offered me a chance to become more aware, more capable of holding myself with compassion, rather than dumping my pain into the relationship and expecting my partner to deal with it or projecting it on to him, getting angry at him for something another man had done forty years earlier. Sometimes, it was hard to stay balanced and not go into a complete meltdown. If I did, I tried to do so in private, sort out what belonged to my childhood and how much of what I was feeling was relevant to the current relationship and needed to be expressed. If I felt grief or anger, I allowed myself to access those emotions and brought myself back to compassion for myself, for my partner, for my father. We were all doing our best. Maybe that wasn't always so skilful, but I don't need people to be perfect to love them. Thankfully, they feel the same about me.

After one particularly challenging month, when it seemed every possible external circumstance which could arise to drive a wedge between us had done so, I was contemplating whether I was being responsible for my own emotional wellbeing by remaining in the relationship. I loved him with a great passion, and I knew he loved me, too—that he found our relationship unlike anything he had experienced before—but there were numerous complicating factors that were outside of my control. I didn't know which way to go. In the absence of a clear intuition, I sensed that my spiritual task was to be present, amid the inner tension that I felt, bearing witness with compassion and to trust that if I needed to act, I would know how and when. That meant dealing with the emotional pressures which would undoubtedly continue to arise as my partner worked through his personal challenges and I worked through my own.

That same evening, I received an email from a spiritual community of which I was a member, saying our beloved Tibetan master's health was in decline. He had been diagnosed with terminal cancer forty years previously and had kept his body alive and functioning well through his spiritual practices, combined with modern medical support. He was kind, funny, down-to-earth and entirely devoted to his work assisting people on the path to enlightenment. From the moment I first encountered him, I was struck by his authenticity and skill. It was easy to recognise a genuine light such as his and loving him was even easier. When I read that news, I realised he could be preparing to leave his form on this earth and move on with his journey. I felt such sadness, yet when I allowed my mind to dwell upon him, I was filled with the joy which was his essence.

That evening, my heart was stretched with pain and love about my relationship and about my most trusted teacher. The joy and bliss, the connection and sweetness, the gratitude and blessings that love brings into our lives sat side by side with grief, sadness, anger, fear and loss. All I could do was just be there, with all the complexity of feeling in my heart. The heart has its own capacity for bearing the mysteries of love and directing us—when things are confusing, challenging and downright devastating—into the light of rebirth, after even the most profound loss. It doesn't make sense, logically. Without a strong connection to the sacred feminine or heart essence, one will lack the courage and inner spiritual support to navigate the deeper initiations that come with being a human on a spiritual path. I knew this. I trusted my heart to guide me.

As I continued to rest in this deep, vulnerable, cracked-open heart space, my own spiritual presence—and clarity and empowerment—became stronger and stronger. Suddenly, I realised Isis was revealing herself to me. Right from the centre of my heart, she was fanning her presence out like rays of the sun. I felt her just as if she was my best friend standing in the room with me. She was the Universal Mother, and she was my sister and friend, just there with me in that moment. She spoke no words, but I was so struck by how powerful her presence was in those moments, I gasped, "Oh! It's you, Ma!" My confusion, pain and uncertainty settled into a blissful ecstasy which brought me peace. Her radiance emanated through my heart and mind, heightening my sense of joy and peace, for days afterwards.

Isis is for those of us who choose to live by the heart's wisdom. She is the guardian priestess on the thresholds of the heart. She doesn't just watch over us when we are going through heartbreak, she *is* the process, she *is* the capacity we have to bear it, to be in it and not turn away — even when we really want to judge another, blame something or someone, switch off and avoid the pain. Not only that, she is the alchemist, the capacity to move through heartbreak and be changed by it in a beautiful way. Without divine alchemy, the change which comes with heartbreak is bitterness, shut down, regret and, perhaps, fear and anger. When we allow Isis to hold us within her heart, an experience of heartbreak can become the means through which we discover an expanded capacity for love, courage, compassion, confidence, and even ecstasy and bliss. We become bolder, braver and more committed to our journey. Rather than becoming more closed, we become more open. We find greater peace within and an understanding of the mechanics of the path of growth, as well as trust in the mysteries of it.

With some exceptions, such as one of my cousins, who seems to pop children out of her birth canal, done and dusted, in all of several minutes, birth is often difficult. It can require great courage and the willingness to break through the pain barrier. It is the intervention of the divine goddess that can help us find the capacity to bear the tension that is so often part of the birthing experience – whether we are speaking of physical birth of a child, a creative work or a new phase in our lives in some other way.

Soul birth can be similarly painful, wild and exhilarating all at once. My mentor and I once discussed the pain that can be involved in writing books. She said, "If it doesn't seem like you are 'pulling rabbits out of hats' and feel very difficult at times, it probably isn't any good!" Whilst I do not believe we have to suffer endlessly to grow, and much can be accomplished with grace, I found some truth in my mentor's statement. It is the nature and divine purpose of the sacred feminine to bring the body into consciousness. That is how we grow our soul. It is a birthing, and true creative birthing takes some spiritual muscle, whether we are talking about a book or a human soul. The dancer who moves with effortless grace built up a lot of strength in mind and body to have those moments in which she appears to exist in the ethers, more than upon the earth.

When we are birthing—in all its mess and glory—we are on the alchemist's path with Isis. Her *cardiognosis* (*heart wisdom*) guides us, even when we are under pressure. Eventually, through the heat of struggle, a synthesis or a birth, the transformation of the old into a new form will occur. With Isis as our ally, there will be enough love in our hearts to accomplish this task, both for the transformation of our own lives and for the benefit of all beings who are in need of our increasing divine presence and light to find their way.

The winged goddess Isis hails from ancient Egypt via the extraordinary star system of Sirius. I have written about Sirius in my book *Crystal Stars 11.11*. As a star system, it is considered a type of cosmic guru or teacher to our solar system. What our sun is for our solar system, Sirius is for our sun. The annual heliacal rising of Sirius, when the star system is seen on the eastern horizon just before dawn after not being visible in the sky for around seventy days, coincided with the flooding of the Nile in ancient Egypt. This event secured an abundant year ahead. Similarly, Isis is associated with fertility, blessings, prosperity and abundance, especially after a time of darkness or emotional 'drought.' One of the promises of the Universal Mother is that she will always be there for us, will always return to us when we have lost our way, will always nurture and provide.

In ancient Egypt, Sirius was called Sothis, and the goddess of Sothis was known as Sopdet, also said to be Isis. Hailing from a solar system held to be more spiritually advanced than our own, Isis is a teacher for adepts, for those already on a path beyond that which the mainstream collective culture can understand. Her wisdom is for one already practicing and embodying a way of the heart, of the soul, of wisdom and compassion. If one approaches Isis via the mind, she cannot be known. As with all true spiritual knowledge, she can only be recognised through the heart. For those of us who know heartbreak in some form—as relationship pains, the loss of a loved one or distress about the state of the world, the plight of humanity or the need for protection for animals and the environment—Isis is our guiding light. For those of us who seek to live in harmony with an inner wisdom the external world cannot understand, and therefore ridicules or denies, Isis is our wayshower.

Isis is a shining example of how to live like a heart-centred queen of light in a world that is too often driven by corruption and abuse of power. Her headdress is a throne. One translation of her name is *throne*. The royal path, represented by the throne, is the higher path. It is the soul, not the ego. It is our true nature, not our limited opinions or identities. The throne is the seat of leadership. When we aspire to the throne, our true motivations can be witnessed. Why do we seek a position of spiritual authority, for example? Is it to serve a higher purpose or gratify a lower need? As a guardian of spiritual leaders, Isis can teach us to assume responsibility for our efforts and become wise guides for others. She helps transform ego-lust for power into devotion and passion to a sacred purpose. She teaches us how to connect to our greater nature with dignity and grace.

Isis also teaches us how to remain pure of heart and not become corrupted by power. Whilst we need to be empowered to do our spiritual work in the world, power can bring out the dark side of human nature, such as when one assumes that power bestows superiority. A powerful leader who serves the people in his or her care can do great work in the world. A powerful leader who treats his or her people as resources for a personal agenda can create devastation on an enormous scale. We need wise people with good hearts in positions of influence and authority. Isis can help this happen without those precious hearts being corrupted.

The wisdom teachings of Isis instruct us how to rise above the forces of jealousy, hate, greed, violence and overcome any expression of extreme negativity. The state of many minds is so askew and disconnected from inner knowledge of the heart that it seems necessary to clearly articulate what our beloved goddess Isis is *not*. Due to media coverage, confusion has arisen around the nature of the goddess Isis and some people seem to think she is connected to a terrorist group. Nothing could be further from the truth. So, I want to clear the confusion.

When I was teaching about the goddess Isis in the United States recently, I heard from people who wandered into their local metaphysical store, saw a flyer for the Temple of Isis workshop I was invited to present and felt intrigued, but also uncertain because of all the negative associations the word *Isis* has generated in the media. At one point, in a room of about eighty people, we went around the group just saying the word *Isis* aloud, reclaiming her sacred name. One woman could not do it. She said *Kuan Yin*, instead. We may absolutely love the mother in the form which resonates for us and it is never a competition or an 'either/or' situation. Yet, I would have loved for her to have welcomed this face of the Universal Mother into her heart, because the only reason she couldn't was because dark forces at work in the world had created confusion around the goddess's name. Fortunately, Kuan Yin is Isis by another name and shall take care of that beautiful soul.

One woman said she was very drawn to the workshop but felt put off by all that had been happening in the media, *even though she knew there was no connection between Isis and terrorists*. We must be careful. Isis teaches us to rescue and protect that which is precious from the destructive forces of hate. Her name is precious. We must keep it pure and clear in our hearts. We must maintain access to our Divine Mother, unfettered, undisturbed, undistorted by the delusions of others. It is the only way we can help ourselves and them. Imagine having a friend who had a terrible relationship with their mother and although you had a great relationship with your mother, your friend's negativity influenced you to hate all mothers, including your own. It is ridiculous to imagine allowing such poison to infiltrate your inner world, yet it can happen. We must be smart. We must be aware. We must refuse to allow our inner Temple of Isis to be corrupted by the ignorance and wounding of those we are on this planet to assist.

That woman had questioned whether she should attend the workshop, mulling it over and over again. After she saw that flyer, although she had known nothing about me before, she suddenly began to see my books in stores, something I wrote popped up on her social media feed and a friend mentioned my *Isis Oracle*. She was still wavering, until the evening before the workshop, when she received a phone call in the middle of the night. It was a wrong number but, as it turns out, it was the right number for her. It was a call from Egypt! The woman was so startled she showed up to the workshop the next day. Hers was the last seat available in a sold-out gathering. The workshop itself was deeply alchemical for her. She had numerous breakthroughs, numerous tears. She came up to me during breaks to tell me what was happening for her. I was so glad she got the message from Isis that guided her to be there. I know the exposure to that sacred feminine energy lifted her from one cycle of her life and set her on her true path.

Interestingly, one of the specific magic teachings of Isis is the power inherent in the accurate use of names. Names hold power. Naming something accurately can release us from its thrall over our body and mind. For instance, in the everyday world, we have the concept of *reputation*. It is given such significance, there are laws to protect our reputation from slander.

It wasn't until people who had my *Isis Oracle* emailed to ask if I thought it was safe for them to carry through airport security (I can report no incidents occurred — the Divine Mother sorted all that out for them) that I realised the extent of the confusion. It seemed so obvious to me that the goddess is about overcoming, rather than perpetuating harm. I could not imagine anyone would be disturbed by a book or card deck that bore her name. I underestimated the capacity of negativity to attempt to defile and destroy what is sacred, when, ironically, this is something Isis cautions us about. So, when people asked me what they should do when the name of the beautiful Egyptian goddess became associated with a group of people dedicated to war, terror, cruelty and violence, I reflected more deeply.

I realised a kind of divine mystery teaching was unfolding, and it was regarding what was needed to overcome the terrorist groups in the world. I wondered if, in some way, Isis had lent her name to remind us what was needed to heal this, as a hint of what was going on at a deeper level. Isis manifests the exact expression of consciousness needed to conquer the workings of terrorism in all its forms. So, in an unexpected way, perhaps that acronym is telling us we need to focus on her, to call her in, to so strongly desire her intervention that her will can be set in motion in the world through us. If there is also a diabolical force beneath the naming of this particular terrorist group with the acronym ISIS, then to that, I respond by sticking out my tongue Kali-style, flipping my middle finger Alana-style, and most of all by loving Isis with all my heart and continuing to share her light, beauty and power with those hungry for her restorative grace, keeping her name sacred in my heart and speaking of her from the heart.

Terrorist groups manifest the qualities of the god Set, who features in the Isis story as the representation of the dark force that wants to destroy all that is loving, kind and good in the kingdom of Egypt including Isis and her husband, Osiris. Set symbolises the same dark forces that exist in these groups, and in our own egos. He represents hate, fear, jealousy and the desire to steal and destroy life based on whether it is serving your ego at any given time. The goddess Isis is the conquering presence of divine good, which seeks to create life, to honour love, goodwill, encouragement and the desire to birth, give, surrender into a greater wisdom of love and affirm the light. These are forces humanity is learning to balance in the soul, and in our world, by finding spiritually intelligent ways to combat negative energy.

Isis teaches us valuable lessons about managing darkness in ourselves and the world. Firstly, we do not try to transform the darkness into something it is not. We do not allow ourselves to be manipulated or exploited by our own good-natured desire to see the good in all things. We instead understand that, *with wisdom we can find a way for all things to work for good*, which is something else entirely. Not all things *are* good. If one pats a hand grenade as though it were a kitten, the nature of the grenade is not changed, nor is its potentially devastating effect. We can accept the grenade for what it is and respond appropriately.

To accomplish this, we must be clear and conscious about what we speak and what we name things. There is an expression about people who speak directly. They call a spade, a spade. We don't need to judge, but we do need to be careful that in our desire to refrain from generating negativity by judging others, for example, we don't end up denying the reality of what is happening and put ourselves in dangerous situations where we can be compromised. This is Isis' teaching on the power of names – we learn to see things as they are, name them, and therefore, respond appropriately.

Isis teaches us discernment. We cultivate discernment and the ability to see things for what they are, not so we can judge others, not so we say certain people are evil and need to be destroyed, but so we can respond with wisdom. Wisdom is compassionate, but it is also effective. To grow our discernment, we strengthen our connection to the light, set wise boundaries, focus on accomplishing our own sacred work and deal with the pain within so we can continue to open to the love within. In these ways, we strengthen the light every being needs so much, especially those who would undermine our progress and destroy our faith, if given half a chance.

Osiris and Isis were in love. As king and queen of Egypt, they ruled with kindness and fairness. The land prospered, and the kingdom thrived. The people loved their kind king and wise queen. There was peace and harmony ... except in the heart of Set, the jealous, jackal-headed god of the desert and brother of Osiris. Set is a powerful god of disorder, storms, war and foreigners. Unlike Kali's divine disorder, which shakes things up to accomplish a loving purpose, Set is the ego let loose. He loves to create a mess, impose his will and make the world turn according to his desire, with no interest in how that affects others. He is an expression of entitlement that separates itself from the feminine fabric of spiritual connectedness and seeks to accomplish its wishes at any cost. A wise, alchemical goddess like Isis can distil something beneficial from such evil, but she suffers intensely in the process. She is willing to endure for the greater good, but she also teaches us how we can avoid setting ourselves up for unnecessary suffering in the first place.

Some years back, I dreamed I was walking along a path with my cat. This was quite a special cat — she was golden, and she could talk. She rested in my arms as I walked. All was good until I noticed a dark alley off to one side. Instead of recognising the darkness and taking heed, I stepped into that side street, curious as to why it caught my attention. The moment I did, I locked eyes with an angry alley cat seated high up on a ledge. She hissed aggressively at me. I had wandered into her territory. She didn't like it one bit. I decided I didn't like it either, and I stepped out of the alley and back on to the path in the bright light of day. That angry cat wasn't appeased. She launched at me, claws out. I quickly repositioned my precious golden cat safely behind me and used the strength of my energy to create a shield between the attacking cat and her intended target, which appeared to be my face. When the cat realised her attack would fail, she retreated to her alley. My golden feline companion and I continued on our way.

That dream was an Isis teaching for me. It came at a time when I had accepted an invitation to work with someone I would have been better to avoid. I was flattered by the invitation and curious about the facilitator and her work. On the surface, she appeared respectful, but something just felt off. In the brief time I spent as a guest in her community gatherings, I finally sensed what lurked in the darkness. She was spreading noxious stories about me whilst being pleasant to my face. As it turned out, the things she said I had done were what she was doing to me.

This dream came when all of this was coming to light. It was confirmation that I was to take care of my sacred feminine offering (the golden cat) and use my energy, my true inner connection to the light, to ward off her negativity and to stay on my path! Her potential attack on my reputation was deflected and my decision to terminate the connection completely was a sensible choice for me. I've been a little more cautious and worldly since that experience.

Set told Osiris he had created a beautiful offering for him. He invited him to come and see it. It was a stunning creation, a box which seemed fit for a king. Set invited Osiris to step into the box and lay down, which trusting his brother, he did. Set promptly sealed the box, effectively turning it into a tomb, and dumped it in the river Nile. When Isis found out, she was wracked with grief. She understood that until he had a proper burial the soul of her beloved Osiris would not be able to rest.

A 'proper burial' means closure. People who have suffered the peculiar devastation of having someone go missing without knowing what has happened to that person, can have a tough time moving on with their lives because of the absence of closure. It *is* possible to find that closure, but it requires a great deal of trust that even though you may not know the details, the Universal Mother will be caring for the precious soul who is no longer with you and caring for those left behind, too.

Closure is so much more than an ending. An ending of itself does not necessarily bring closure. That is why divorced people might still be re-enacting the wounds of their marriage, years after it is legally over, or why we may struggle with the emotional legacy that burdens your heart even after the person connected to that issue has died. Closure is true inner resolution. It happens by accessing the wisdom in our heart that knows how to process what has taken place and create freedom to move on with peace in one's soul.

Closure is needed in all sorts of circumstances such as the loss or ending of a job, a relationship, a life, an identity or a phase of one's life. A spiritually healthy culture will have meaningful ceremonies to help us navigate our way through transitions of all kinds, finding closure and freedom to move into a new cycle with grace. One of the deficiencies of modern culture is the absence of supportive rituals to honour the numerous rites of passage in our lives. Supportive ceremony can provide closure and help us gain wisdom and spiritual maturity as we process our experiences. The practitioners of my *Soul Guidance and Sacred Mentoring*™ modality can facilitate *threshold blessings*. These are soul-level healings, a form of sacred interactive ceremony that support those who are moving through transitions of any kind – whether joyful or deeply challenging. If your heart feels connected to such a thing and you want to find a practitioner in your area, you can search the list of *Soul Guidance and Sacred Mentoring*™ practitioners on my website. Many of the practitioners also offer special healing sessions dedicated to growing a connection with the goddess Isis. This can also help to bring closure and open your heart to a new phase in your life.

Isis wanted and needed closure for the death of Osiris — for herself, for her people and for her husband. She searched for his body as part of that process. This took her far from her palace. Eventually, she needed to rest. Just then, a servant woman approached her and offered her refreshment. Isis accepted her kind gift and was invited into the household. Her story and her quest became known. People began to talk of the missing tomb of Osiris. During her time in the household, she helped care for an infant boy. During the night, she would pass him in and out of the fire. One evening, the mother of the child came to check on him and witnessed the actions of the goddess with fear and anger. She scolded her, and Isis replied, "You don't understand. I was turning him into an immortal. One last pass through the flames and it would have been accomplished."

This mysterious passing in and out of the flames refers to the heat of initiation. When you are going through it, the emotional and psychological pressure can make you feel like you are being cooked! The tension between what you are becoming and where you are—and the challenge of what you need to do to bridge the gap—can seem like it's breaking you down. In a way, it is. Like Kali's positive destruction, which has a liberating effect, Isis shows us that the Universal Mother, kind as she is, won't infantilise her children. She sees our potential and knows that we need certain pressures to grow, just as a seed needs pressure to germinate and crack open. This is how the body adapts to fitness programs. You need enough pressure to break through past limits, otherwise you remain as you were. With insufficient pressure, there is stagnancy or even regression. With too much pressure, there is breakdown rather than breakthrough. Isis, as the initiator on the threshold between humanity and divinity, negotiates the fine line between them. She teaches us to avoid unnecessary suffering but encourages us to go through what *is* necessary to bring out the best in us and fulfil our destinies.

A wealthy man found the tomb of Osiris. Not knowing what it was, but admiring its beauty, he had kept it in his home. Upon hearing of her plight, he returned the tomb to Isis, freeing her to take it back to the kingdom for public grieving and a respectful formal burial. When she returned to the palace with the tomb of the beloved dead king, Set erupted in a ferocious rage and cast Osiris' remains all over Egypt. Isis went about the task of reclaiming those remains, unwavering in her commitment to gain closure and refusing to bow down to the negativity of Set. She travailed until she reclaimed every part of her husband's remains, except his phallus, which was consumed by a crocodile in the Nile River. Isis created a new phallus, which she fashioned out of gold and wax. She used magic to transform herself into a hummingbird and conceive a child with her husband before releasing him with love to become King of the Underworld.

Hummingbird is a potent symbol of goodness. In shapeshifting into a hummingbird, Isis embodied the metaphysical power of that tiny, beautiful winged creature. Hummingbird wisdom includes the power to evolve and adapt so as to triumph in challenging conditions and the capacity to reach deep for the innermost sweetness (which means the soul, the 'taste' of which is said to be sweet, in the spiritual teachings of Ancient India). Hummingbird represents the qualities of happiness and hope, a positive portent for overcoming the apparently impossible.

Isis birthed the child she conceived through her sacred shapeshifting and alchemical healing of her husband's soul. That child was born a saviour, a warrior and a future king who would defeat and dethrone Set. This falcon-headed god known as Horus assumed leadership of Egypt. He ruled with the fairness of Osiris, the love of Isis and the wisdom that can come through being taken down by dark energies and learning how to rise again, smarter and more empowered.

Osiris trusted Set when he shouldn't have. It cost him his life and threw his beautiful and true kingdom of Egypt into turmoil. Yet that error also led to spiritual growth for himself and Isis which in turn resulted in the creation of a more powerful force of goodness in the form of Horus. This is the power of wisdom. It can take even terrible events and find a way to make the light grow stronger through the healing that follows.

The valuable teaching Osiris and Isis give us is that negativity, if given an inch, will take a mile. This doesn't mean we need to be paranoid. It does mean that, when something doesn't feel right, it is best not to talk ourselves out of our wisdom. Being nice does not always equate with being wise. It's fine to be polite to others and have respect. It is a good rule of thumb, but you can still set a boundary and say, "Thanks but no thanks," when needs be. Fortunately, there is always the comfort of knowing that, if we do ignore our inner wisdom, we can still find our way back to love, even if it is a more difficult journey. Since it may be that something of value could only arise through that more challenging path, it is good to let there be peace in our hearts about how our life journeys unfold, rather than thinking that if things get tough, we have made a mistake.

I had a dream of a beautiful but tiny light. I was aware that all around the light were creatures of darkness. They hovered around the edges and then, suddenly attacked from every angle. They were ruthless and relentless. They attempted to destroy that light, and in my dream, I witnessed this with a feeling of horror in my heart. Suddenly, the light rose up and expanded until it was thousands of times its original size. It then transformed into a mighty winged horse. It was huge and radiant! It slammed one of its hooves on the ground and the power of that action was so intense—like thunder and lightning combined—that I heard it reverberating through me as I was dreaming. It forced those relentless evil forces to scurry off in all directions. I was stunned by how swiftly the battle turned and how rapidly the light had become powerful. My terror transformed into bliss, and I woke with a sense of wonder at what had taken place.

From this dream, I realised that there is never a time to indulge the darkness of ego, and never a time to ignore the preciousness of the light. It needs to be protected, especially when it is small and vulnerable. Whether I interpret my dream to relate to the interplay of good and evil on the planet, or to the need to protect our small victories of spirit and mind from doubt, despair and naysayers, it taught me the value of guardianship and *why* negativity seeks to act whenever it can. It has no interest in a fair fight. The power of light is so great that, when it is in full flight, it cannot be overcome. That is Isis. The consciousness that operates against the light will strike whenever it can. We must neither underestimate this nor be fearful about it. We just need to be realistic. We need to take care of ourselves, to clean off the effects of negativity as soon as we notice them creeping in to our hearts and minds. This can become a habit just like cleaning our teeth or taking a shower.

Skilful guardianship of the light is what Isis teaches us. When we are in touch with the seeds of something new and positive within—perhaps self-love or a decision to meditate or explore healing or the realisation that everything is going to be okay—we need to protect and foster those seeds. This is what the mother does. She provides the womb space, so a seed can grow into fullness and be birthed into the world. It is why the child archetype features so strongly in the depictions and stories of the Universal Mother, from Jesus and Horus, to the bare-breasted goddesses like Tara who represent the Universal Mother as willing and able to nourish her children.

Isis teaches us to keep unconditional faith and be active in doing so. We need to have trust and confidence to make it through the darkest times and not cower in a corner and let them defeat us. If we trust in the power of the light, we can accomplish much, even against what appear to be odds stacked against us. We might feel vulnerable, but if we open our hearts to her, that vulnerability can become the crack in our defences that allows her greater access—therefore, the greatest capacity—to empower our hearts with the needed higher wisdom and grace to overcome whatever lies before us. Our vulnerability can become a source of spiritual strength.

The dark night of the soul is, by its nature, a time when confidence, faith, hope and love are farthest from our reach. The wisdom teachings and spiritual empowerment of Isis are relevant in everyday matters but can be especially comforting during those times when all feels lost, when there seems to be no hope and when the enemy of love appears to have the upper hand. We may have moments when we look at someone who appears to be prospering and think (as the ancient Chinese divination tool known as the *I Ching* would put it) that *the inferior man is rising to power*. Isis teaches us to recognise when that is happening, but not believe it is the final chapter. If the light hasn't won, the story isn't over.

The challenges Isis faced were devastating. Yet, despite her pain, she refused to give up or give in. She consciously chose to act with confidence. She knew no matter what was sent her way, she would find her way through it with authenticity, courage and grace. From that place, she is extremely inventive. She is the part of the soul which never gives up, which will always find another way if an obstacle arises. Calling on her connects us to the courage and power within our hearts. We need to be stubborn about the *right* things on the spiritual path. Stubbornly demanding something work out according to our desire is the ego. It doesn't get us anywhere. On the other hand, stubbornly continuing until we find the path Spirit has laid out for us, ensures we are never blocked from our destiny. Nothing can stop Isis because her faith and will are such that she never even considers it. We have such grit within our souls, too.

The triumph of Isis and her son Horus, born out of the loss and death imposed by Set, resulted in the rebirth of spiritual leadership which saved Egypt, bringing it back into the light with more wisdom than ever before. This is a reminder for our own souls of what is possible through divine love and a hefty dose of determination. If, for whatever reason, we find ourselves off the path of grace and on the path of hard knocks for a while, we don't need to panic or judge ourselves. Sometimes, people think they are doing something wrong when the spiritual path is tough, as though it would be effortless if they were doing everything right. I think it depends on what is needed at the time. Grace always gets the job done, but sometimes grace is hidden beneath the challenge because we need to learn something, and that's the only way we are going to do so.

For instance, we learn we can survive what we once feared. Then we go from strength to strength because we have become confident in ourselves — like the rapid, empowering transformation of the light in my dream, from tiny seedling to massive heroic force within moments. If someone is about to give up, or has already given up, and needs tenderness and the power of love to reignite their trust and courage, Isis is medicine for the soul.

The missing phallus is a teaching about sacred, conscious masculinity. The phallus is a symbol of masculine energy. In Osiris, the masculine energy was developed in some ways. His goodness, responsibility and leadership were strong enough to support his people during good times. He wasn't developed enough in discernment and boundaries, in understanding the ruthless and relentless nature of negativity, to be able to withstand the dark times. The teaching here is that learning to deal with negative situations can help us become wiser and more courageous. It can strengthen our light, rather than wearing it down or making us bitter.

The old phallus was swallowed by a crocodile in the river Nile because it needed to be digested and transformed into a new form. It was not equipped for the requirements of the new world. The crocodile-headed god of ancient Egypt was Sobek. He was associated with military strategy, pharaonic power, protection and fertility. The masculine consciousness of Osiris, which had been destroyed, needed to be born anew, needed to develop in a new way to overcome the powers which had conquered it. That included figuring out a way to manage conflict and challenges to spiritual authority from sources of negativity like Set, or in our case, our own ego.

The released masculine energy of Osiris was replaced by a golden phallus. Gold represents the alchemist's highest aspiration, which is the transformation of one energy into a golden, or higher, expression. Gold is a symbol of divinity. The birth of Horus, through Isis's magical alchemy with gold, represents what can happen when our efforts—which may not quite be enough to get the job done on their own—are integrated with divine energy. Magic and healing can take place. We evolve in such a way that we are transformed. I truly believe we are called to a task because of what is in our hearts but are given the capacity to accomplish it by divine dispensation. Isis is the giver of divine blessing, the one who recognises our capacity, but also knows the blessings required to evolve it into a divine expression.

From Osiris and the golden phallus, with Isis's alchemical magic, is born Horus. He is the new masculine consciousness for those who want to effectively deal with the negative powers Set represents. Horus sets boundaries and is willing to back them up. He decides what is acceptable and takes action to gain respect for his values. When this is in loving response to the intuition and values of the feminine soul, it is the hallmark of developed conscious masculinity.

Underdeveloped masculine energy—in men and women—doesn't yet have the capacity to esteem the values of the soul which differ from what others may value. A person may be capable of superficially winning at this game of life—playing by social rules in such a way they seem to have it all—but if their life choices are not in harmony with the inner truths of their heart, they will not be on their soul path and, inside, the most beautiful and valuable part of them will be withering from lack of respect, attention, care and protection. Set will be destroying the Osiris within, and they'll need the wild sacred feminine power of Isis to transform their inner masculine into the take-no-nonsense boldness of Horus.

The sacred masculine is the energy within us which recognises what matters, listens to the heart and is willing to tell naysayers to bugger off. Thus, it protects the sacred feminine as she incubates the soul essence. The sacred masculine trusts the sacred feminine to know when things need to happen and, at the correct time, carries out the relevant actions with courage and determination. The conscious masculine and feminine like each other, love each other and support and empower each other. She gives him meaning to defend, and he protects her space to continue to deepen that meaning. The healing of their relationship within us means our head and heart are no longer at war with each other. We live with a sense that all parts of us are moving in the same direction, working together, not at odds with each other, pulled in multiple directions, causing confusion, tension and exhaustion.

As we empower the sacred feminine within us, we learn what our real values are and pull back from those which do not resonate. We allow our hearts to grow full with dreams, vision and yearning, as well as with compassion for our suffering and the suffering of others. Our path becomes clearer. We know what we really want because we know who we are in a deeper sense. We realise that, although we can assume certain identities in order to make our way through life and relate to others, those identities are not who we are but they serve the purpose of connection and relationship, which do matter.

As the feminine grows stronger, the masculine must evolve to meet her needs. The more radically unique and authentic her vision, the less likely there is to be a path already created for her. The world may not even understand, let alone support, what it is she wishes to birth. Therefore, the masculine will have even more need to respect her and stand up to the disparaging forces that resist her uniqueness, originality and creativity. He doesn't have to become aggressive or violent. Mahatma Gandhi taught us the power of inner will can be enough to make the external expression of collective resistance give way.

In the course of my work, I meet some amazing souls with truly beautiful ideas which could profoundly benefit our world. However, without a developed masculine sense of discernment and honouring of the feminine, they will not set aside the time nor make their intuitive vision a high enough priority in their life to get it off the ground. They'll dream about it. They'll yearn for it. But without the masculine consciousness necessary to pick up the sword and take on opposition (most of which will be in their own habits and belief systems), it cannot go any further. The need of the sacred feminine to birth something genuinely of their souls is not met. Connecting with Isis can help us build our feminine soul values *and* the masculine strength of our will so the energies of goodness within us cannot be overcome.

During a talk I gave on the sacred masculine and feminine energies, a woman in the audience said she had never considered the masculine to have such value. A beautiful woman who was a high-flyer in the world of corporate finance, this woman had made exceptional progress in her field through a combination of skill at her job and a warm, engaging feminine charisma that generally went over well with her colleagues. Networking was a breeze for her, and she attracted supporters for her efforts, which

benefitted the company for which she worked. Everyone was happy. Except for her female superior, who hated her with a passion likely fuelled by jealousy, and who was determined to get this woman out of the company. Her boss was the Set to her Isis, which shows that toxic masculinity can exist in women as well as men. Her boss instigated a witch hunt fuelled with such vitriol that even her numerous influential connections could not protect her. At this point, she sought me out and began paying deeper attention to her spiritual journey.

Amongst this woman's admirable traits was a refusal to become a victim. She continuously identified and set aside the negativity directed at her, listening to her body and processing her emotions. Her intuition and connection to her inner world blossomed as a result. The more challenged she felt, the more she would meditate, record her dreams and ask the Universe for guidance. Eventually, she realised she wanted out of the corporate world, at least for a time. She shared her considerable skills with not-for-profit organisations. Her journey continued to unfold, and her spirituality continues to deepen.

The real beauty in this story is not that she shifted from corporate to not-for-profit, for certainly the corporate world needs conscious men and women who have access to their inner light. The beauty is that, when under attack, she didn't collapse. She explored, she opened up, she knew when to stay and when to move on in order to sustain, nourish and strengthen her light. She used the same combination of feminine warmth and masculine adventurousness which helped her thrive in her job to move out of that position with dignity and embrace new opportunities for growth. Her light continues to shine, and she touches the lives of those fortunate enough to be around her.

Combatting forces of darkness within us and around us is part of our work as healers and guiding lights. When we grow our ability to heal through forgiveness and love's true empowerment, we become bearers of the real Isis in our souls. Her presence encourages us to understand and embody purity, determination and cleverness. She empowers our souls with an ignition of the divine spark within — that bold, valiant determination which sustains us even when everything seems lost. She is the spiritual reminder that, if things become difficult, there is always a way through based on love and wisdom. No matter how difficult things get, or how viciously someone may attempt to block, or even attack, us, we can always take refuge in the heart and triumph. We never need give up on ourselves nor betray our values to accomplish a task. The right way will always present itself if we remain connected to our hearts, trust in divine timing and commit to act when the way becomes clear. It may not be what we expect but that's usually when the fun begins, as we are handing over the steering wheel of our lives to a higher spiritual intelligence.

Sometimes we don't realise just how close someone is to losing their connection to the light. They may seem to be going about their business, perhaps even experiencing more success than ever before, yet not be able to show the face of their pain to the world. In the event of suicide, most of the people connected to the person who died express a deep sense of shock.

I think one of the least helpful responses to suicide—that the person who killed themselves was being selfish—comes from the fear those around the person feel. They may fear they made a mistake, that they should have sensed something, but didn't. But suicide is not evidence of selfishness, nor of a failure of people to love each other. It is what happens when one's soul is dying. Others' shock is evidence of how little we, as a society, acknowledge the reality of the soul. The tragedy of modern culture is the great difference between how things appear and how they really are. We buy into the surface and don't sink into the depths.

I believe we avoid those darker places because, even though they house marvellous treasures like wisdom and compassion, they also house past pain. I have met educated, clever people who are at the top of their field but have so little emotional intelligence they believe just leaving something alone and not 'going there' will nullify the negative influence of unresolved wounding. This is the equivalent of living in a tiny corner in an attic, whilst the rest of their soul house turns to rot and crumbles and in their determined ignorance, they proclaim all is well (even though they cannot shake their anxiety, fear, doubt, numbness, panic, grief, obsession or addiction). If we are caught up in all that glitters, rather than discerning the real gold, we will try to nourish ourselves with that which cannot sustain us, and the starvation will continue.

The great tragedy here, and the great promise, is this doesn't have to happen. A connection with legitimate, authentic sources of light can cast out damaging negativities that undermine the health of the soul. Even a dying soul can be revitalised and nourished into fullness with divine love. The sacred feminine knows what will nourish, knows how to feed and grow the seed into full bloom. The sacred masculine knows how to cut off forces which would distort and diminish our soul, that steal our inner peace and sense of spiritual value. As we learn how to do this for ourselves, we can support others in learning how to do this for themselves, too.

We must remember we are not meant to be gods and goddesses. We are spiritual beings — divine beings, yes, but we are expressing through human form. That means having compassion for the times our bodies and minds forget divine truth and get seduced by ego. Recognising that we are not in authenticity is part of the breakthrough. It is easier to know when we are in authentic self when we are connected to our bodies. We can more readily sense if love, or ego, is ruling what is going on in our heads and hearts and then take appropriate action.

Isis has a special place in my heart. Her celestial light shines truly as divine love. She is determined to continue where lesser spirits would abandon the path. This renders her a powerful guide for taking darkness and, through our own connection to our hearts, finding the way, so it ends up serving the light.

To connect with Isis, even if you don't practice *The Kuan Yin Transmission*™ modality with me, you can listen and sing along to the Isis mantras and practice the guided processes on *The Kuan Yin Transmission*™ album. A short version of a mantra or prayer to call in Isis is *Jai Ma Isis Namo Namaha* (sounds like *JAY MAH ISIS NUMB-OH NUMB-AH-HAH*), which essentially means, *Victory to the Universal Mother of Love, Peace and Magic, I bow to you in respect. May you thrive for the greater good.*

I have created an oracle deck dedicated to Isis, *The Isis Oracle*, and an album of meditations to connect you to her teachings called *Isis: Power of the Priestess*. There is a chapter dedicated to her in my book *Crystal Goddesses 888*, along with healing processes, a section devoted to the healing power of Isis quartz crystal and a crystal mandala. If you are interested in enrolling in my year-long online training program for healers, called *Soul Guidance and Sacred Mentoring*™, there is a special program dedicated to Isis for those who complete the initial year of training successfully. That program includes workshops and healing sessions you can conduct for individuals and small groups using an oracle deck and meditations, music and sacred rituals. If you would like to find a practitioner and attend one of those sessions, you are welcome to look through the *Soul Guidance and Sacred Mentoring*™ practitioner listing on my website to find a qualified practitioner in your area.

May you know the unwavering love and courage of Isis within your own heart.